# "A VERY STABLE GENIUS!"

@realDonaldTrump

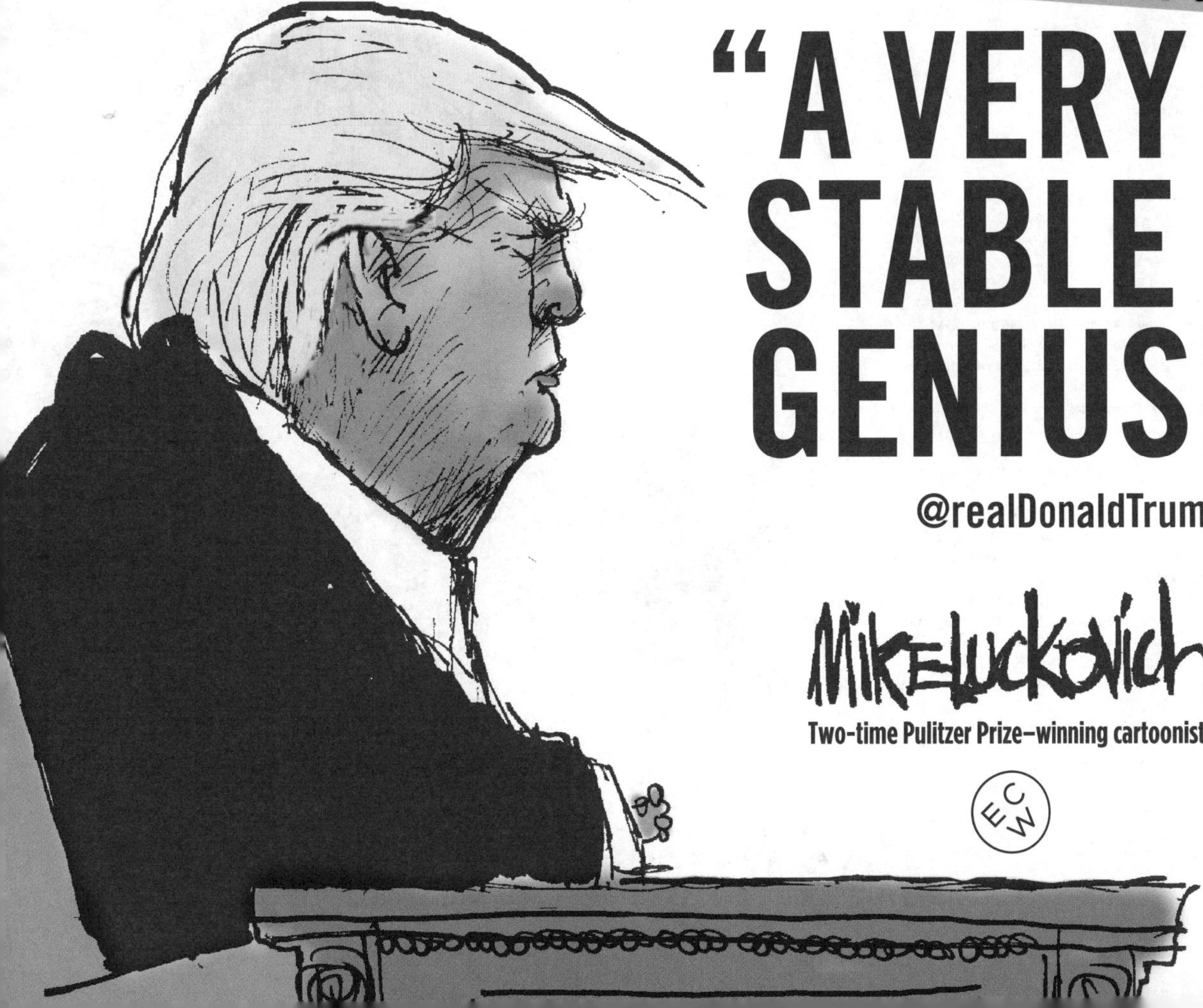

MIKE LUCKOVICH

Two-time Pulitzer Prize–winning cartoonist

ECW

Published by ECW Press
665 Gerrard Street East
Toronto, Ontario, Canada M4M 1Y2
416-694-3348 / info@ecwpress.com



LIBRARY AND ARCHIVES CANADA CATALOGUING IN PUBLICATION

Luckovich, Mike, 1960–, author, illustrator
"A very stable genius!" @realDonaldTrump / Mike Luckovich, two-time Pulitzer Prize-winning cartoonist.
ISBN 978-1-77041-478-5 (softcover)
1. Trump, Donald, 1946– — Caricatures and cartoons. 2. American wit and humor, Pictorial. 3. Presidents — United States — Humor. 4. Editorial cartoons — United States. 5. United States — Politics and government — 2017– — Caricatures and cartoons. 6. Cartoons (Humor) I. Title.
NC1429.L82A4 2018 973.93302'07 C2018-903591-9

PRINTING: FRIESENS 5 4 3 2 1
PRINTED AND BOUND IN CANADA

MIX
Paper from responsible sources
FSC® C016245

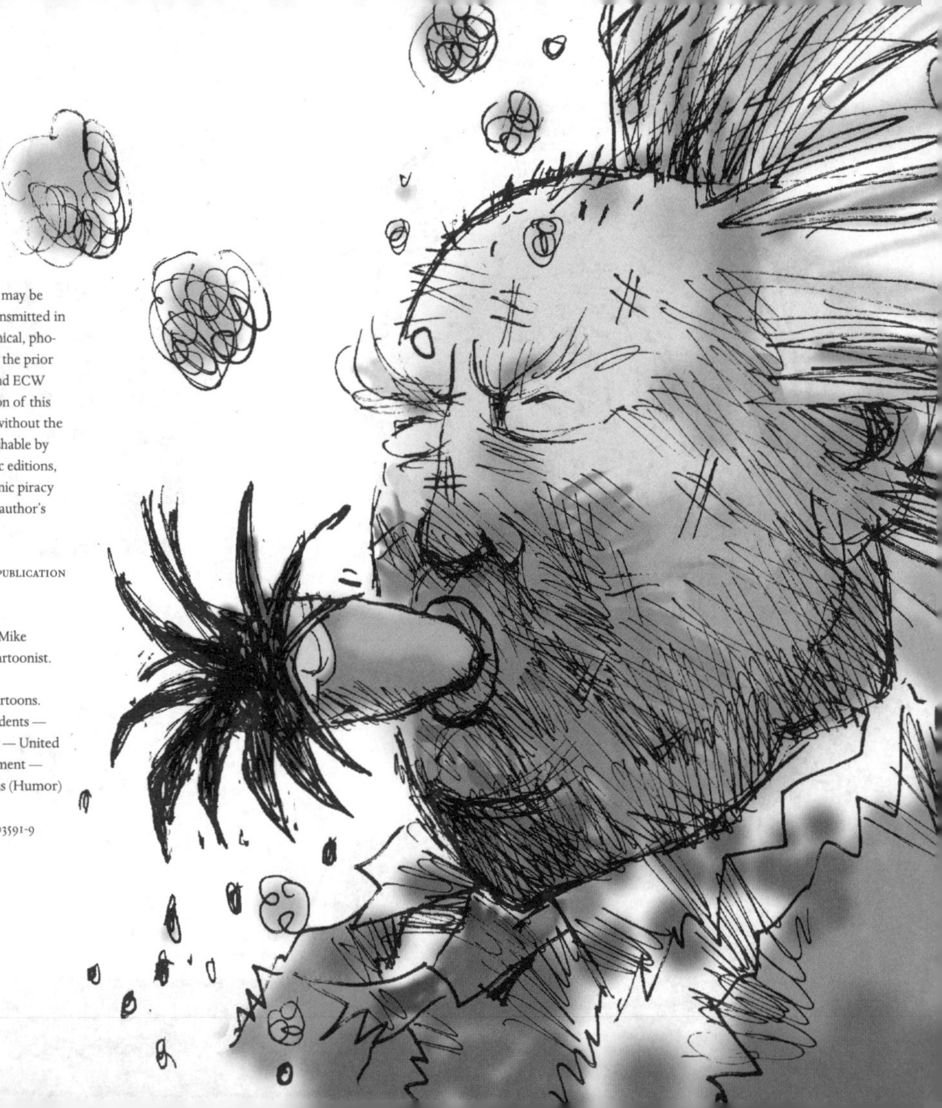

# INTRODUCTION

People come up to me all the time and say, "Boy, with Trump in office, you've got lots of material." To this, I always reply, "Yeah, but it's like being married to a nymphomaniac: fun at first, but it quickly becomes a nightmare." Many friends tell me they've stopped paying attention to the news to distance themselves from Trump's daily deluge of nonsense. As much as I might want to, I can't do that. It's my job to follow everything he says and does. It's actually harder coming up with cartoons now. When Bill Clinton, Barack Obama or even George W. Bush were in office and said or did something I disagreed with, my cartoons would exaggerate their statement or action, making it more absurd in order to mock it. With Trump, his absurdity level is already so off the charts, it's hard to top it in a cartoon.

Here's an example of a typical day dealing with Trump. I arrive at work a little before noon and he's usually already tweeted something irrational like, Cheetos mock me! Lock them up! So, I ask myself: Do I draw a bag of Cheetos working in a chain gang?

Naw. I decide to wait a little while until he says or does something even crazier. I know that as Trump emits more verbal baloney throughout the day, his earlier tweet threatening incarceration of Cheetos will be forgotten. Then later, I'm in my office and receive a breaking news alert: At the White House luncheon, Trump literally poops in the punch bowl! It's still early, and I'm thrilled I've already gotten today's cartoon topic. I start to draw what will assuredly win me a Pulitzer Prize, sketching a large United States–shaped punch bowl, and floating in the middle, labeled "Trump," is a big orange . . . and then there's another breaking news alert: Trump gives the Pope a glass of punch! Bummer, I think, now I have to switch focus to papal hydration.

The three networks plus MSNBC and CNN feature nonstop "Defecategate" coverage. On CNN, Jake Tapper's interviewing presidential historian Michael Beschloss asking, "So, Michael, did Abe Lincoln ever poop in a punch bowl?"

Unsurprisingly, Fox News isn't even mentioning it. Complete silence. Instead, Sean Hannity's railing about Bill and Hillary Clinton being in a love triangle with a Nazi dwarf.

The next day, as readers open their papers or check their devices, they see most of America's cartoonists have drawn a bald eagle with a tear in its eye as it watches the Pope consume punch, except for the few conservative cartoonists who've drawn bald eagles with tears in their eyes perched on bedposts, watching Bill and Hillary cavorting in the sheets with a torch-carrying, *Sieg Heil*–shouting dwarf.

 **Donald J. Trump**
@realDonaldTrump

# OMG,
# HE'S RUNNING!

| RETWEETS | LIKES |
|----------|-------|
| 3,582 | 9,935 |

↰ 1.7K  ⇄ 3.6K  ♡ 99K ...

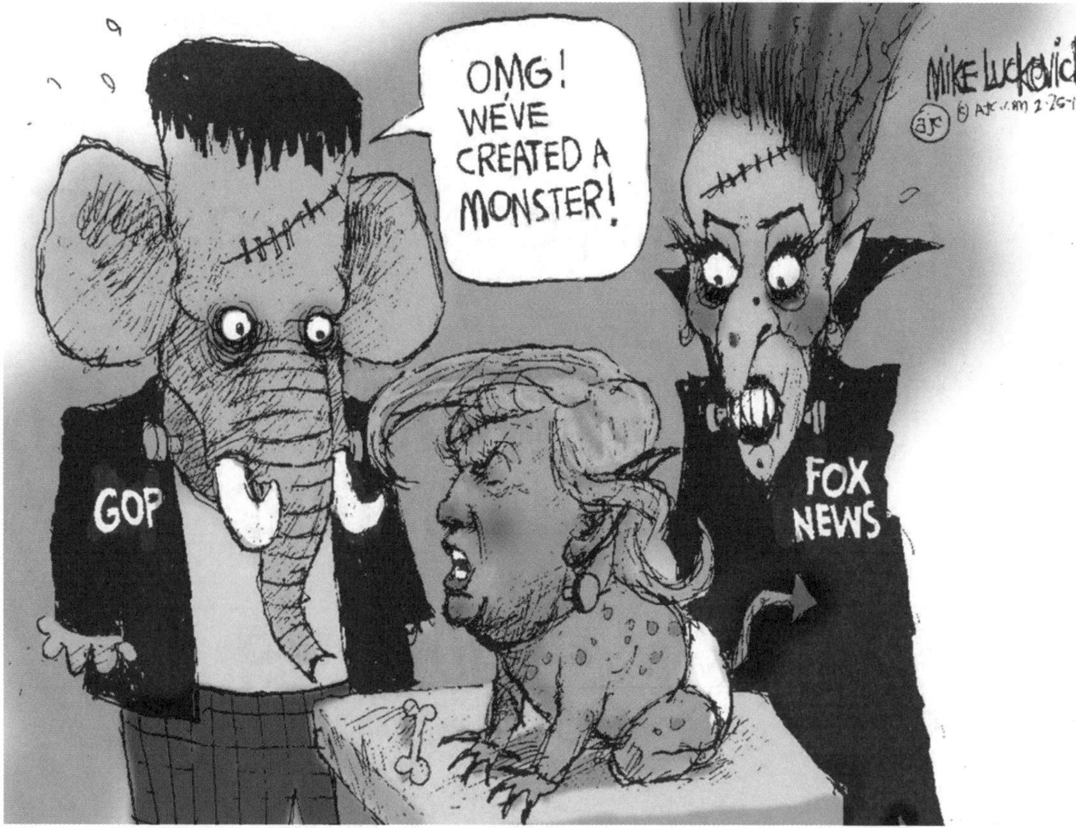
OMG! WE'VE CREATED A MONSTER!
MIKE LUCKOVICH
GOP
FOX NEWS

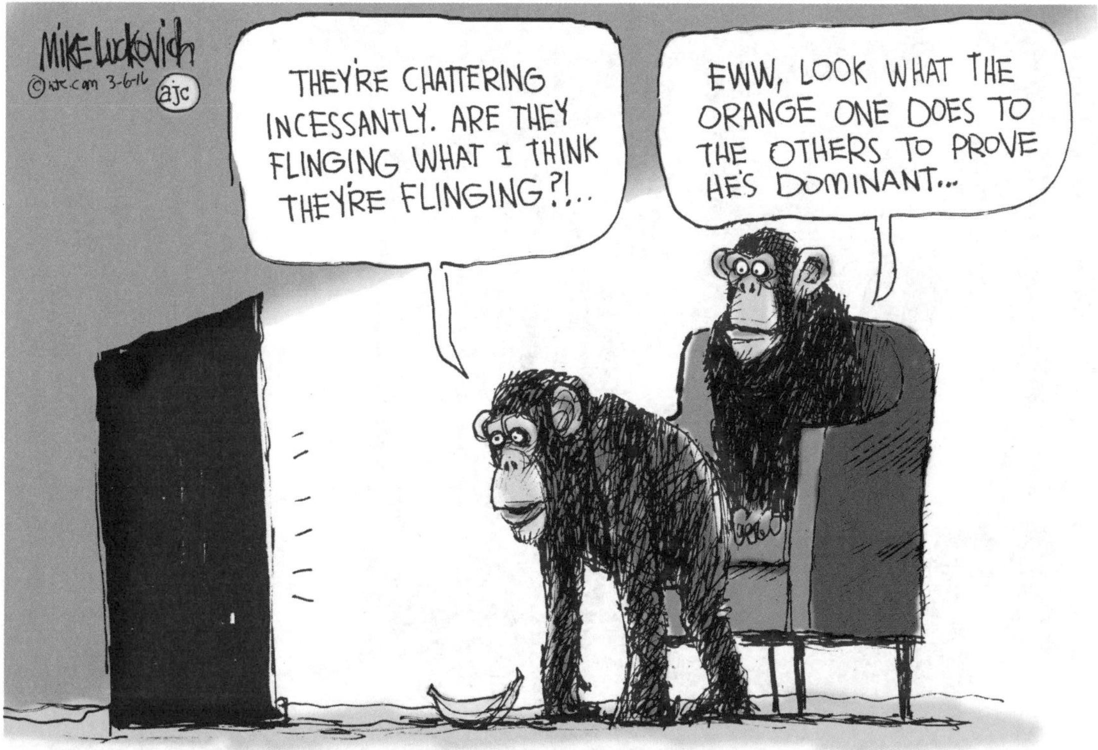
MIKE LUCKOVICH
©ajc.com 3-6-16
ajc
THEY'RE CHATTERING INCESSANTLY. ARE THEY FLINGING WHAT I THINK THEY'RE FLINGING?!...
EWW, LOOK WHAT THE ORANGE ONE DOES TO THE OTHERS TO PROVE HE'S DOMINANT...

WATCHING THE REPUBLICAN DEBATE

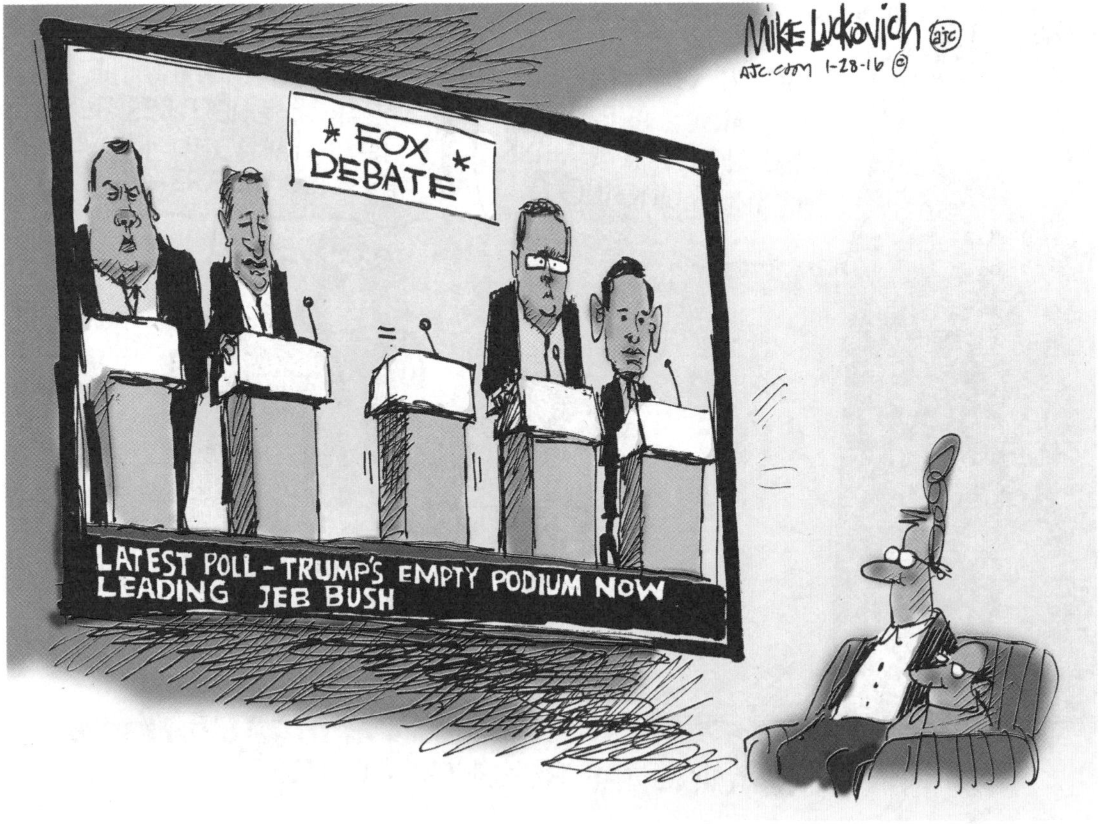
MIKE LUCKOVICH ajc
AJC.com 1-28-16 ©
* FOX DEBATE *
LATEST POLL - TRUMP'S EMPTY PODIUM NOW LEADING JEB BUSH

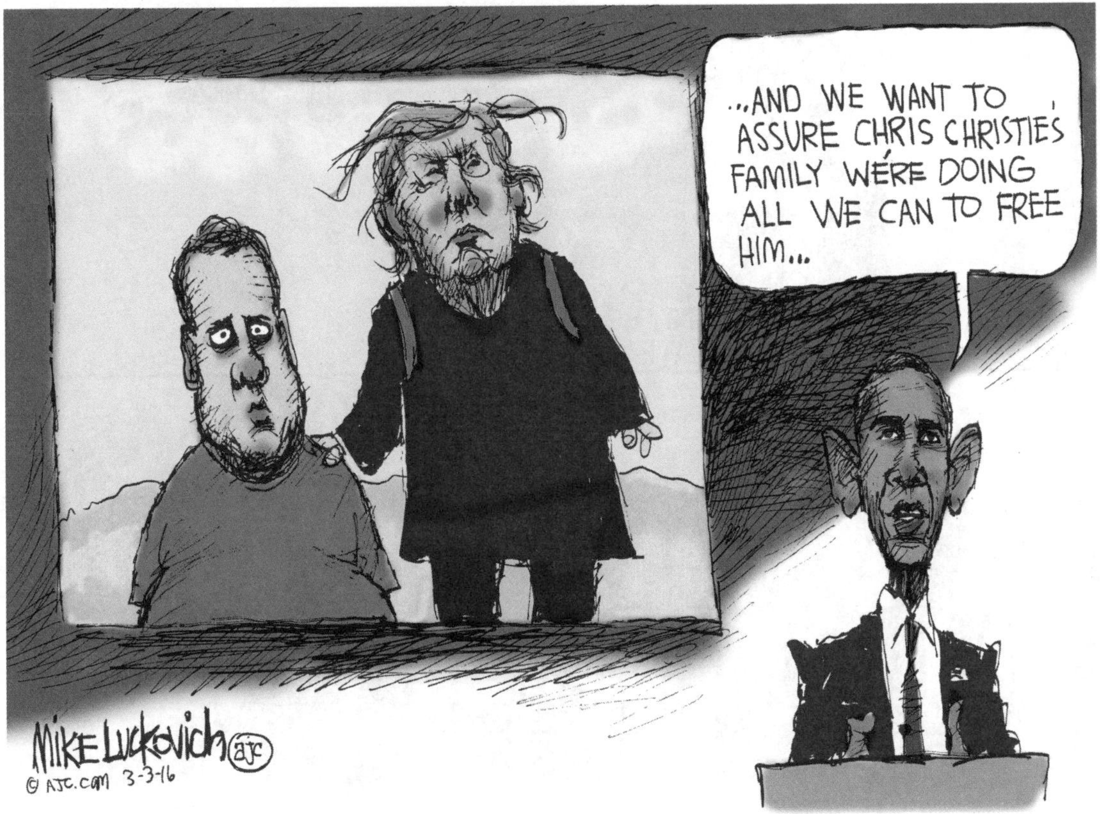
...AND WE WANT TO ASSURE CHRIS CHRISTIE'S FAMILY WE'RE DOING ALL WE CAN TO FREE HIM...
MIKE LUCKOVICH ajc
© AJC.com 3-3-16

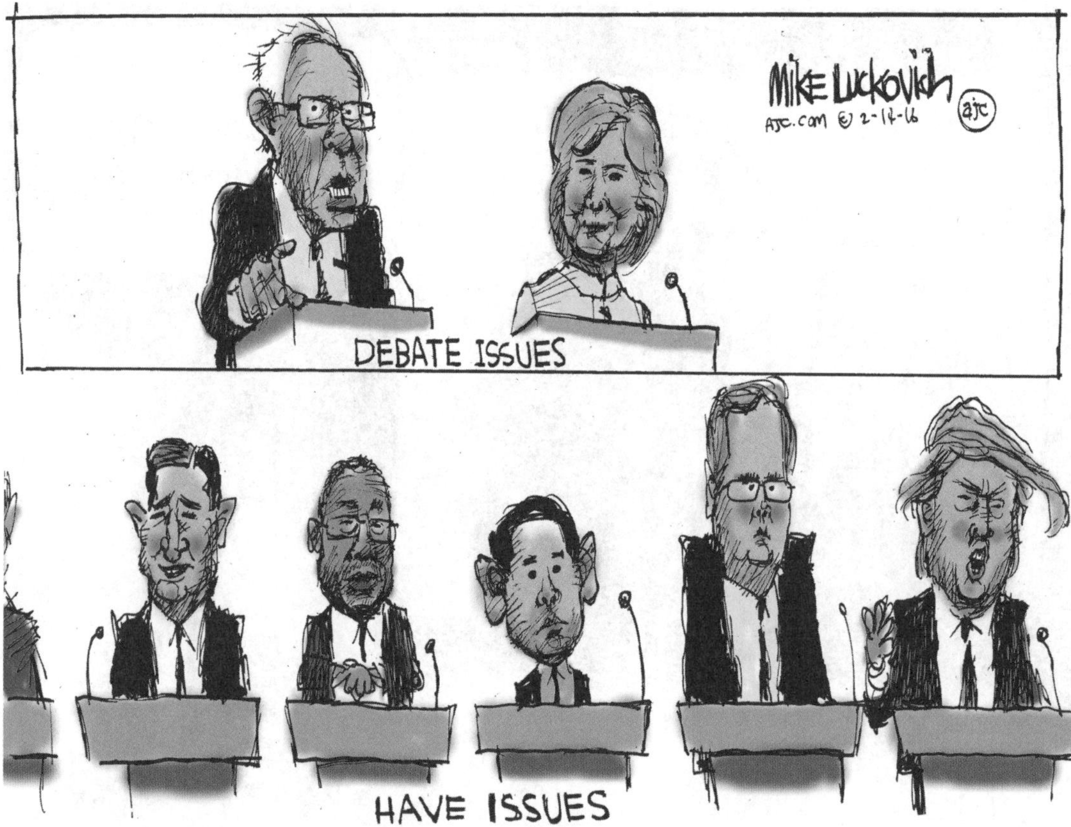
MIKE LUCKOVICH
AJC.com © 2-14-16
ajc
DEBATE ISSUES
HAVE ISSUES

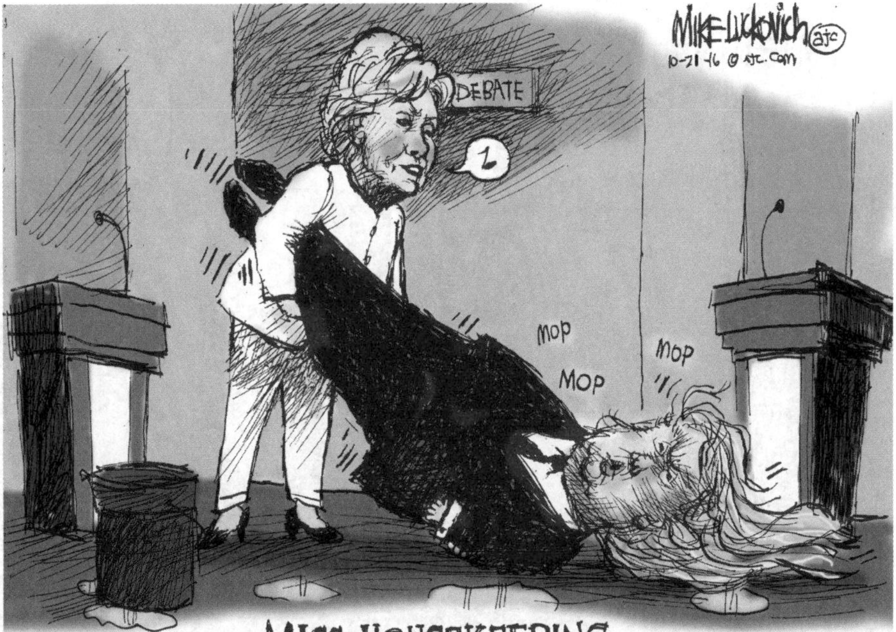
MIKE LUCKOVICH ajc
10-21-16 © ajc.com
DEBATE
MOP
MOP
MOP

MISS HOUSEKEEPING

After former beauty queen Alicia Machado, an avid Hillary supporter, threatened to write about Trump's bad behavior, he mocked her weight gain and her Hispanic heritage, calling her "Miss Piggy" and "Miss Housekeeping." I drew this after Hillary mopped the floor with him during the debates.

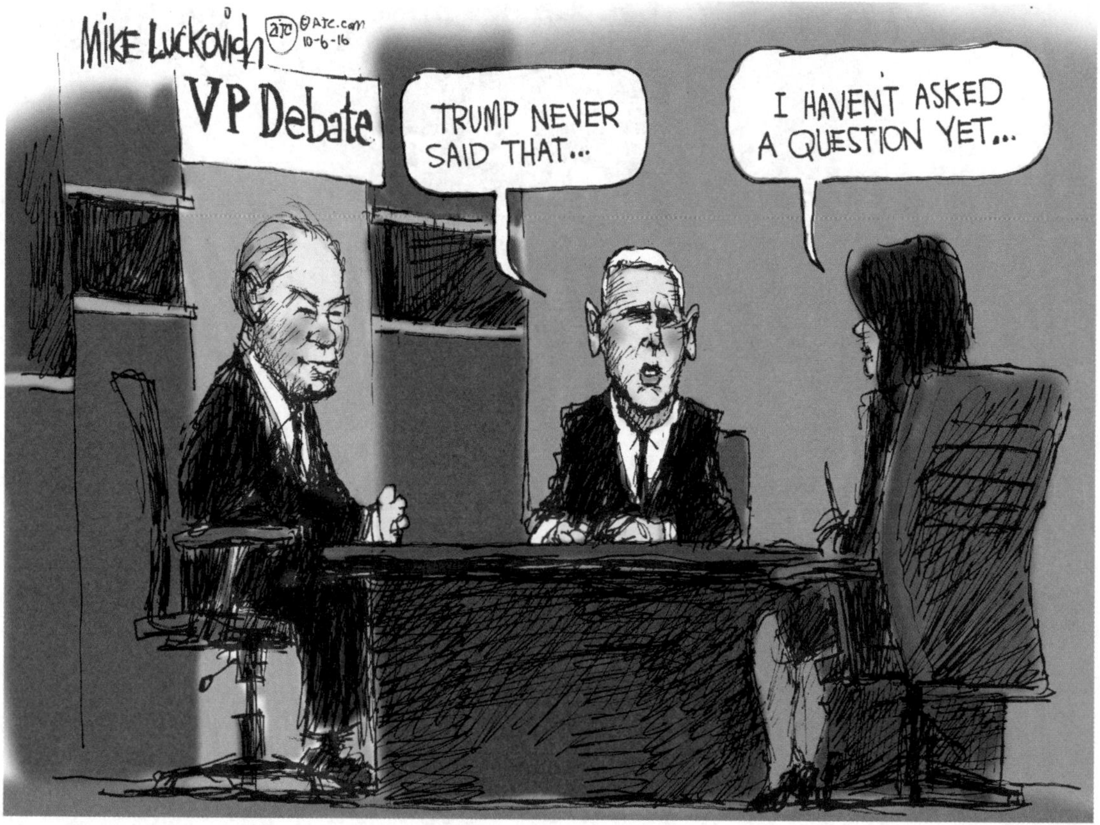
MIKE LUCKOVICH
ajc ©AJC.com 10-6-16
VP Debate
TRUMP NEVER SAID THAT...
I HAVENT ASKED A QUESTION YET...

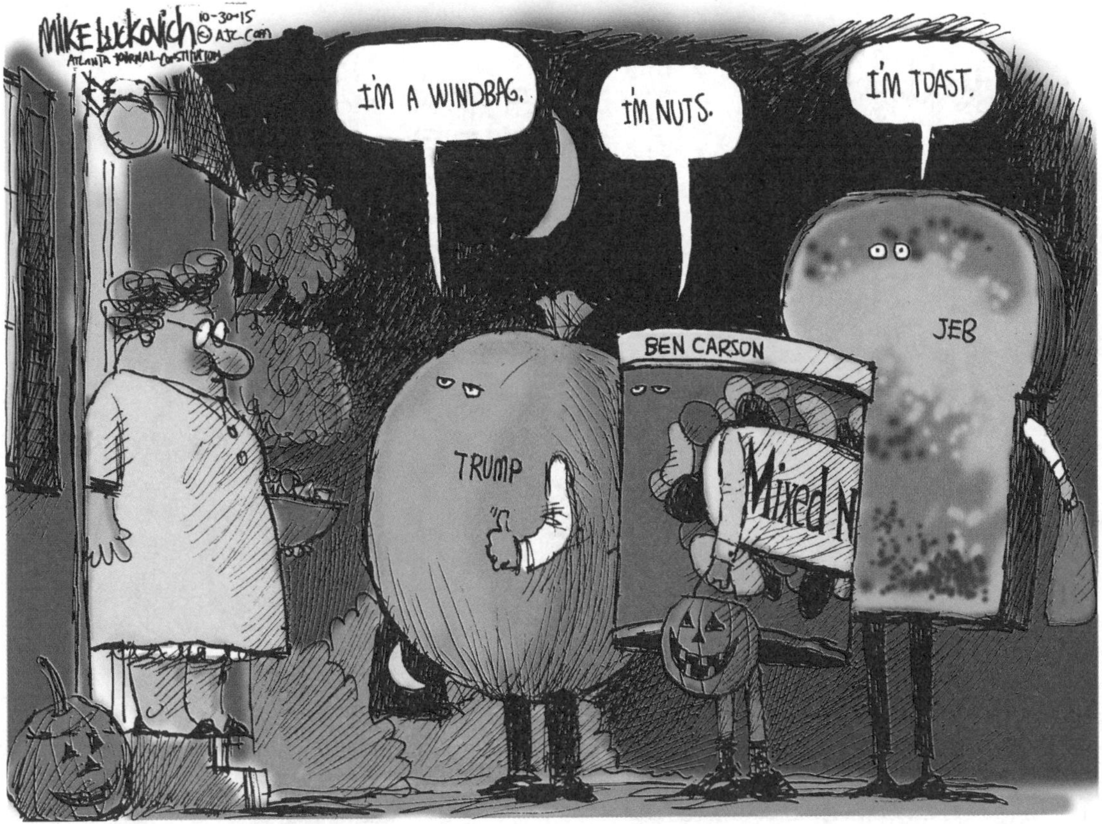
MIKE LUCKOVICH
10-30-15
© AJC.com
ATLANTA JOURNAL-CONSTITUTION
I'M A WINDBAG.
I'M NUTS.
I'M TOAST.
TRUMP
BEN CARSON
Mixed N
JEB

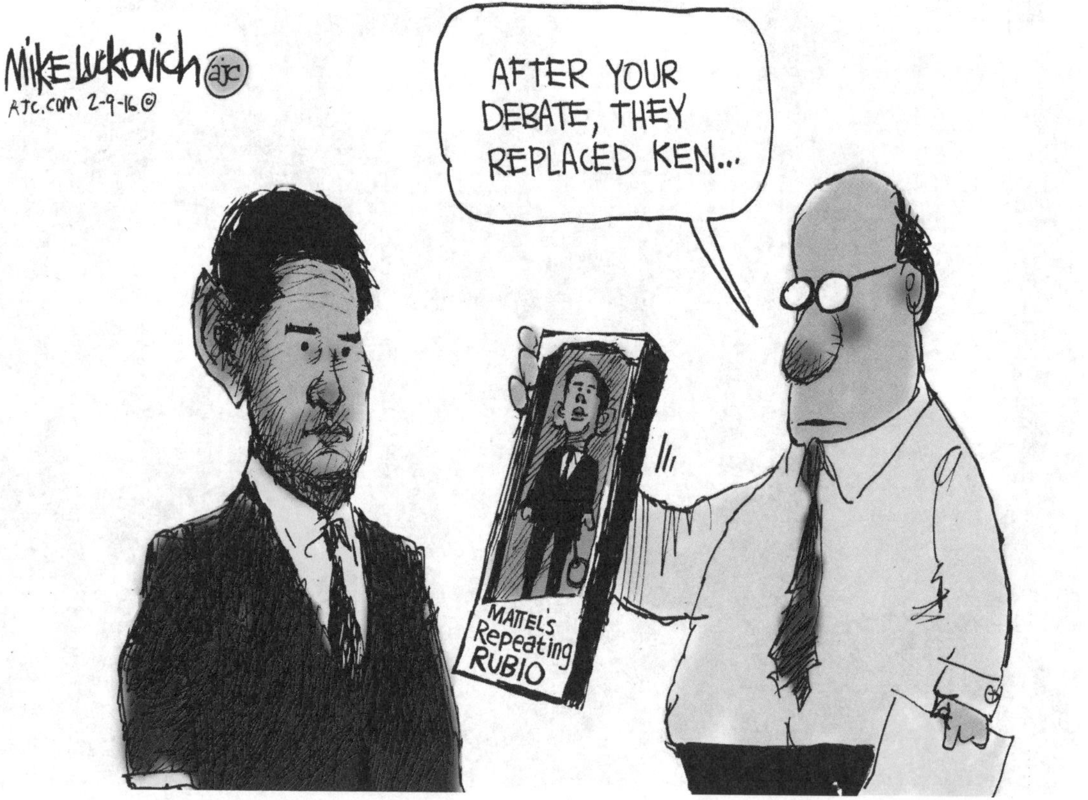
MIKE LUCKOVICH ajc
AJC.com 2-9-16 ©
AFTER YOUR DEBATE, THEY REPLACED KEN...
MATTEL'S Repeating RUBIO

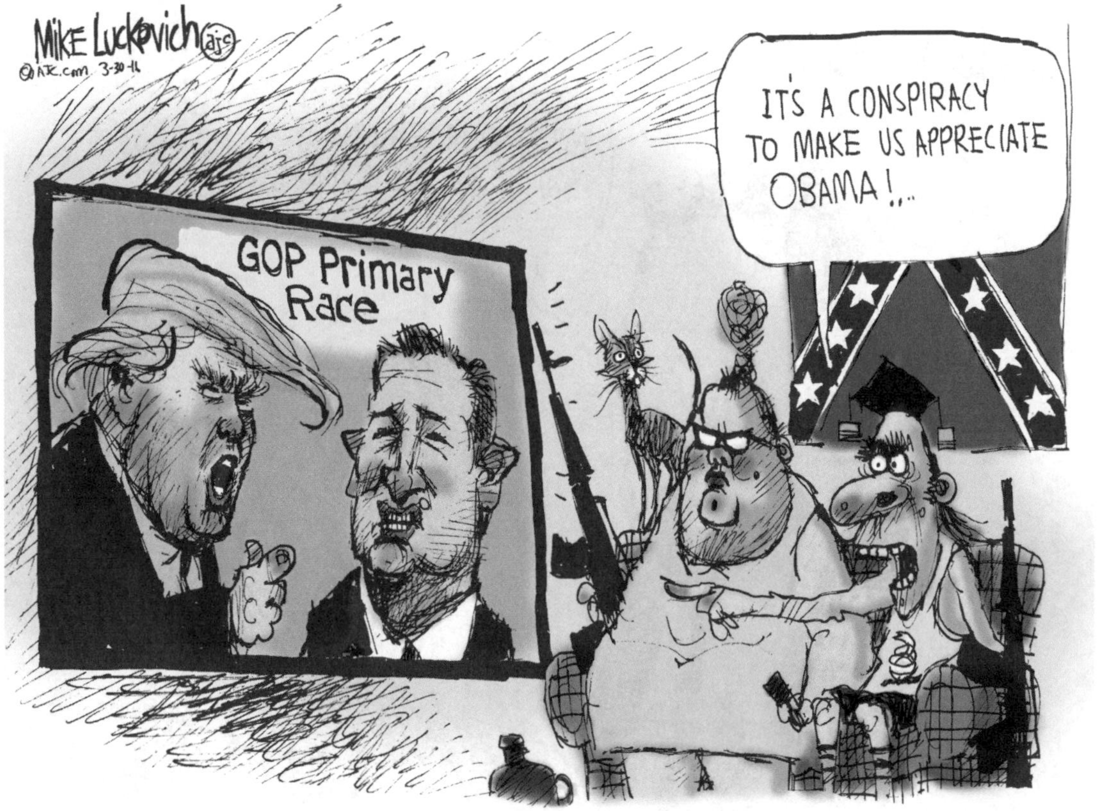
MIKE LUCKOVICH
©AJC.com 3-30-16
GOP Primary Race
IT'S A CONSPIRACY TO MAKE US APPRECIATE OBAMA!...

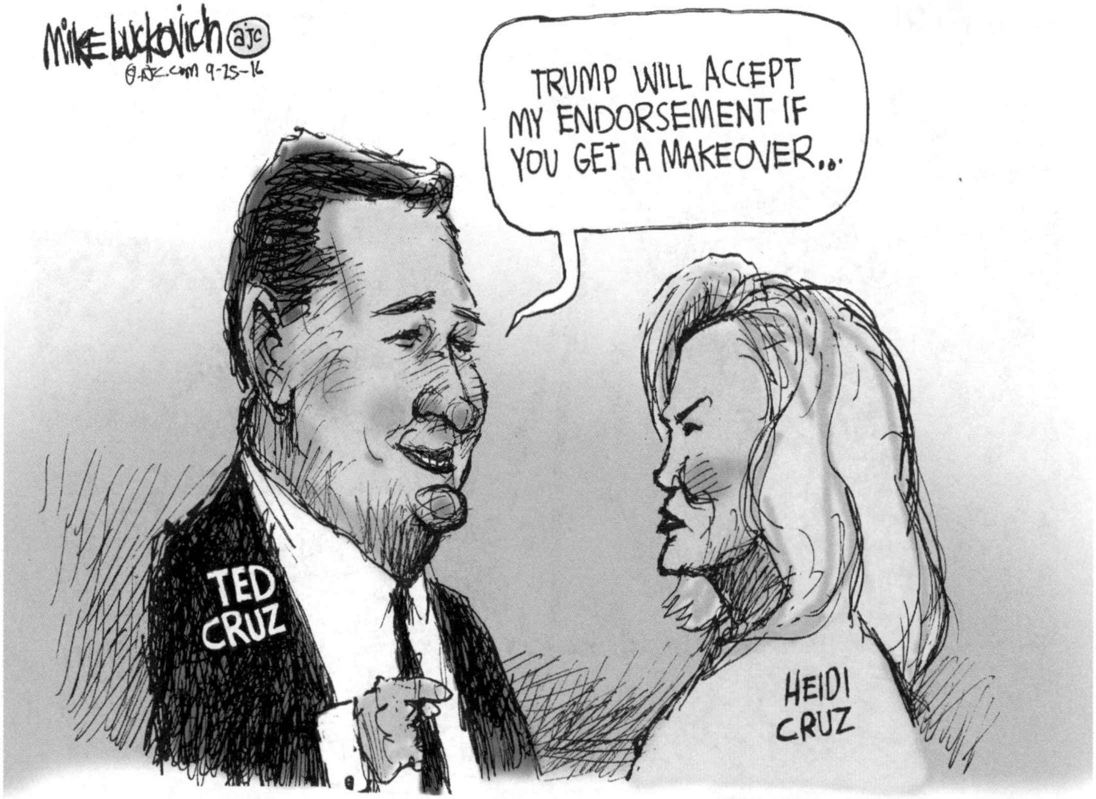
MIKE LUCKOVICH ajc
TRUMP WILL ACCEPT MY ENDORSEMENT IF YOU GET A MAKEOVER...
TED CRUZ
HEIDI CRUZ

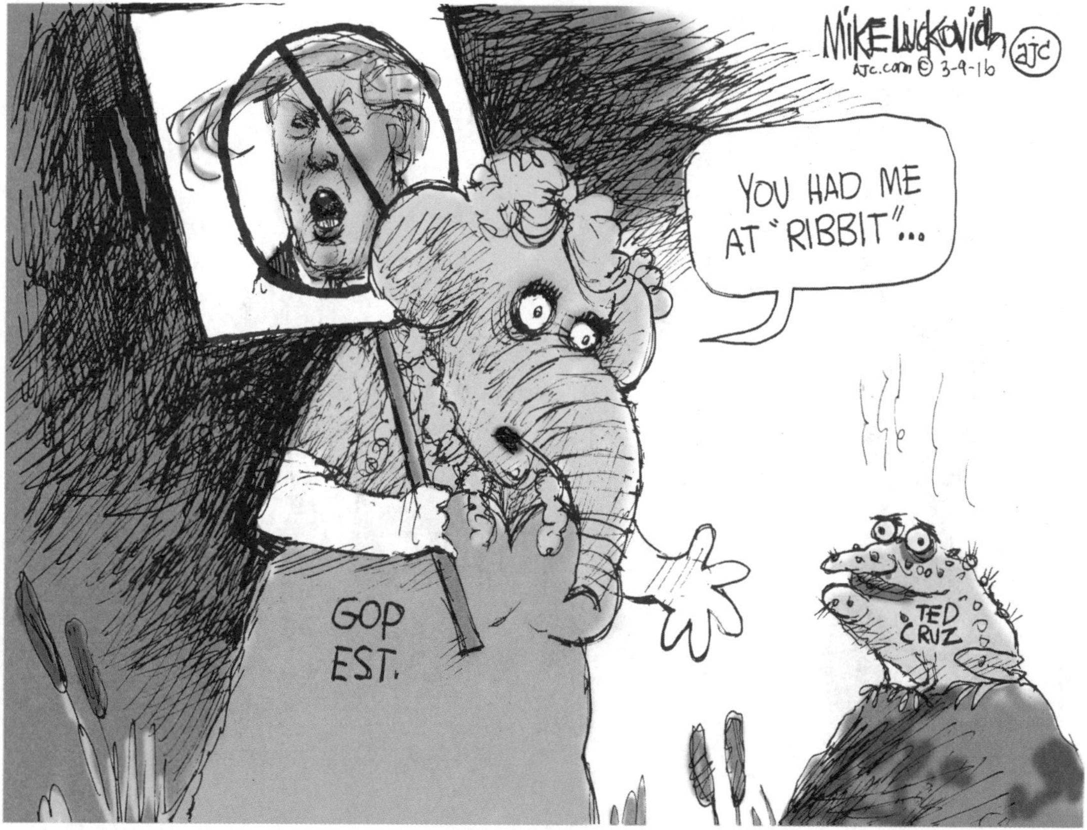
MIKE LUCKOVICH
AJC.com © 3-9-16
ajc
YOU HAD ME AT "RIBBIT"...
GOP EST.
TED CRUZ

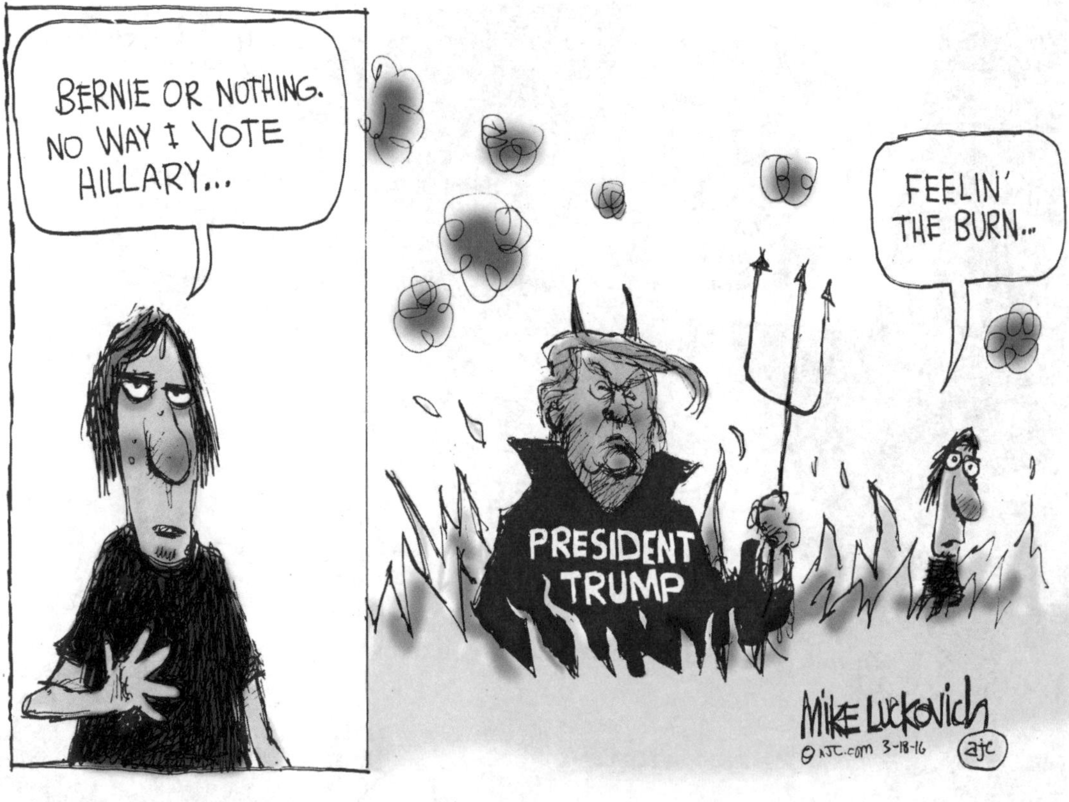
BERNIE OR NOTHING. NO WAY I VOTE HILLARY...
PRESIDENT TRUMP
FEELIN' THE BURN...
MIKE LUCKOVICH
©AJC.com 3-18-16
ajc

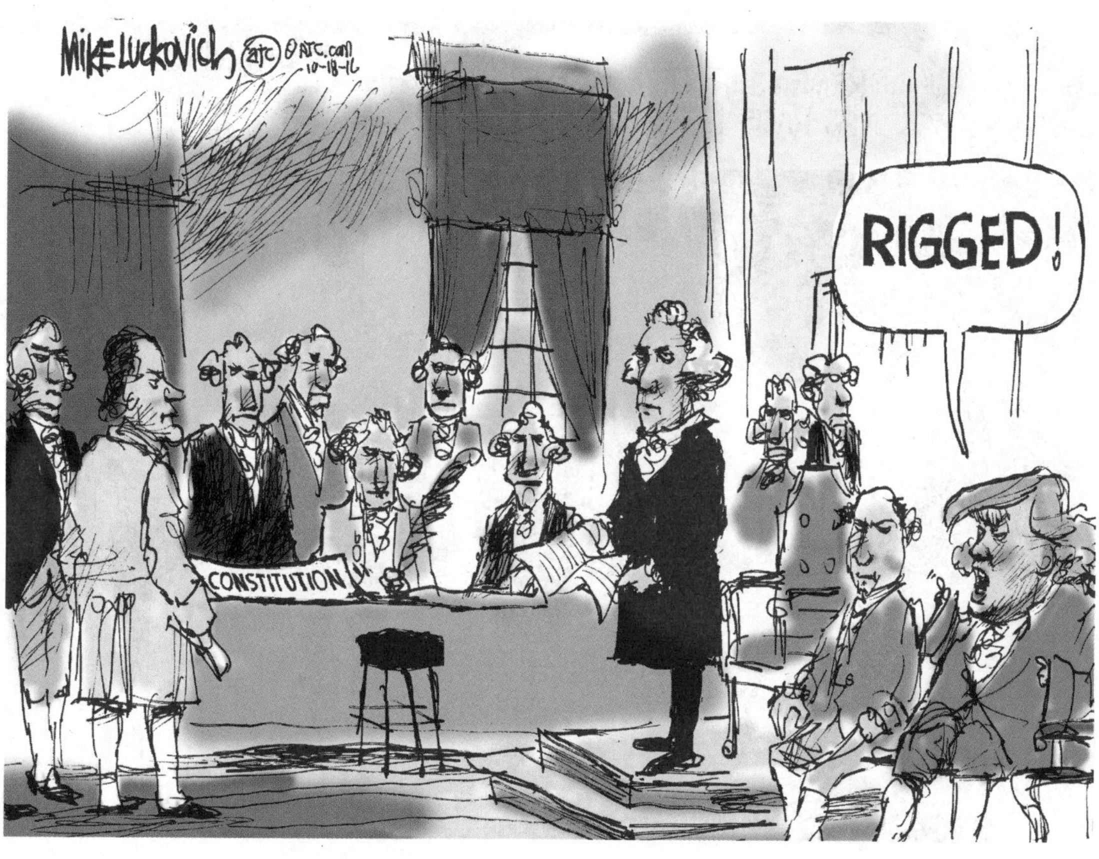
MIKE LUCKOVICH
ajc
©AJC.com
10-18-16
RIGGED!
CONSTITUTION

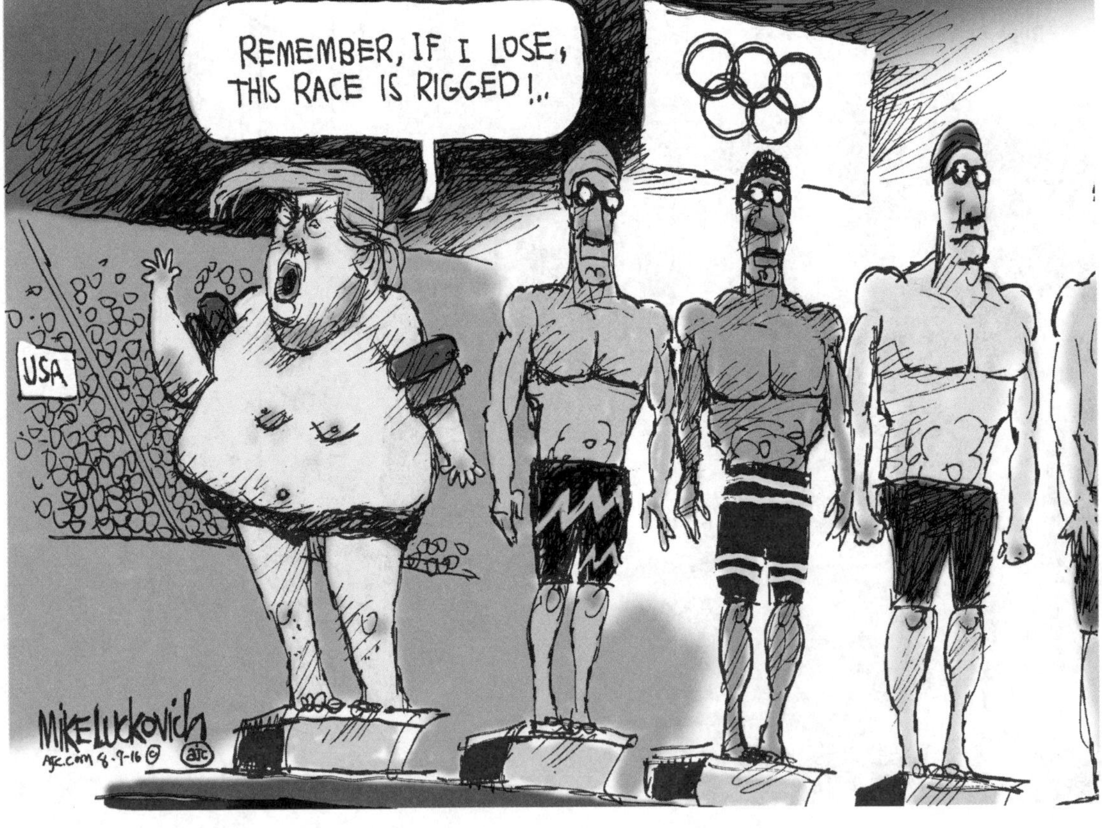
REMEMBER, IF I LOSE, THIS RACE IS RIGGED!..
USA
MIKE LUCKOVICH
ajc.com 8-9-16 ©
ajc

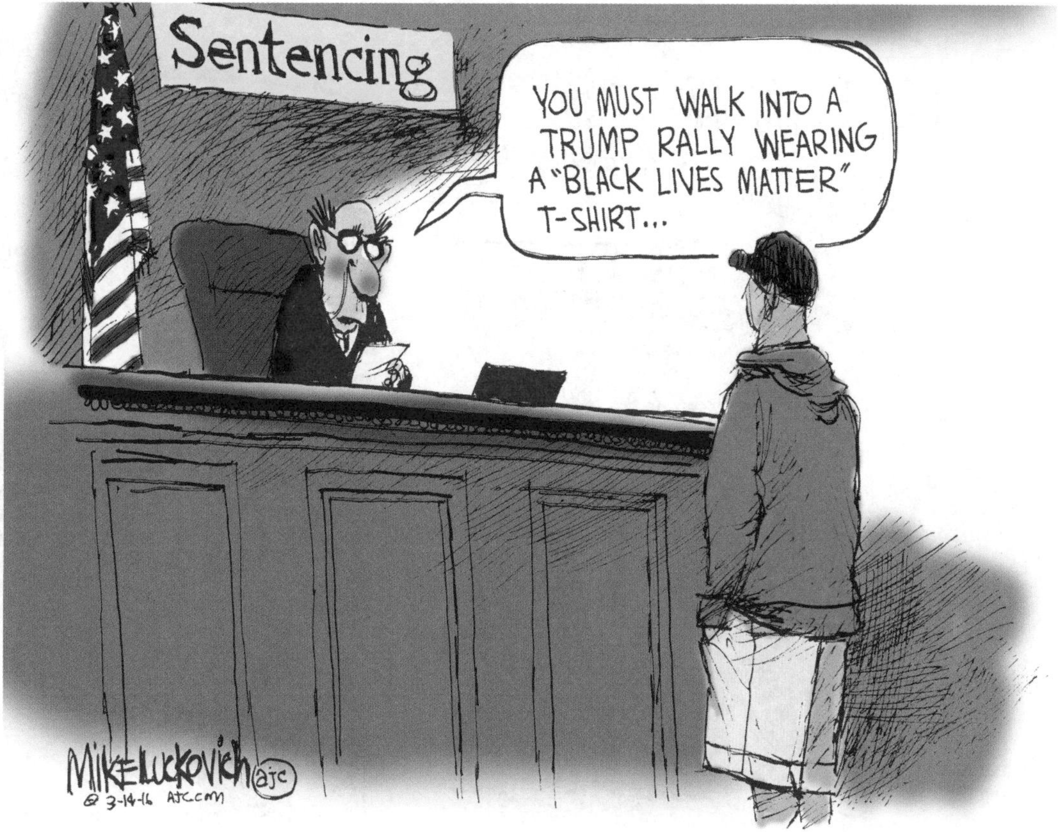
Sentencing
YOU MUST WALK INTO A TRUMP RALLY WEARING A "BLACK LIVES MATTER" T-SHIRT...
MIKELUCKOVICH ajc
© 3-14-16 AJC.com

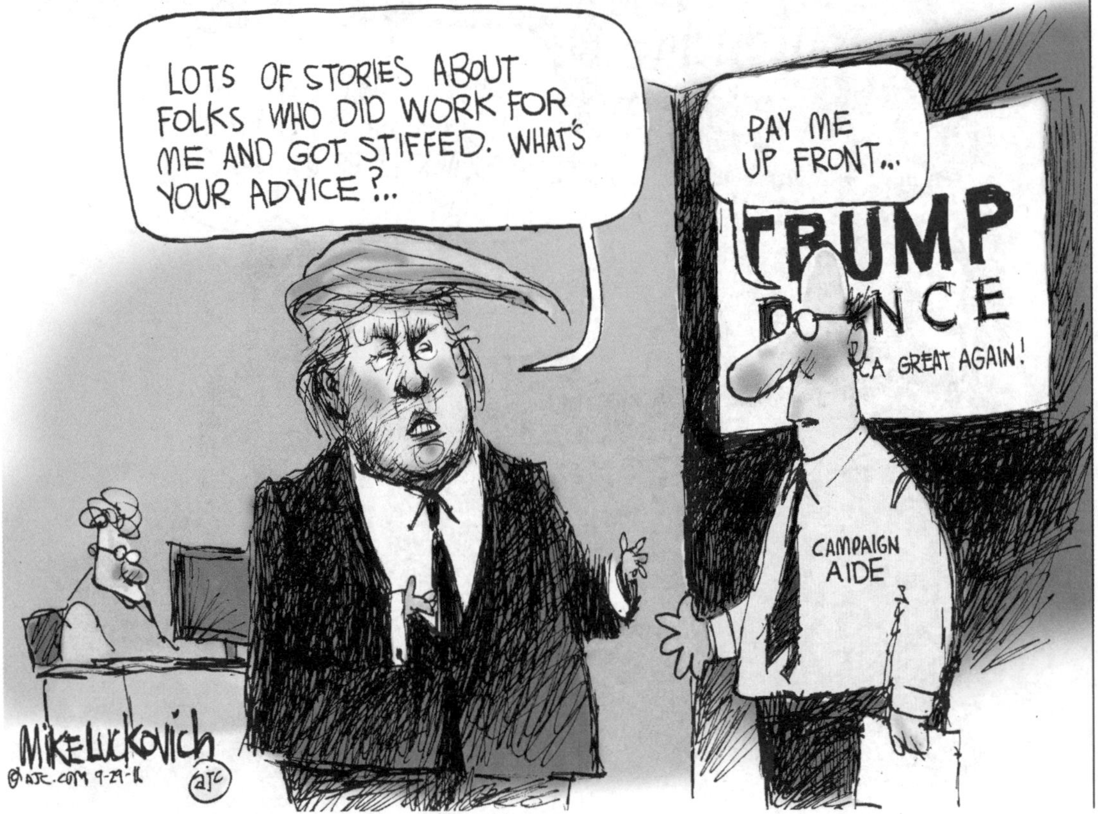
LOTS OF STORIES ABOUT FOLKS WHO DID WORK FOR ME AND GOT STIFFED. WHAT'S YOUR ADVICE?..
PAY ME UP FRONT...
TRUMP
CA GREAT AGAIN!
CAMPAIGN AIDE
MIKE LUCKOVICH
©AJC.COM 9-29-16
ajc

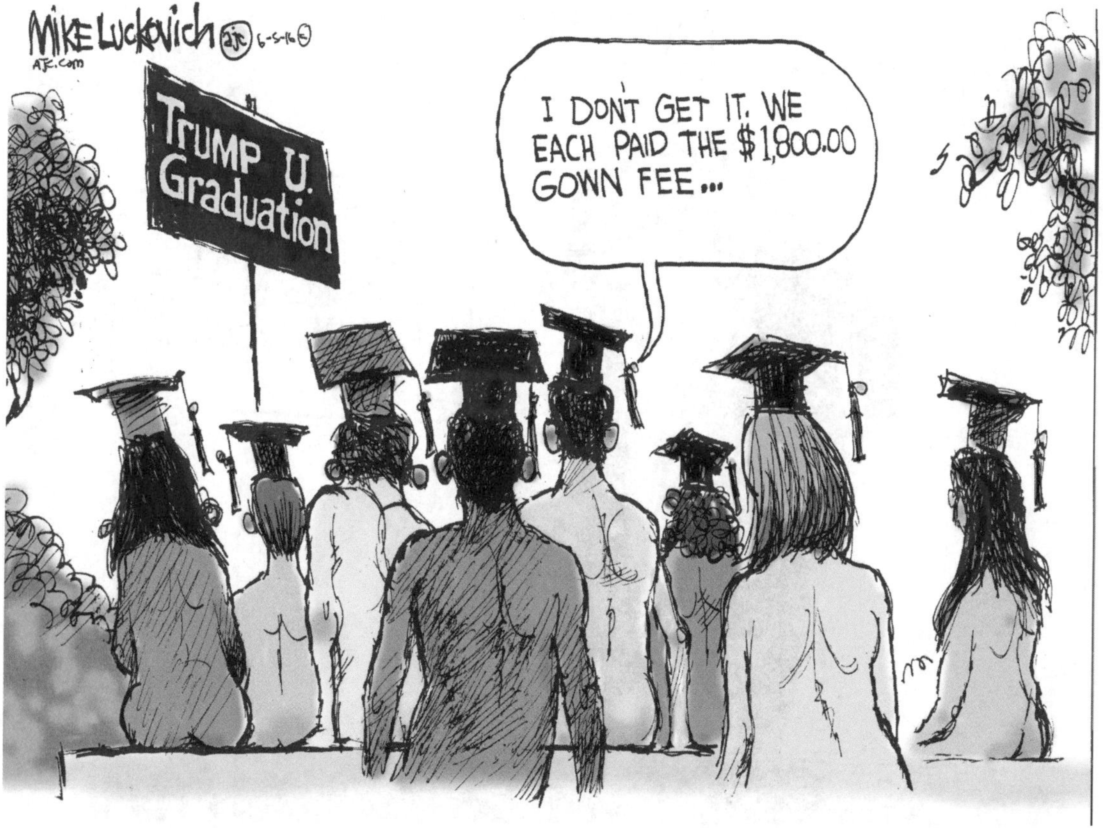
MIKE LUCKOVICH AJC 6-5-16
AJC.com
Trump U.
Graduation
I DON'T GET IT. WE EACH PAID THE $1,800.00 GOWN FEE...

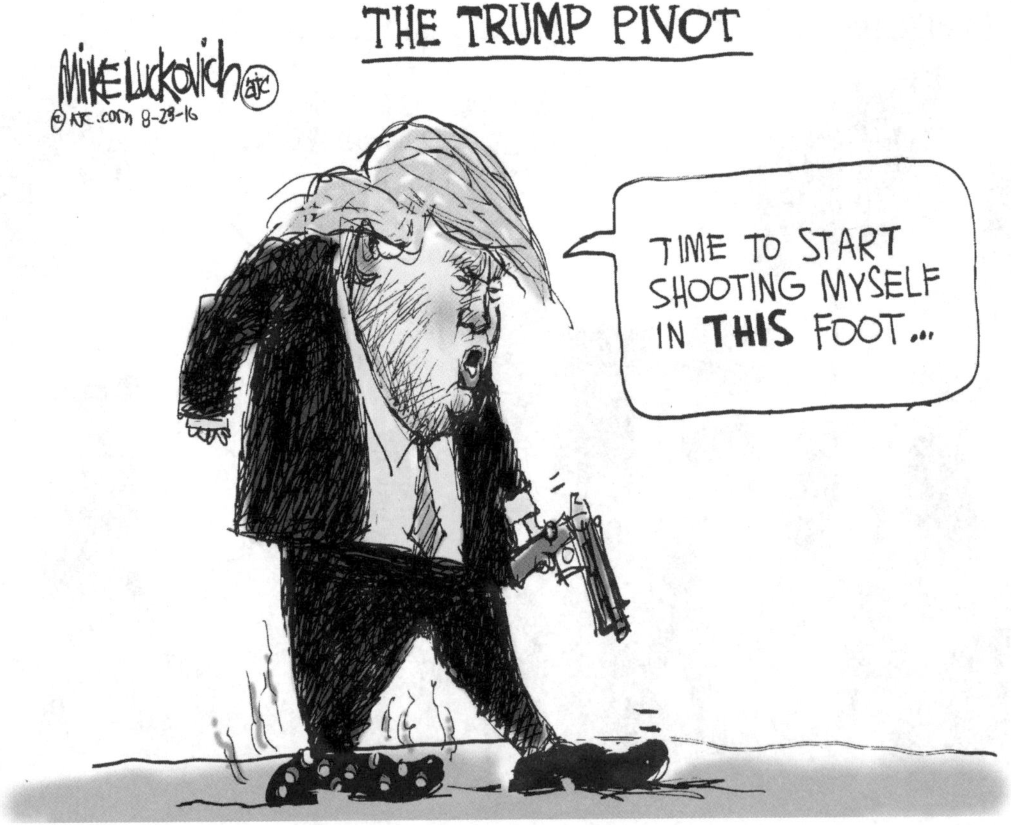
THE TRUMP PIVOT
MIKE LUCKOVICH ajc
© AJC.com 8-28-16
TIME TO START SHOOTING MYSELF IN THIS FOOT...

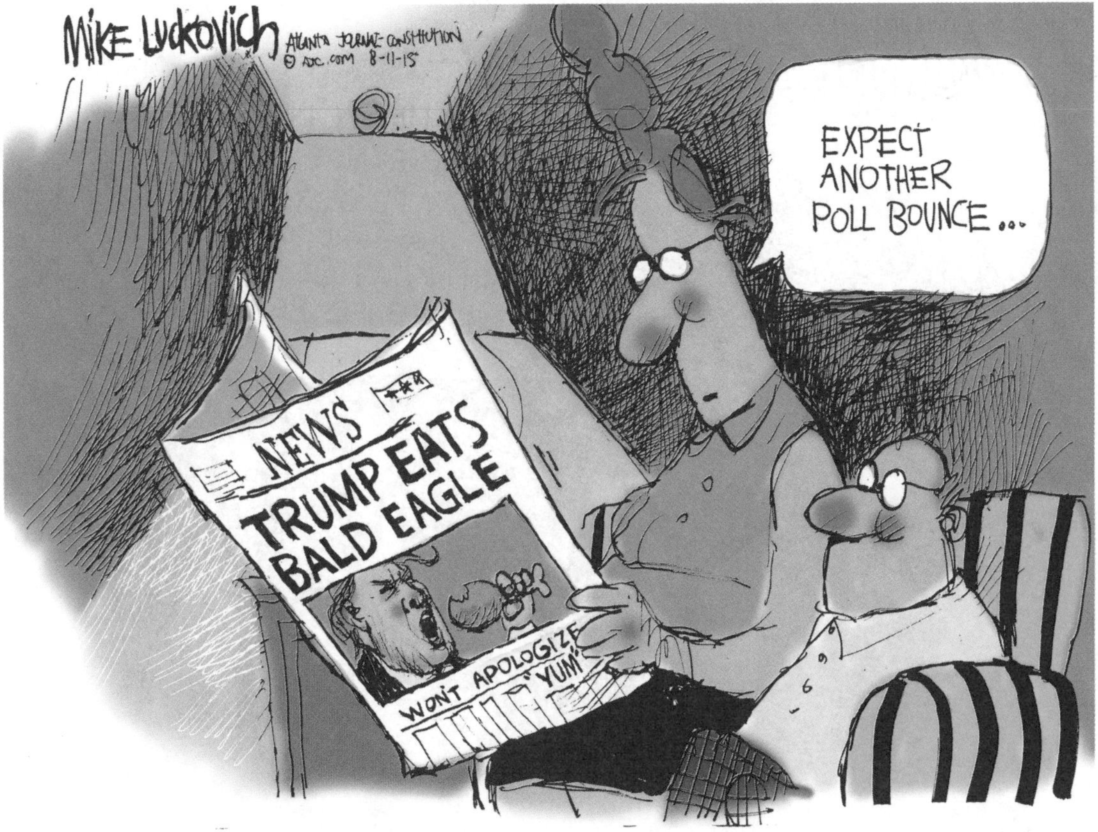
MIKE LUCKOVICH
ATLANTA JOURNAL-CONSTITUTION
© AJC.COM 8-11-15
EXPECT ANOTHER POLL BOUNCE...
NEWS
TRUMP EATS BALD EAGLE
WON'T APOLOGIZE
"YUM"

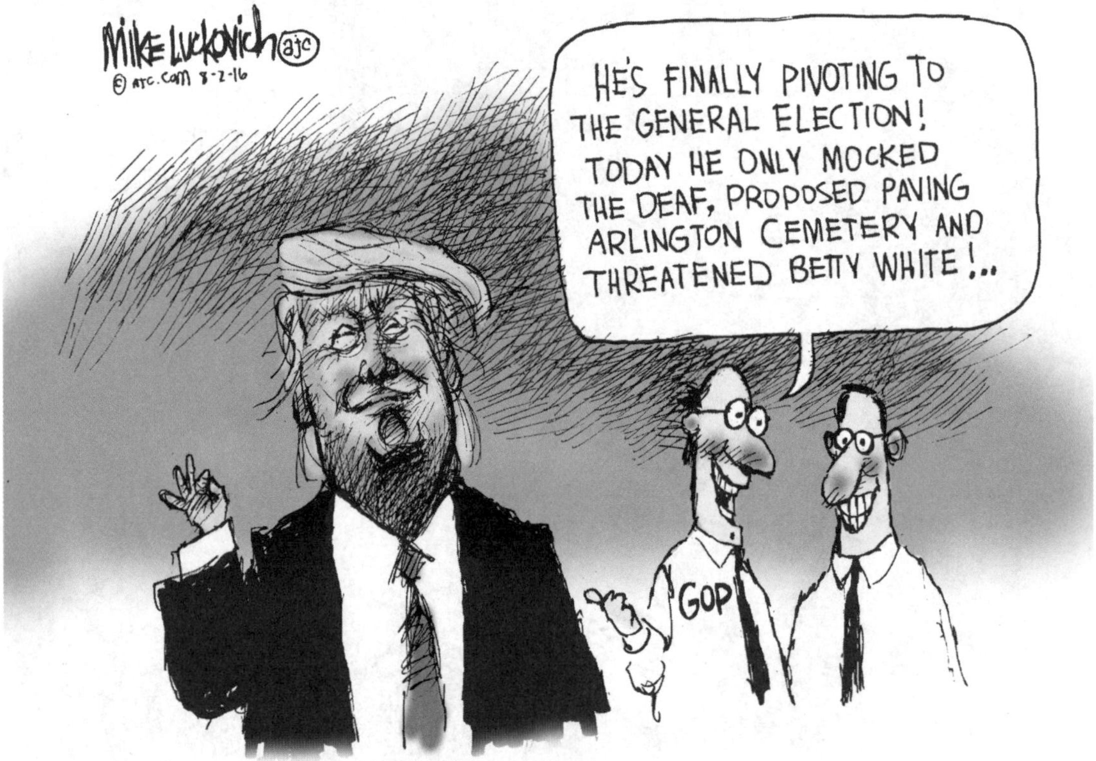
MIKE LUCKOVICH ajc
© AJC.com 8-2-16
HE'S FINALLY PIVOTING TO THE GENERAL ELECTION! TODAY HE ONLY MOCKED THE DEAF, PROPOSED PAVING ARLINGTON CEMETERY AND THREATENED BETTY WHITE!..
GOP

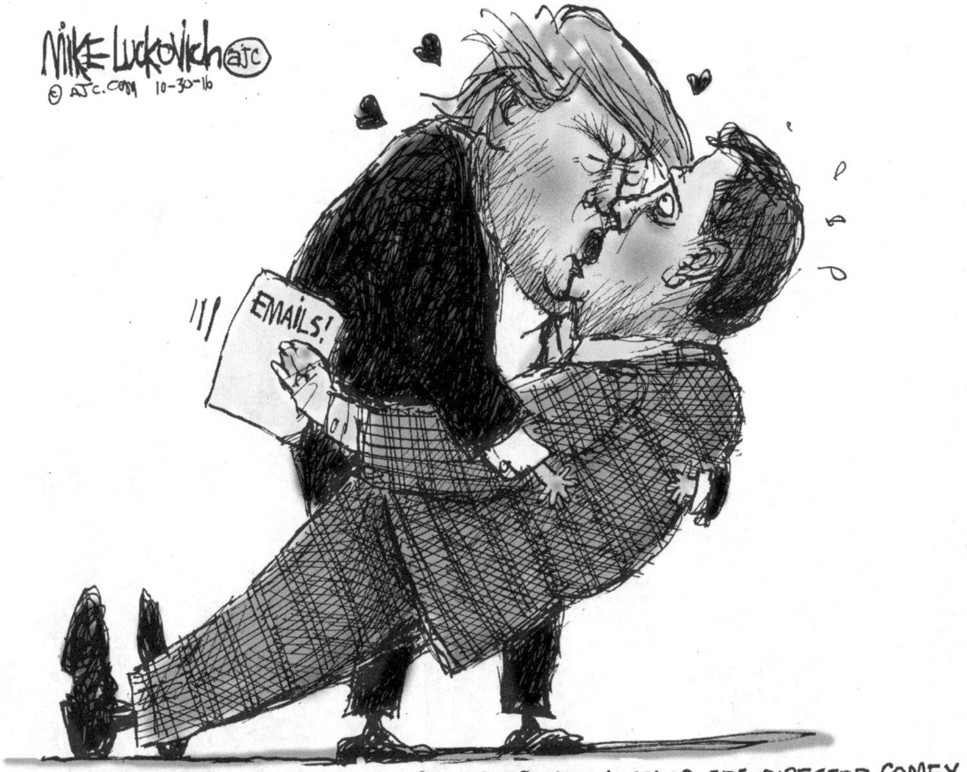
MIKE LUCKOVICH AJC
© AJC.COM 10-30-16
EMAILS!

NEW VIDEO SURFACES OF TRUMP GRABBING AND KISSING FBI DIRECTOR COMEY.

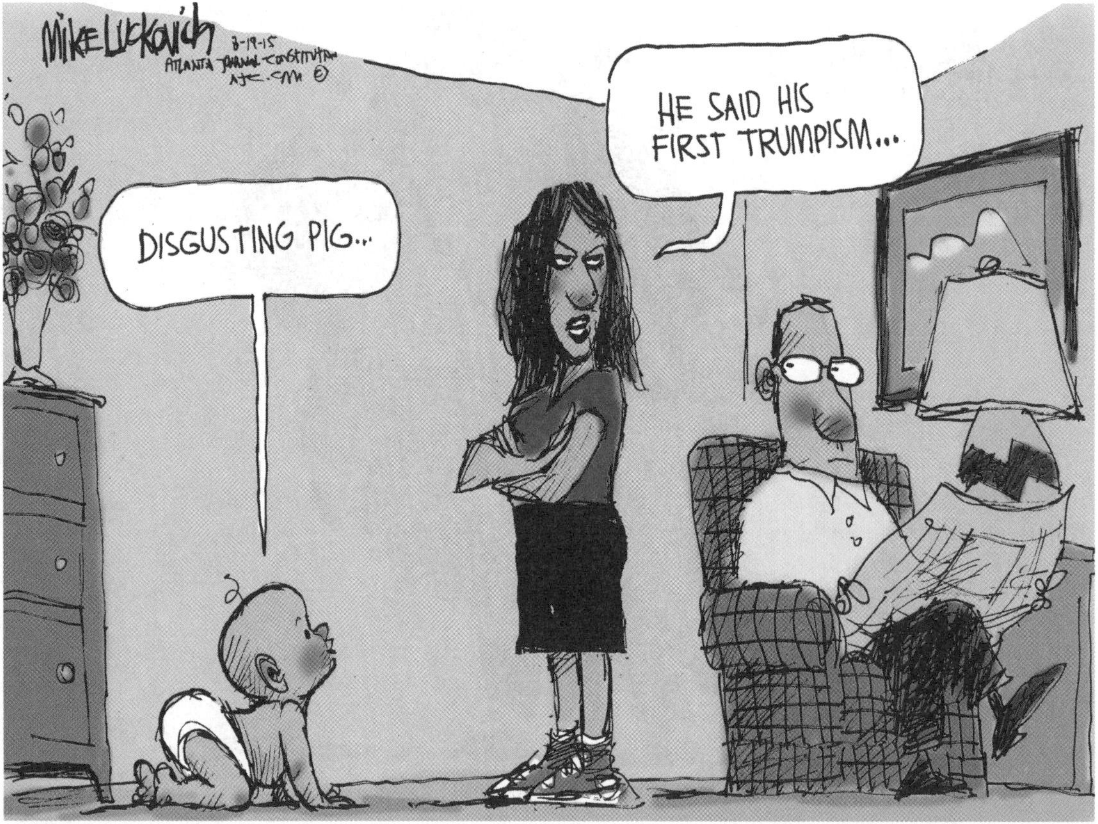
Mike Luckovich
8-19-15
Atlanta Journal-Constitution
AJC.com ©
HE SAID HIS FIRST TRUMPISM...
DISGUSTING PIG...

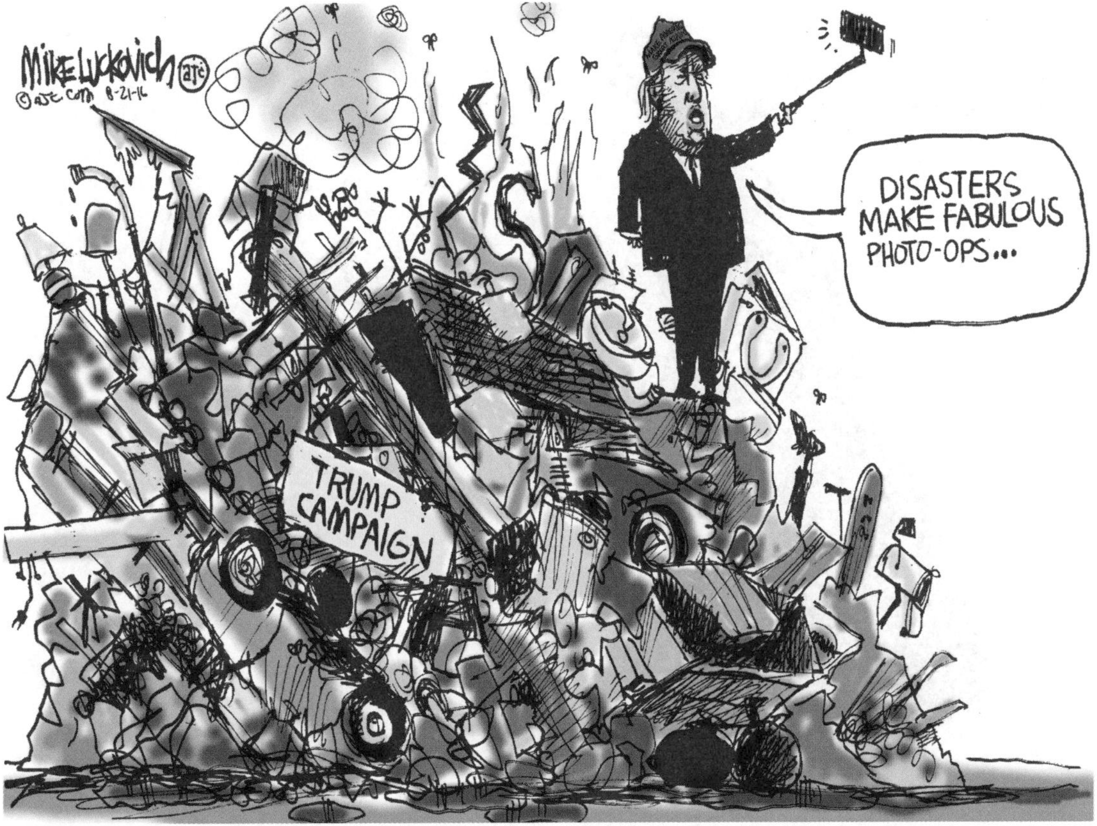
MIKE LUCKOVICH
© ajc.com 8-21-16
DISASTERS MAKE FABULOUS PHOTO-OPS...
TRUMP CAMPAIGN

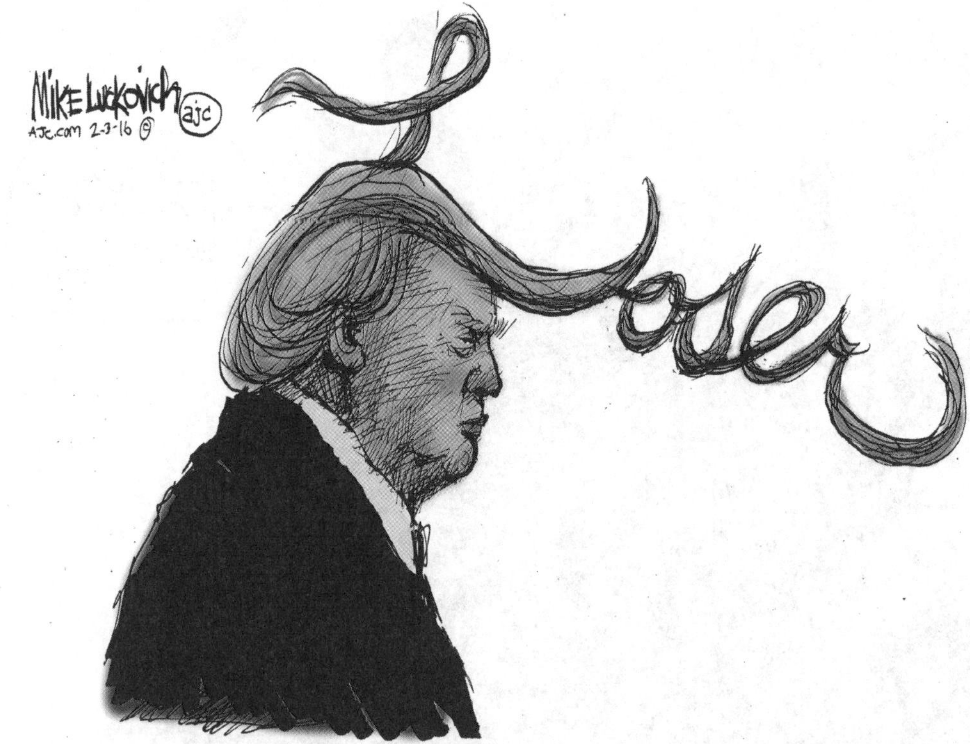
MIKE LUCKOVICH
ajc
AJC.com 2-3-16 ©
Loser

I drew this after Trump lost the Iowa Caucus vote to Ted Cruz by a large margin.

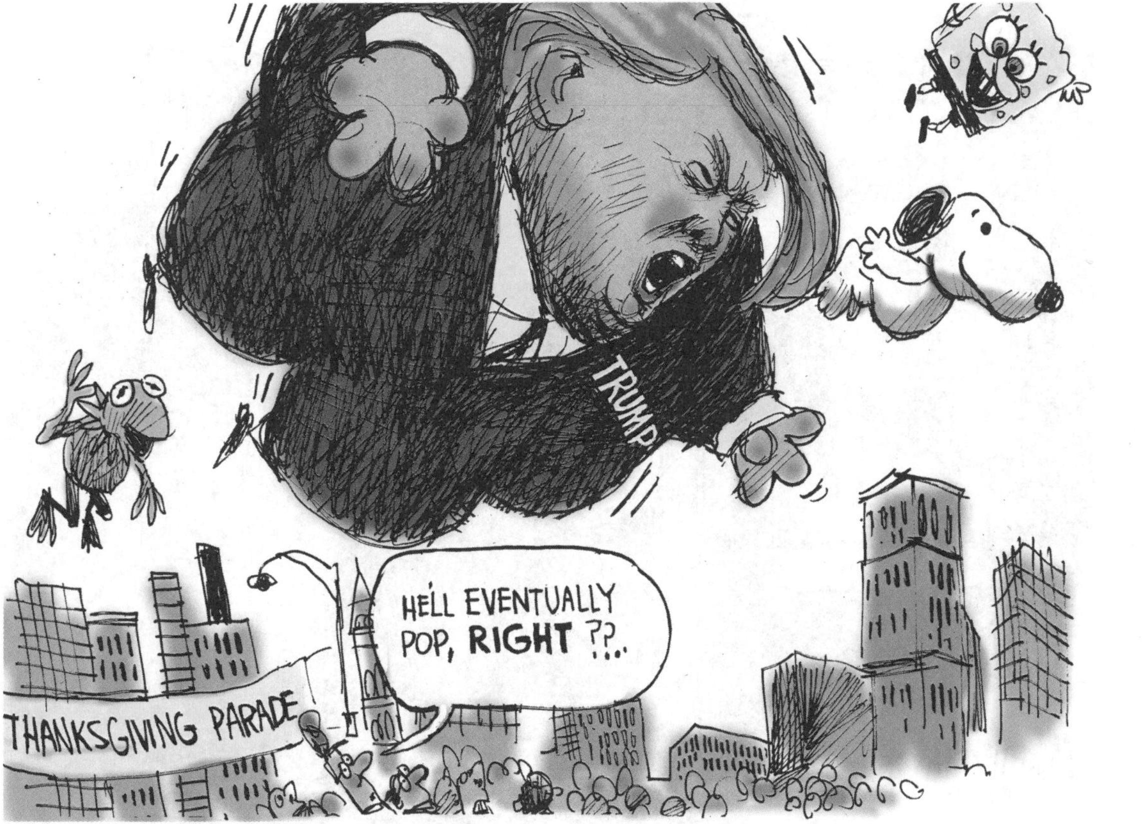
TRUMP
HE'LL EVENTUALLY POP, RIGHT ??..
THANKSGIVING PARADE

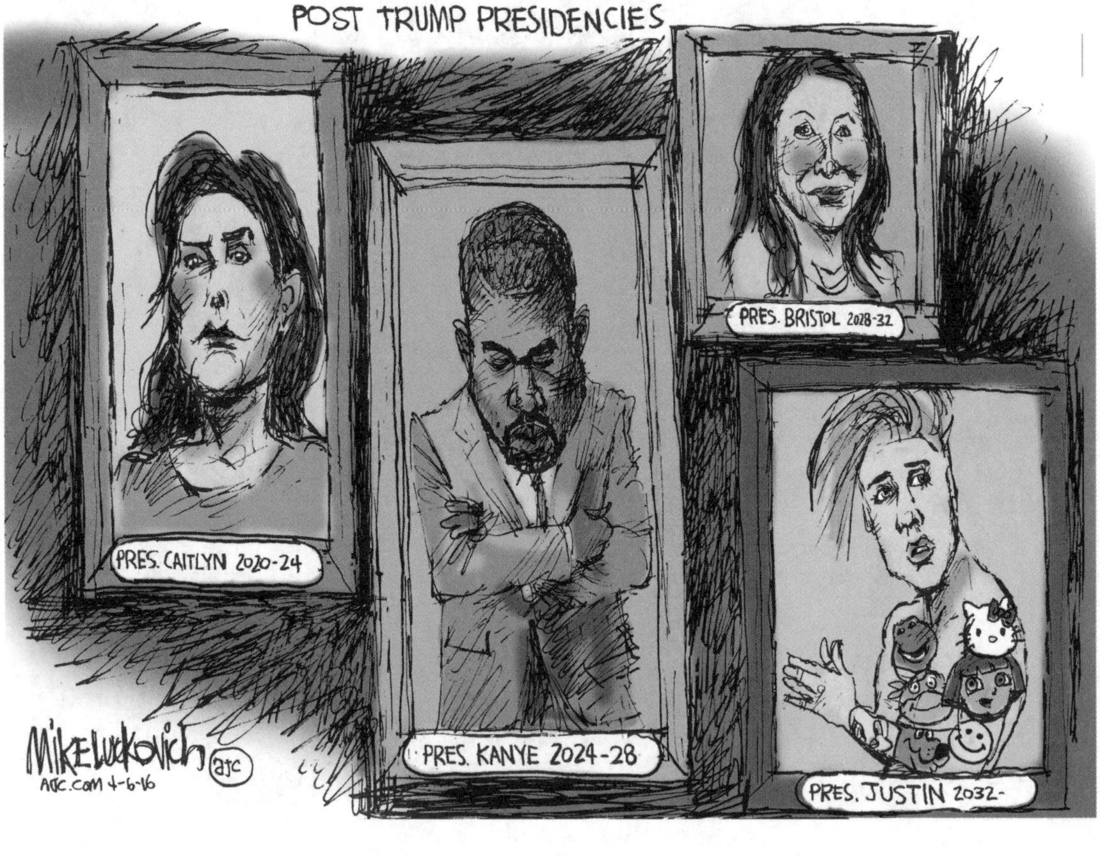
POST TRUMP PRESIDENCIES
PRES. CAITLYN 2020-24
PRES. KANYE 2024-28
PRES. BRISTOL 2028-32
PRES. JUSTIN 2032-
MIKELUCKOVICH
ajc
AJC.COM 4-6-16

This is one of my favorite Trump cartoons. I did this during the campaign when it was apparent Trump had authoritarian tendencies and, like Hitler, looked for scapegoats he could vilify — Trump's being African-Americans, Muslims and Mexicans. I like this drawing because it conveys my fears in a simple yet unsettling way. Trump is testing American democracy's guardrails. He's like one of those dinosaurs in *Jurassic Park*, constantly probing the electric fence for weaknesses. Thankfully, Trumpasaurus rex is an idiot with a short attention span. I'm hopeful our form of government survives this and that we Americans take voting seriously to prevent empowering a new demagogue who may not be so stupid.

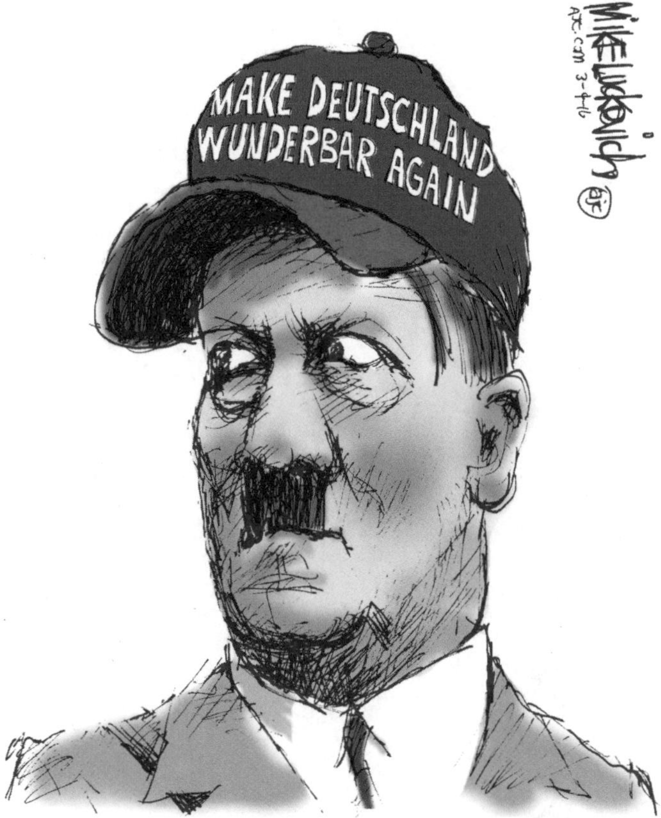
MAKE DEUTSCHLAND
WUNDERBAR AGAIN

 **Donald J. Trump**
@realDonaldTrump

# OMG,
# HE WON!

---

| RETWEETS | LIKES |  |
|----------|-------|--|
| 3,582 | 9,935 | |

↑ 1.7K  ⇄ 3.6K  ♥ 9.9K  •••

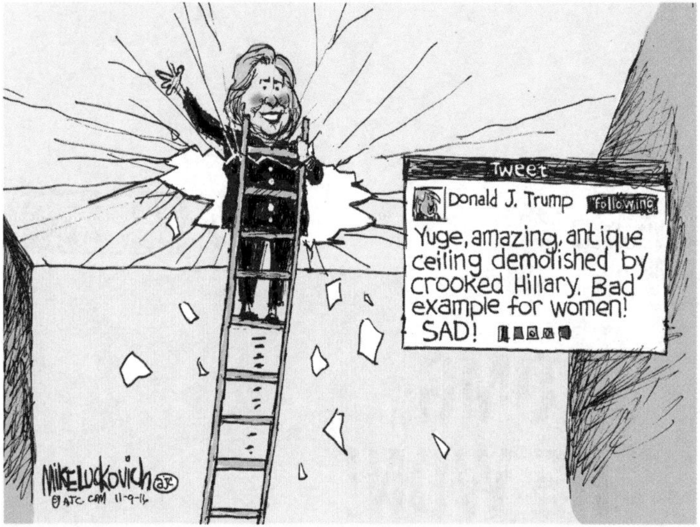
Tweet
Donald J. Trump
Following
Yuge, amazing, antique ceiling demolished by crooked Hillary. Bad example for women! SAD!
MIKELUCKOVICH

On election night, I was nervous about the prospect of a Trump presidency but hopeful Hillary would win. The polls confirmed she would. I was still at the office around 7 p.m., so I drew this cartoon of Hillary breaking the glass ceiling as Trump tweeted nonsense about his election loss. Then I went home to watch the results. At first everything looked good, but as the night wore on, it became obvious things were headed south. At 9:30 p.m., I turned to my wife and numbly told her that I might need to redraw my cartoon. As the results rolled in, I headed back to the office with a growing sense of dread.

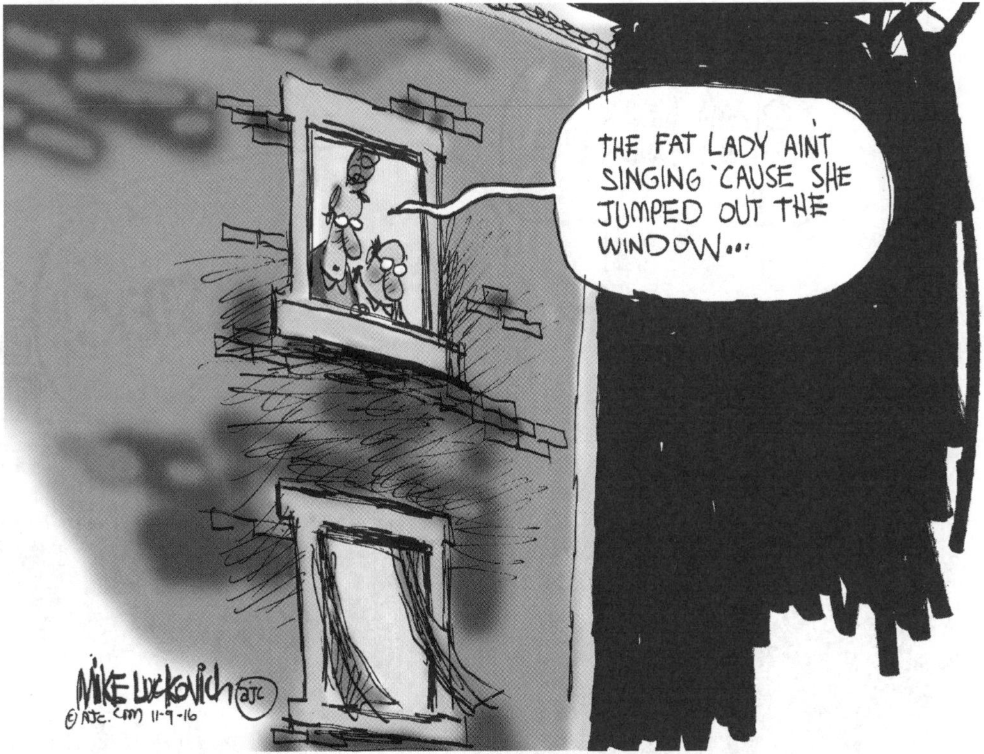
THE FAT LADY AIN'T SINGING 'CAUSE SHE JUMPED OUT THE WINDOW...
MIKE LUCKOVICH AJC
© AJC.COM 11-9-16

This is the cartoon that ended up running. Definitely one of the most depressing days of my life.

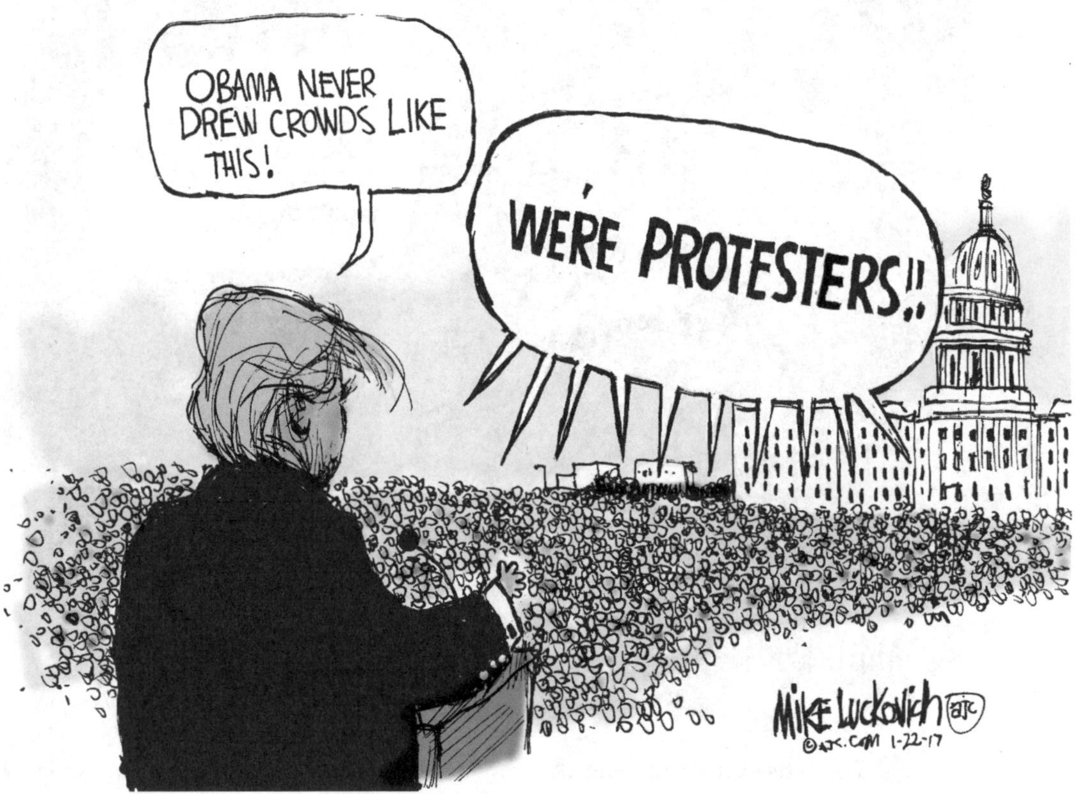
OBAMA NEVER DREW CROWDS LIKE THIS!
WE'RE PROTESTERS!!
MIKE LUCKOVICH
©AJC.COM 1-22-17

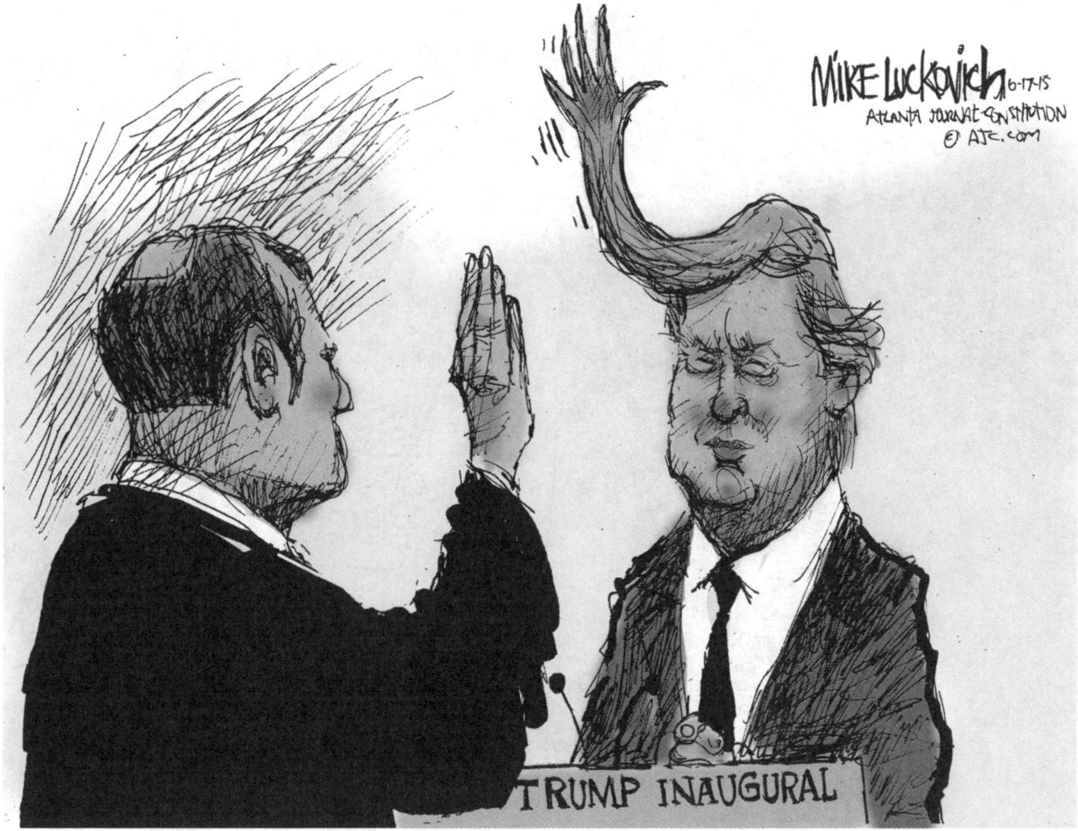
MIKE LUCKOVICH 6-17-15
ATLANTA JOURNAL-CONSTITUTION
© AJC.com
TRUMP INAUGURAL

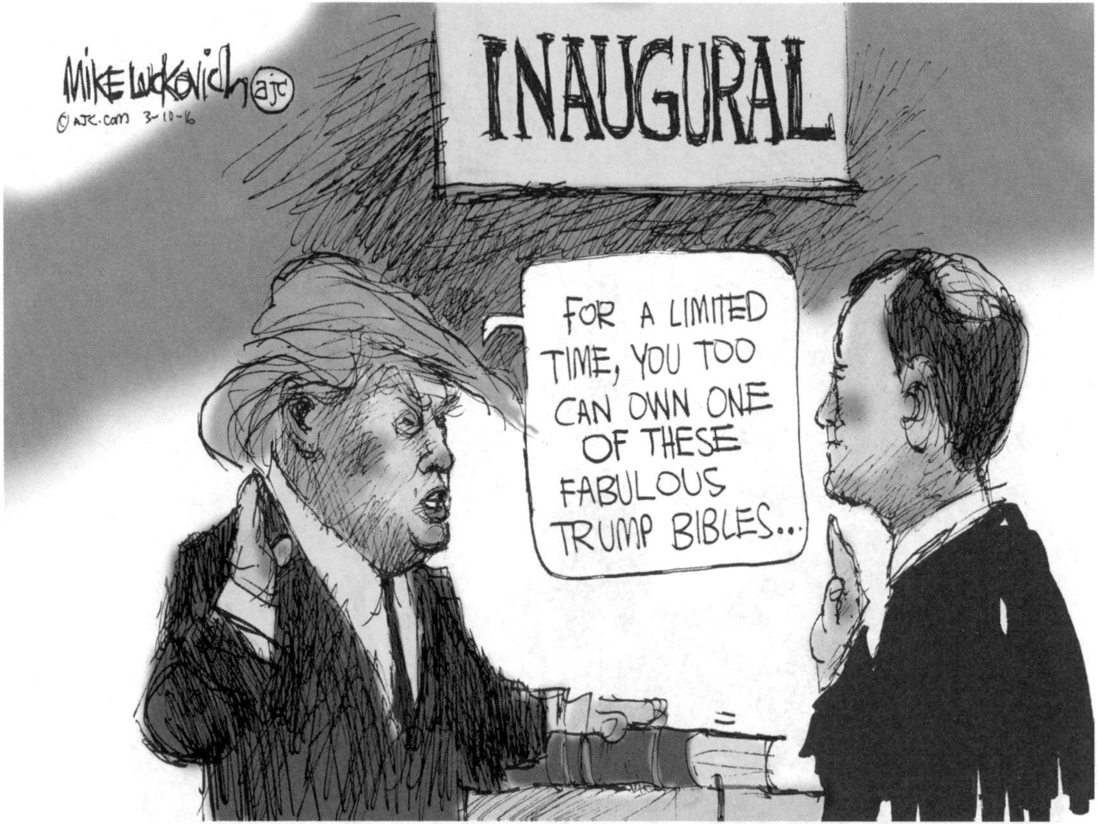
MIKE LUCKOVICH ajc
© AJC.com 3-10-16
INAUGURAL
FOR A LIMITED TIME, YOU TOO CAN OWN ONE OF THESE FABULOUS TRUMP BIBLES...

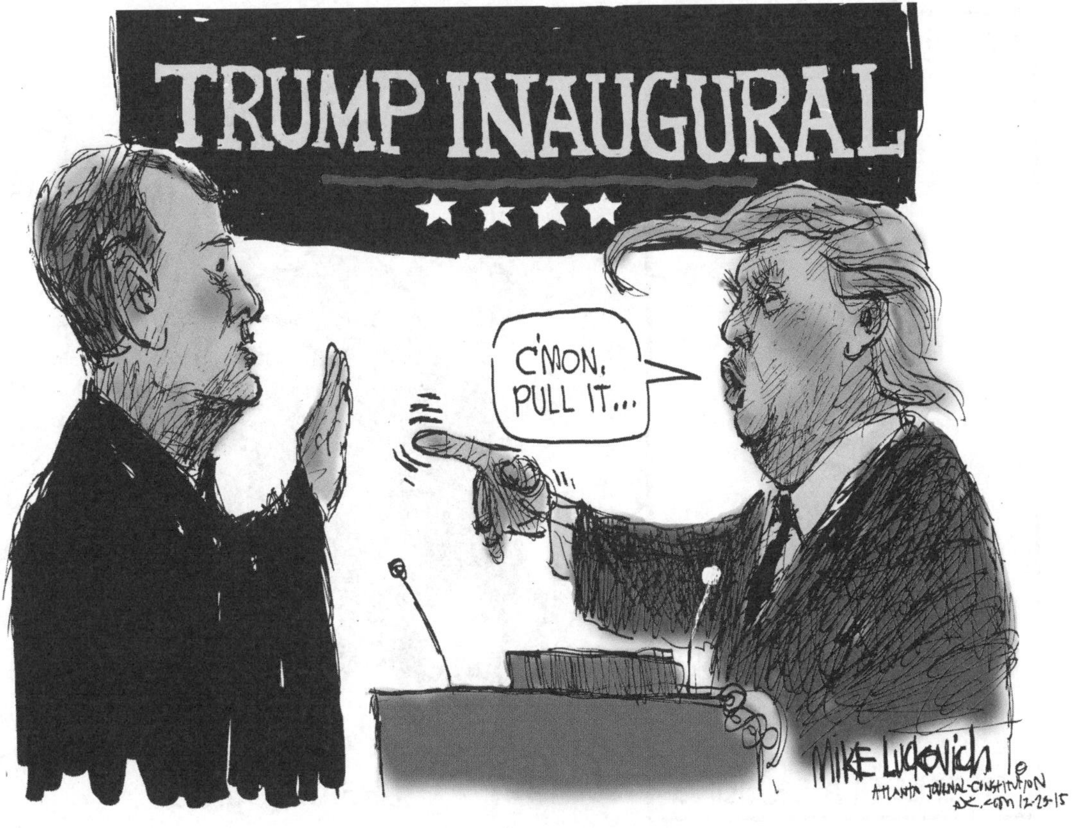
TRUMP INAUGURAL
C'MON. PULL IT...
MIKE LUCKOVICH
ATLANTA JOURNAL-CONSTITUTION

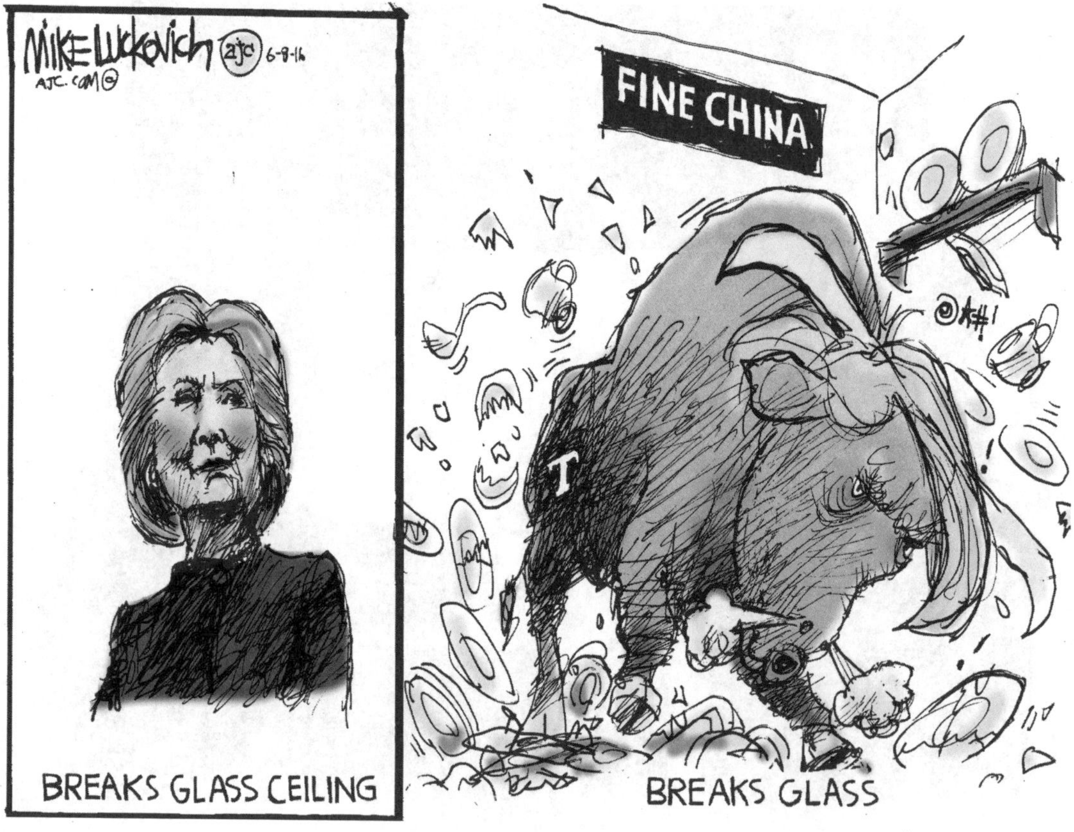
MIKE LUCKOVICH
ajc
6-8-16
AJC.COM©
BREAKS GLASS CEILING
FINE CHINA
T
@*#!
BREAKS GLASS

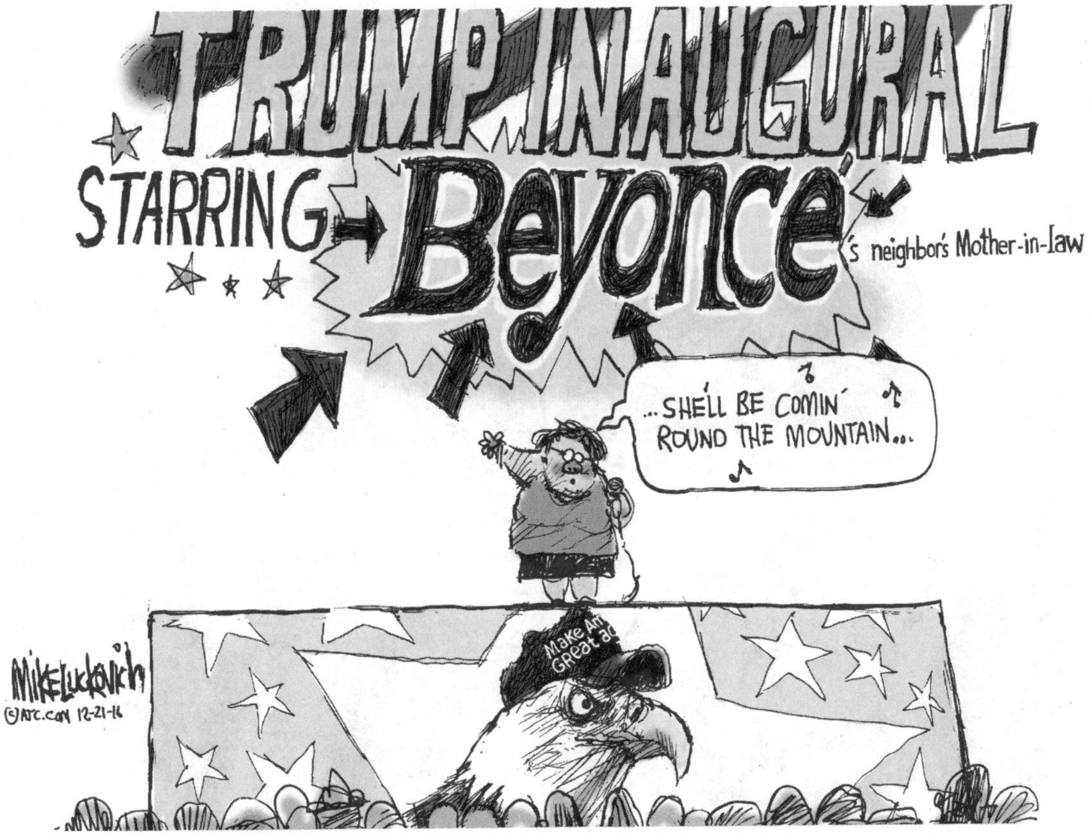
TRUMP INAUGURAL
STARRING
Beyoncé's neighbor's Mother-in-law
...SHE'LL BE COMIN' ROUND THE MOUNTAIN...
Make Am
GReat ag
MikeLuckovich
©AJC.com 12-21-16

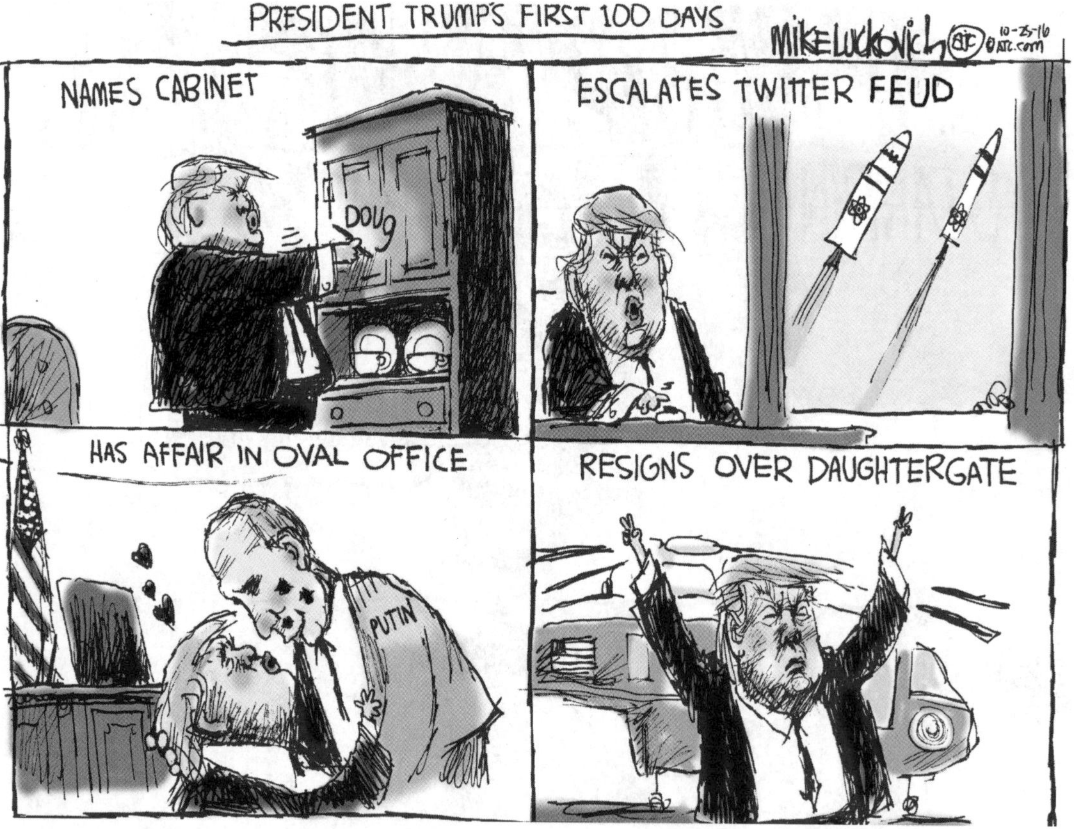
PRESIDENT TRUMP'S FIRST 100 DAYS
MIKE LUCKOVICH
10-25-16
©AJC.com
NAMES CABINET
DOUG
ESCALATES TWITTER FEUD
HAS AFFAIR IN OVAL OFFICE
PUTIN
RESIGNS OVER DAUGHTERGATE

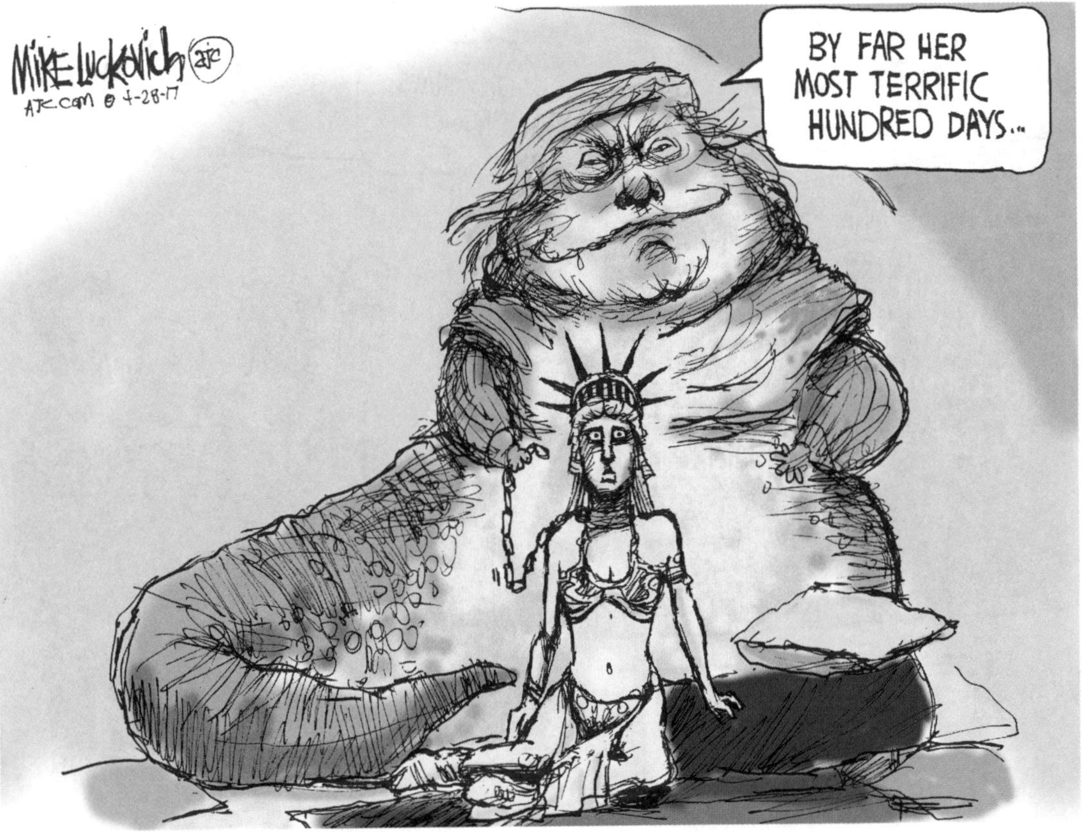
MIKE LUCKOVICH ajc
AJC.com © 4-28-17
BY FAR HER MOST TERRIFIC HUNDRED DAYS...

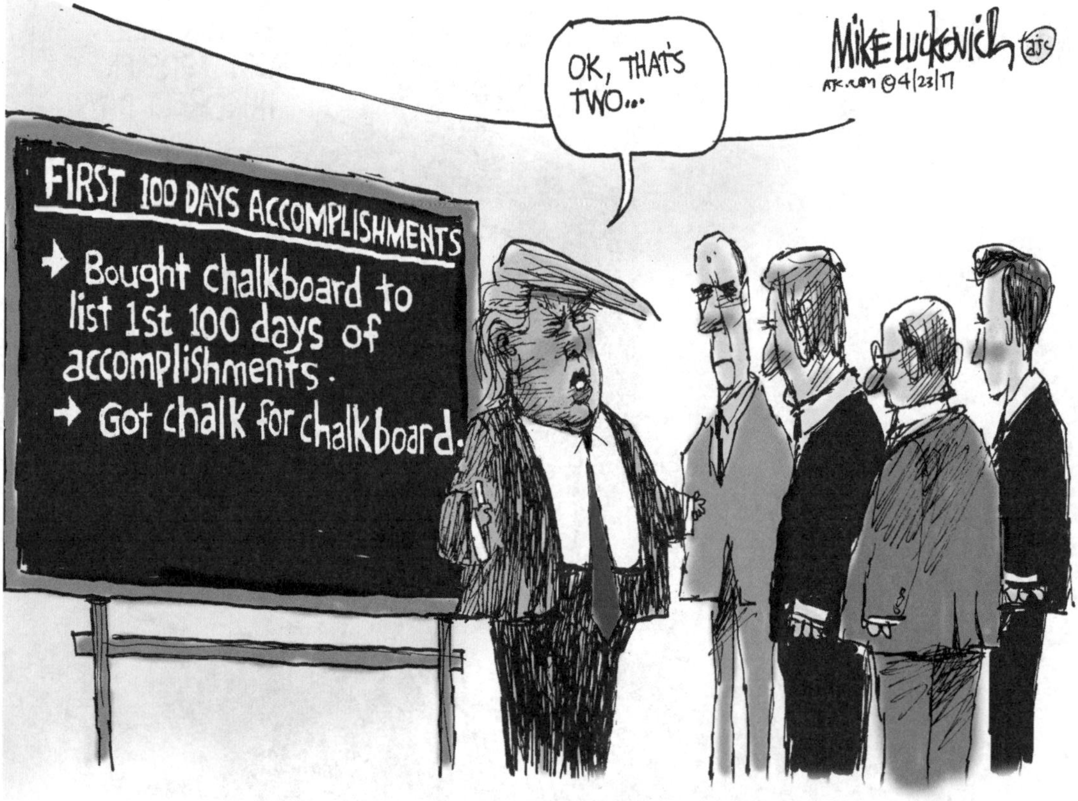

MIKE LUCKOVICH AJC
AJC.com ©4/23/17
FIRST 100 DAYS ACCOMPLISHMENTS
→ Bought chalkboard to list 1st 100 days of accomplishments.
→ Got chalk for chalkboard.
OK, THAT'S TWO...

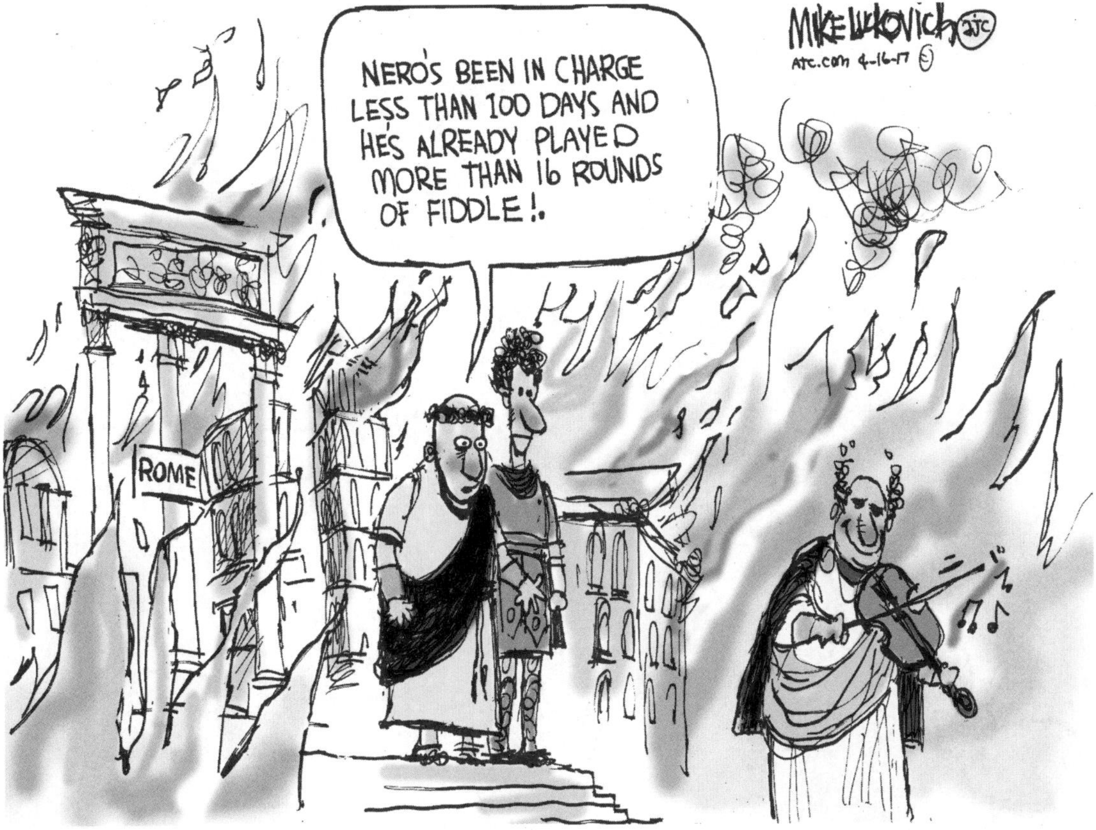
NERO'S BEEN IN CHARGE LESS THAN 100 DAYS AND HE'S ALREADY PLAYED MORE THAN 16 ROUNDS OF FIDDLE!.
MIKE LUCKOVICH AJC
AJC.com 4-16-17
ROME

 **Donald J. Trump**
@realDonaldTrump

# OMG,
# HE'S THE PRESIDENT!

RETWEETS 3,582   LIKES 9,935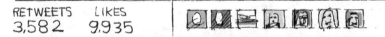

1.7K   3.6K   99K …

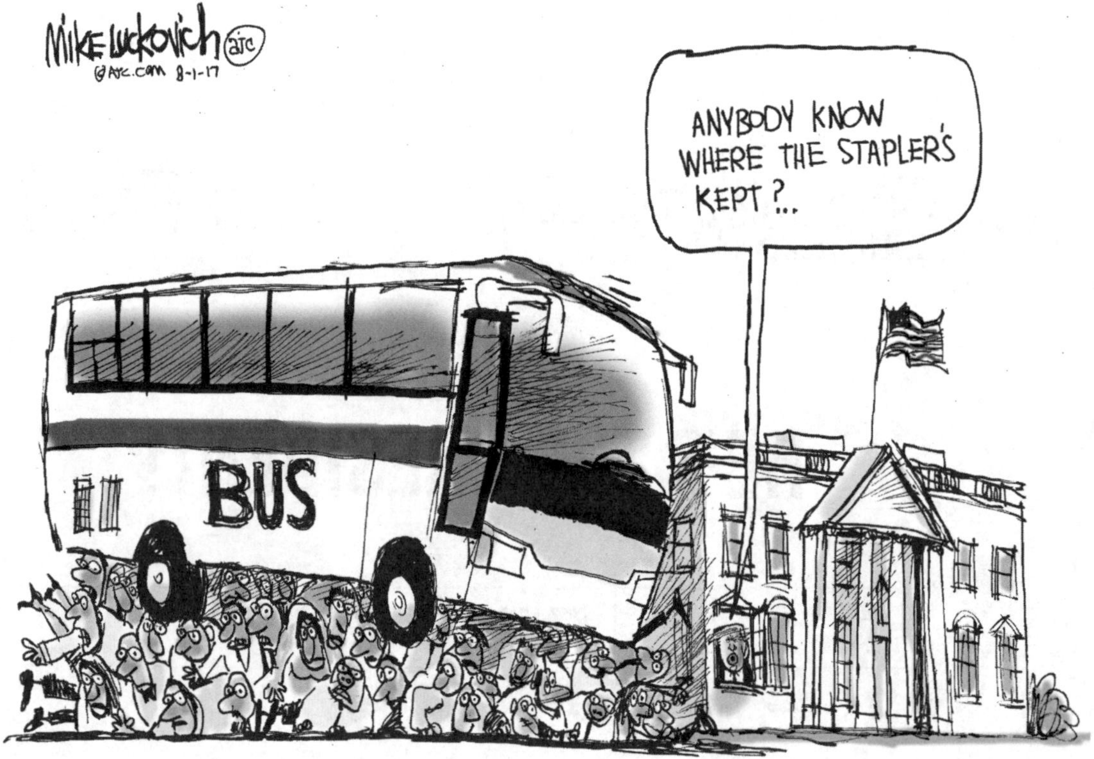
MIKE LUCKOVICH AJC
@AJC.COM 8-1-17
ANYBODY KNOW WHERE THE STAPLER'S KEPT?..
BUS

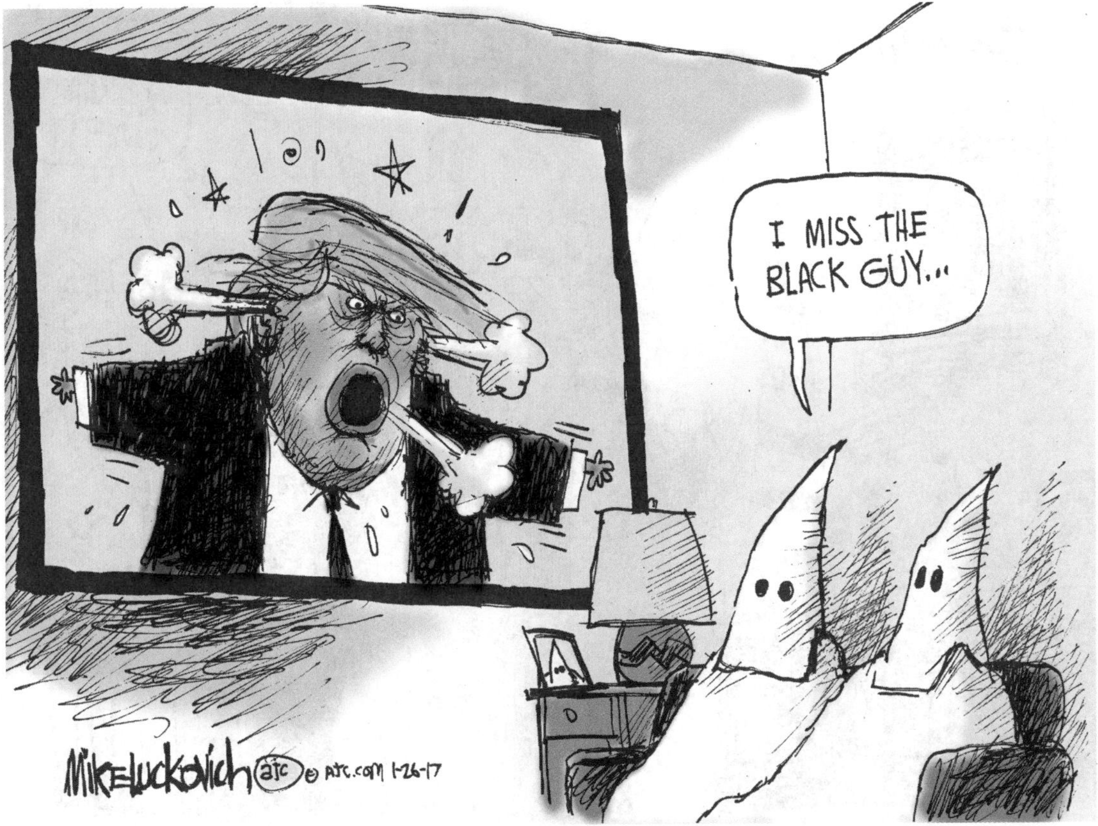
I MISS THE BLACK GUY...
MIKELUCKOVICH ajc © AJC.com 1-26-17

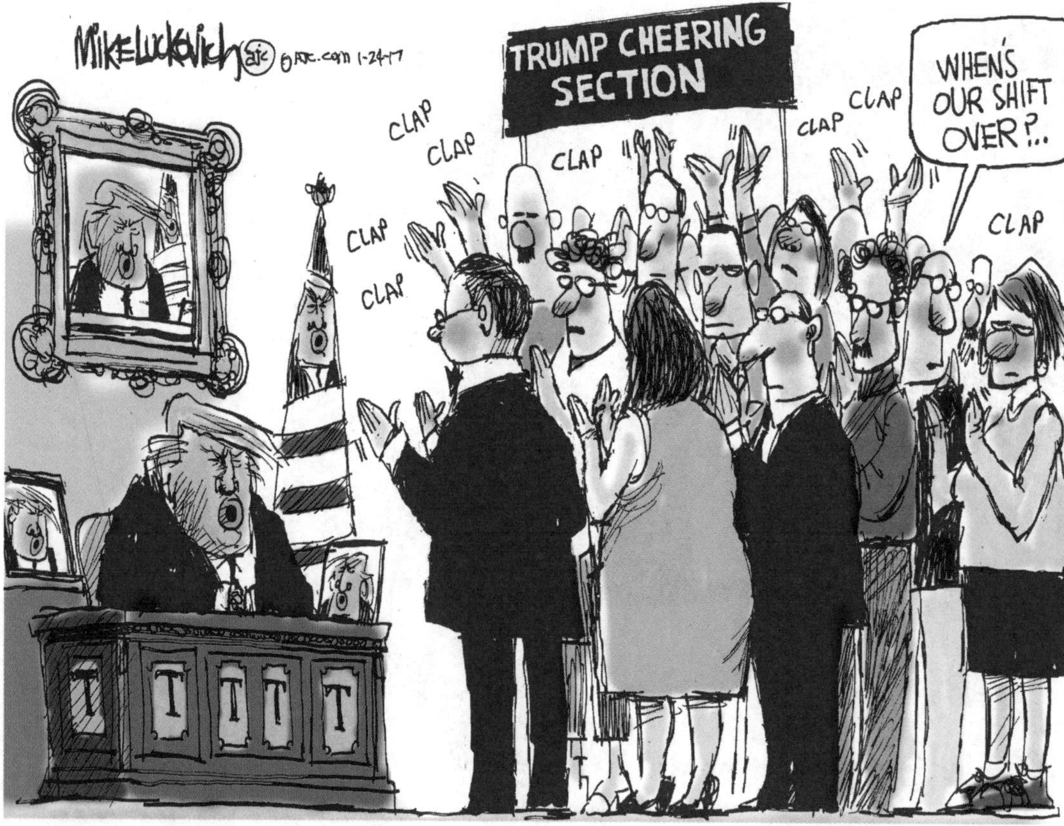
MIKE LUCKOVICH ajc ©ajc.com 1-24-17
TRUMP CHEERING SECTION
CLAP
CLAP
CLAP
CLAP
CLAP
CLAP
CLAP
WHEN'S OUR SHIFT OVER?..
CLAP

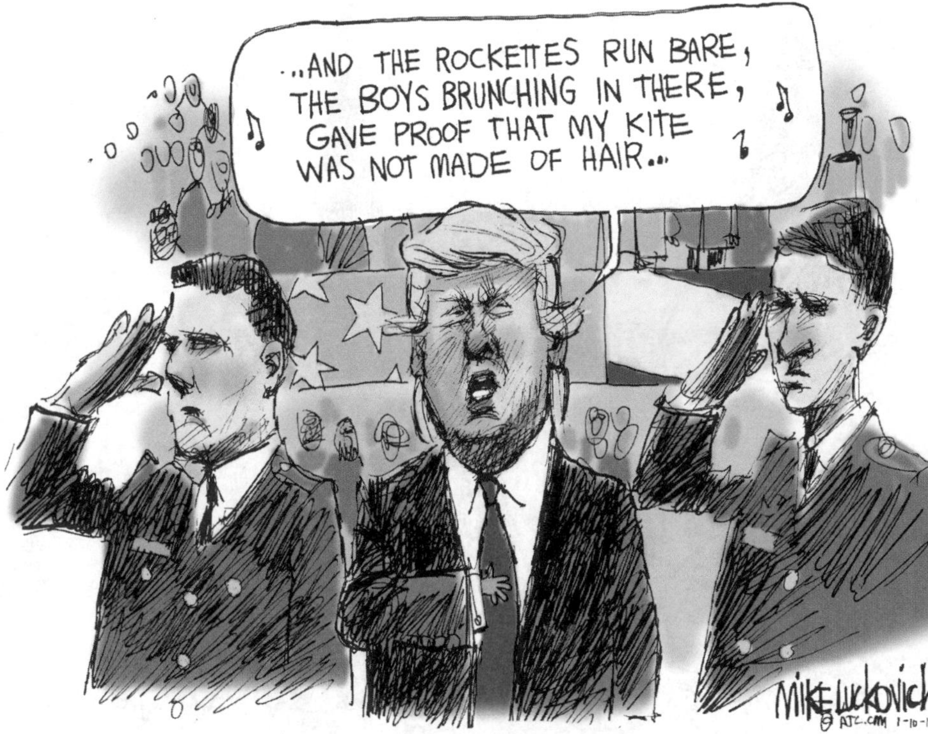
...AND THE ROCKETTES RUN BARE, THE BOYS BRUNCHING IN THERE, GAVE PROOF THAT MY KITE WAS NOT MADE OF HAIR...
MIKE LUCKOVICH
AJC
© AJC.COM 1-10-18

At the start of the 2018 College Football National Championship, it was obvious Trump didn't know the words to the national anthem.

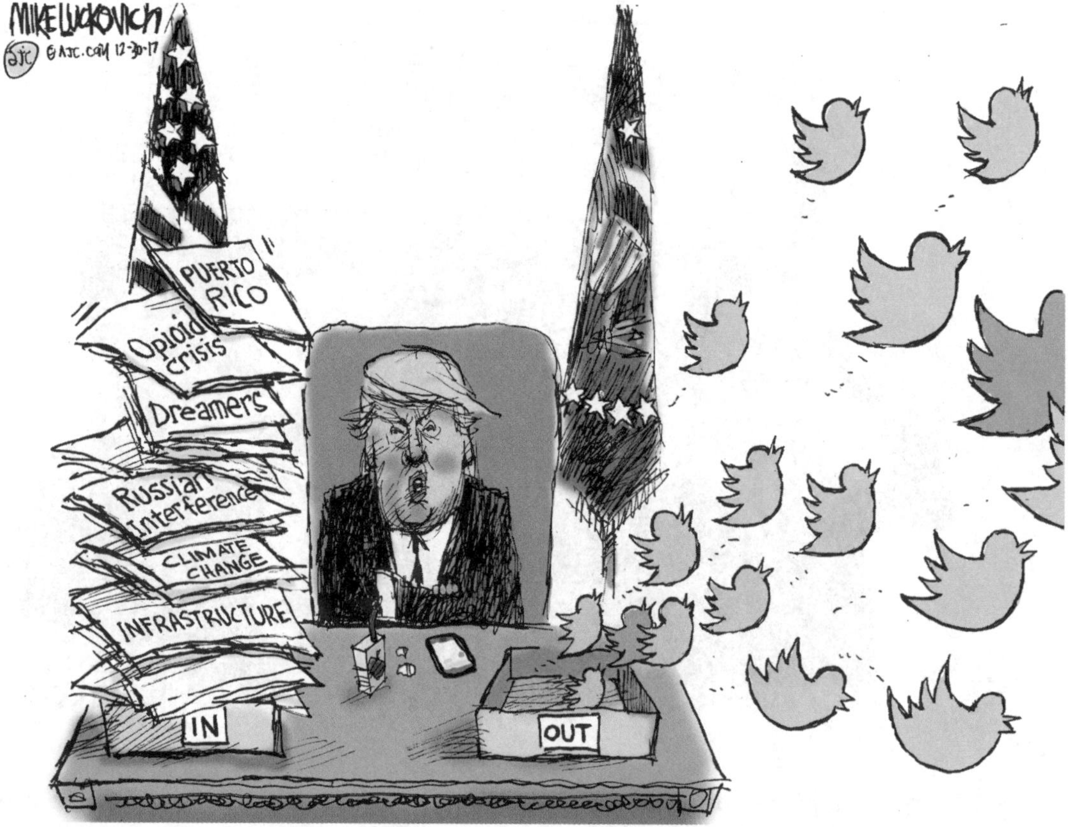
MIKE LUCKOVICH
AJC.COM 12-30-17
PUERTO RICO
Opioid crisis
Dreamers
Russian Interference
CLIMATE CHANGE
INFRASTRUCTURE
IN
OUT

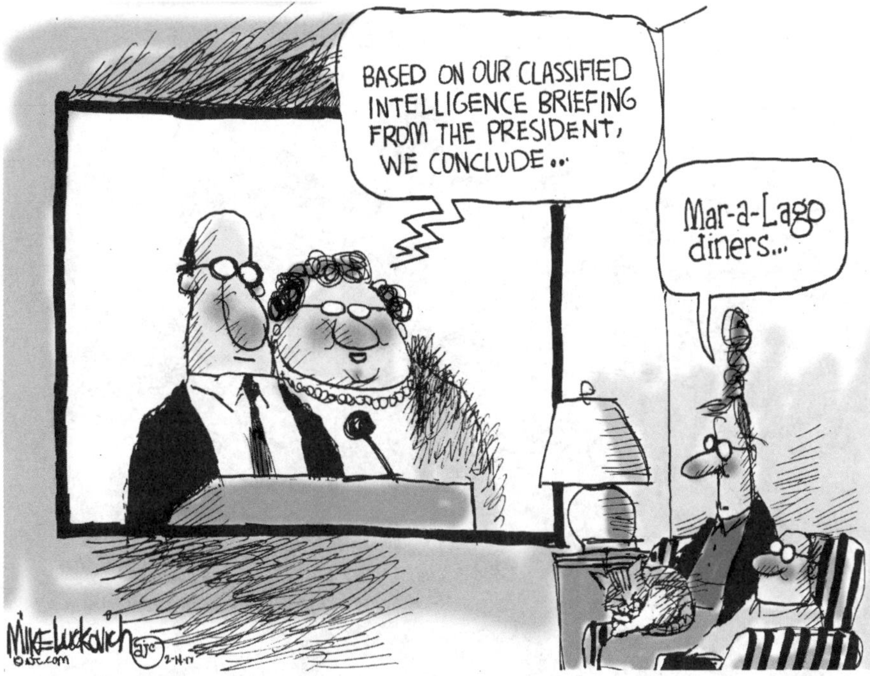
BASED ON OUR CLASSIFIED INTELLIGENCE BRIEFING FROM THE PRESIDENT, WE CONCLUDE...
Mar-a-Lago diners...
MIKE LUCKOVICH
©AJC.com
AJC
2-14-17

While vacationing in Mar-a-Lago, Trump discussed the firing of a North Korean missile with his advisers and with Japanese Prime Minister Shinzo Abe while surrounded by guests at his resort. Imagine being one of the lucky diners in the middle of a top-secret foreign-policy discussion as you eat your crème brûlée.

HOW TO MAKE TRUMP NOTICE

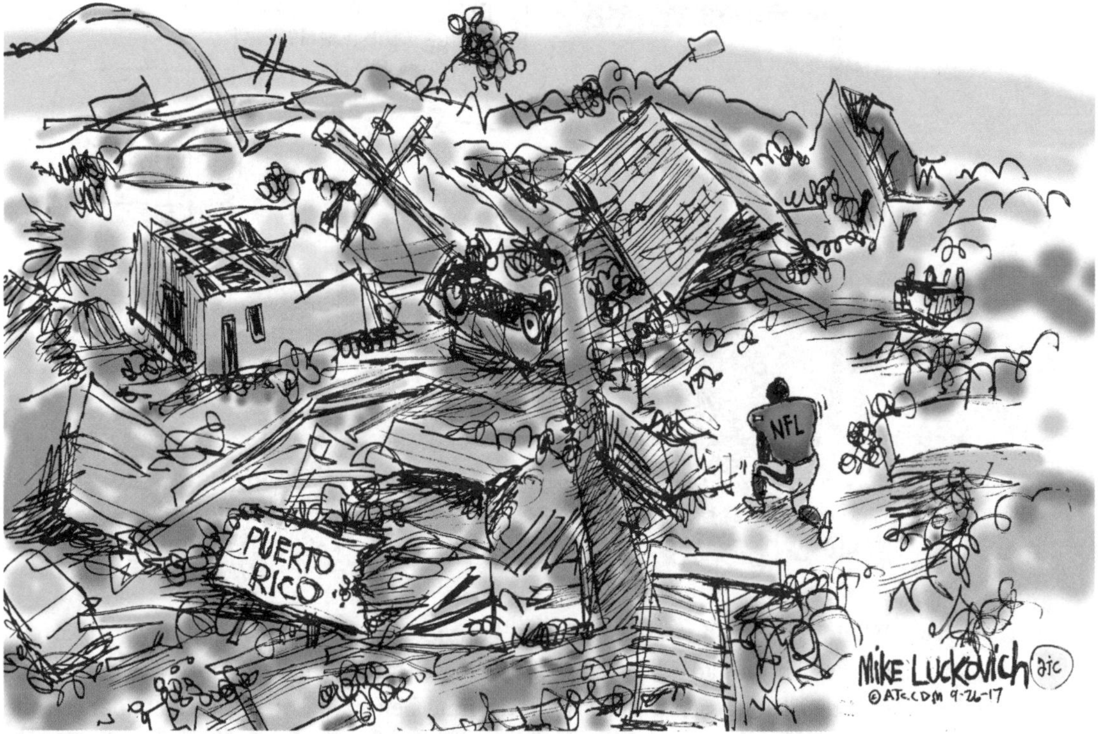
NFL
PUERTO RICO
MIKE LUCKOVICH ajc
©AJC.CDM 9-26-17

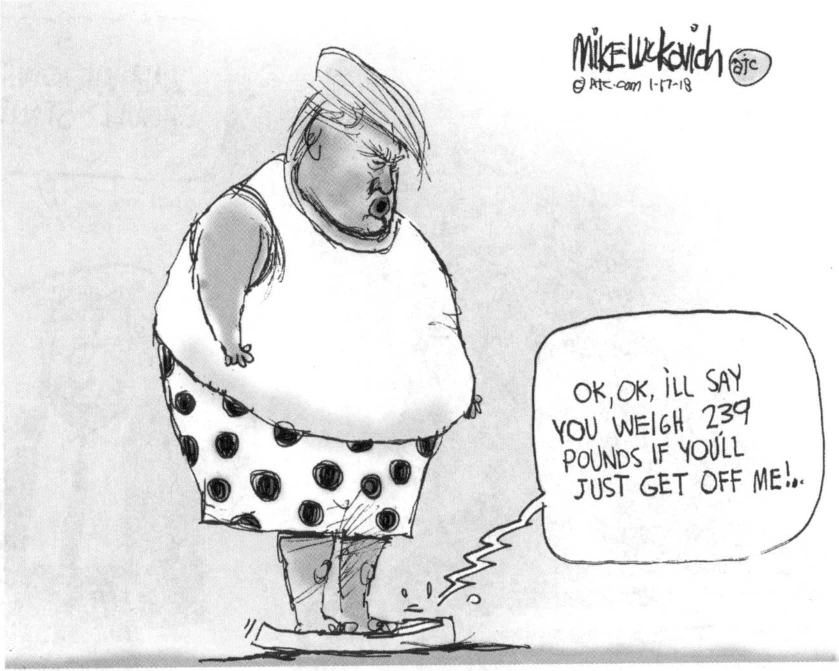
MIKE LUCKOVICH ajc
© AJC.com 1-17-18
OK, OK, ILL SAY YOU WEIGH 239 POUNDS IF YOU'LL JUST GET OFF ME!..

After performing Trump's first formal medical exam since taking office, former White House physician Dr. Ronny Jackson declared Trump was a svelte 239 pounds.

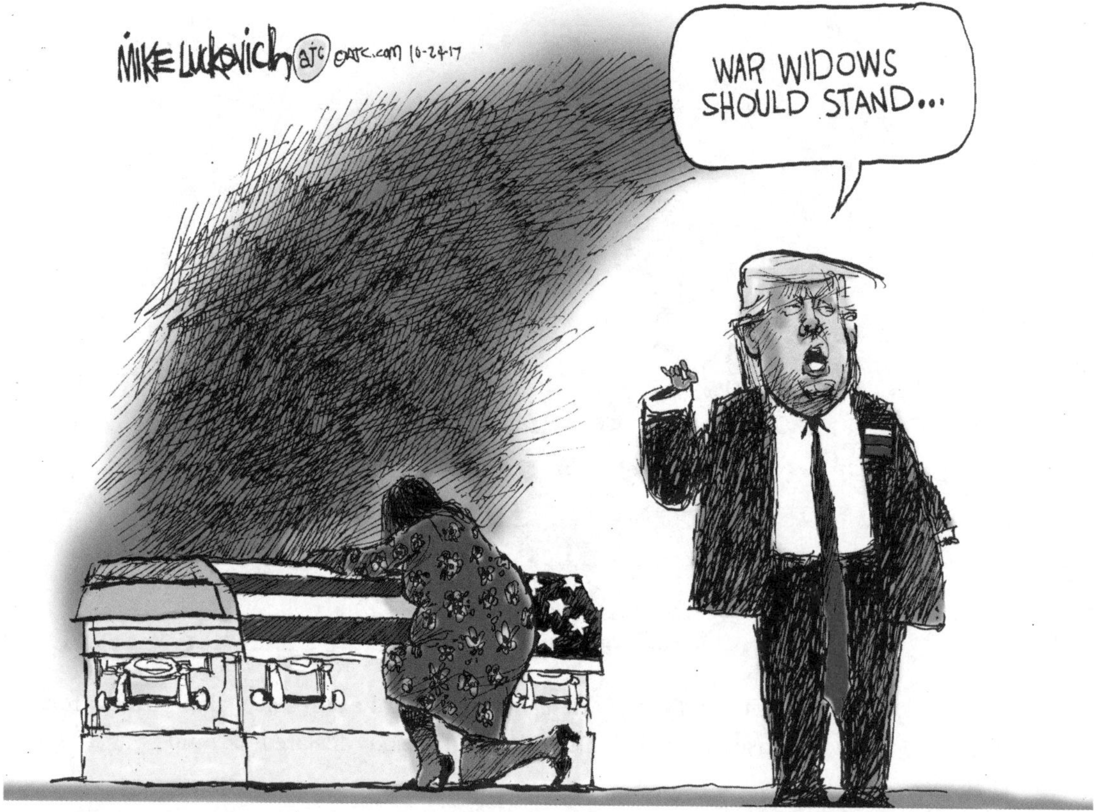
MIKE LUCKOVICH ajc ©AJC.com 10-24-17
WAR WIDOWS SHOULD STAND...

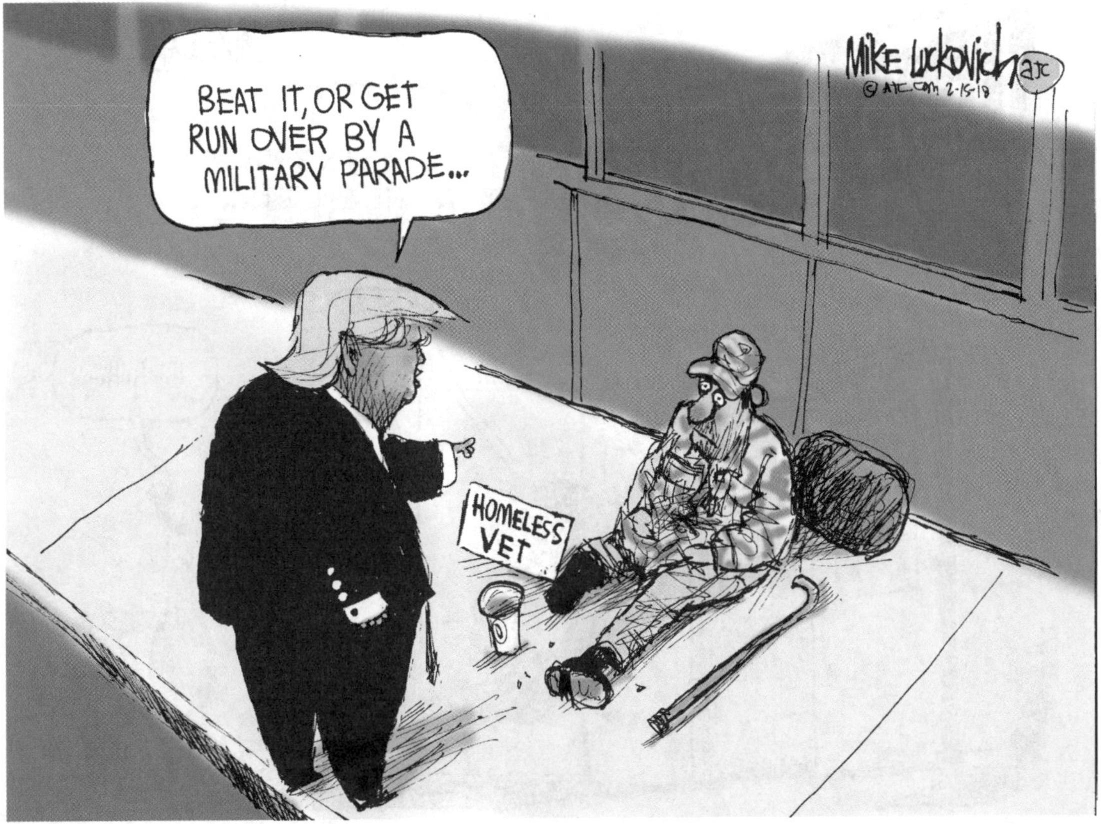
BEAT IT, OR GET RUN OVER BY A MILITARY PARADE...
MIKE LUCKOVICH
AJC
HOMELESS VET

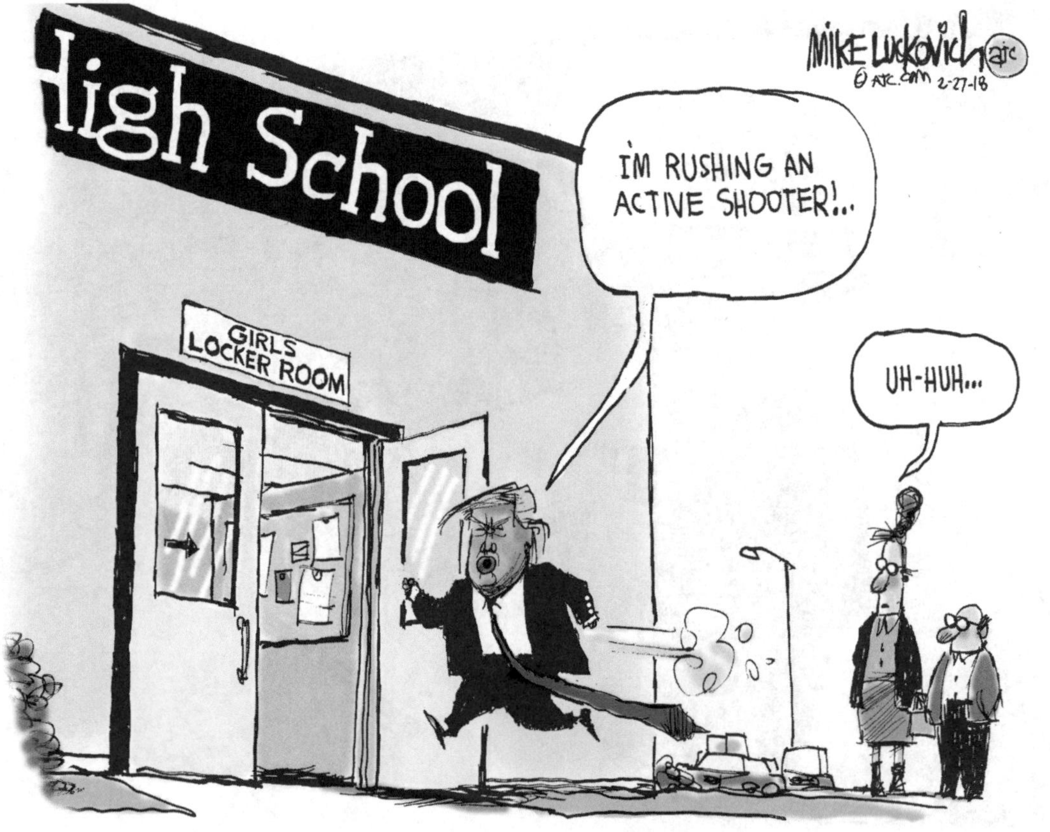
High School
GIRLS
LOCKER ROOM
I'M RUSHING AN
ACTIVE SHOOTER!..
UH-HUH...
MIKE LUCKOVICH ajc
© AJC.com 2-27-18

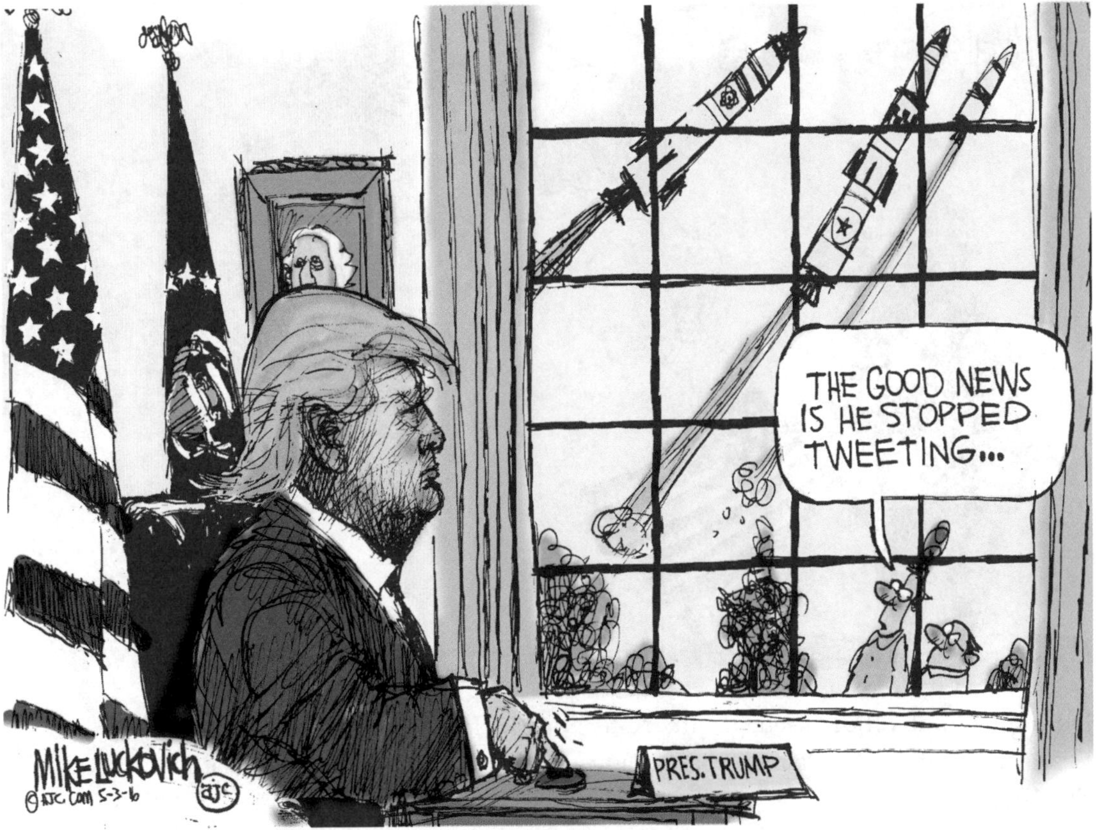
THE GOOD NEWS IS HE STOPPED TWEETING...
PRES. TRUMP
MIKE LUCKOVICH
©AJC.com 5-3-16
ajc

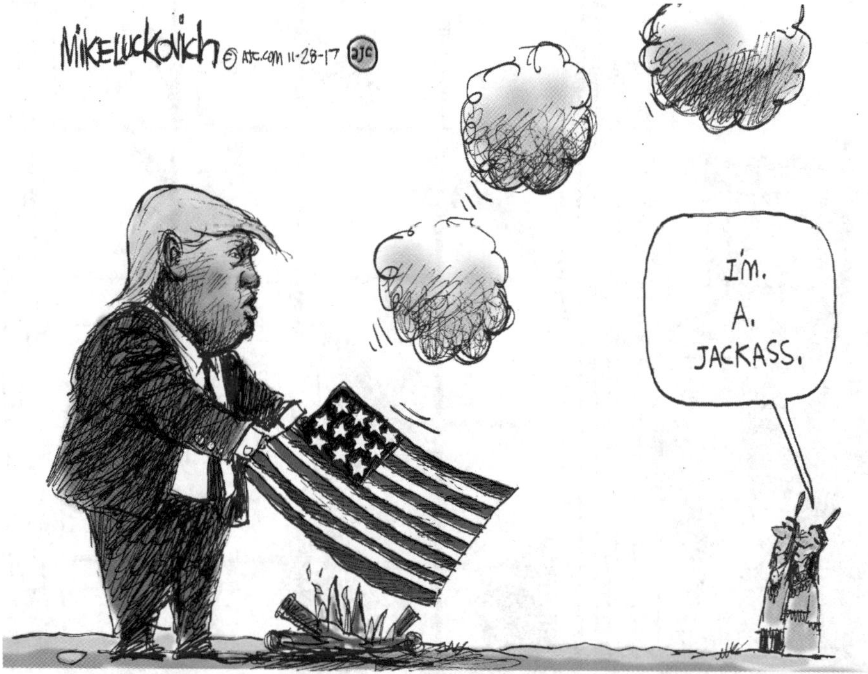
MIKELUCKOVICH © AJC.COM 11-28-17 AJC
I'M.
A.
JACKASS.

During an oval office meeting with Native Americans, Trump referred to Elizabeth Warren, who claims to have Native American heritage, by the racial slur "Pocahontas."

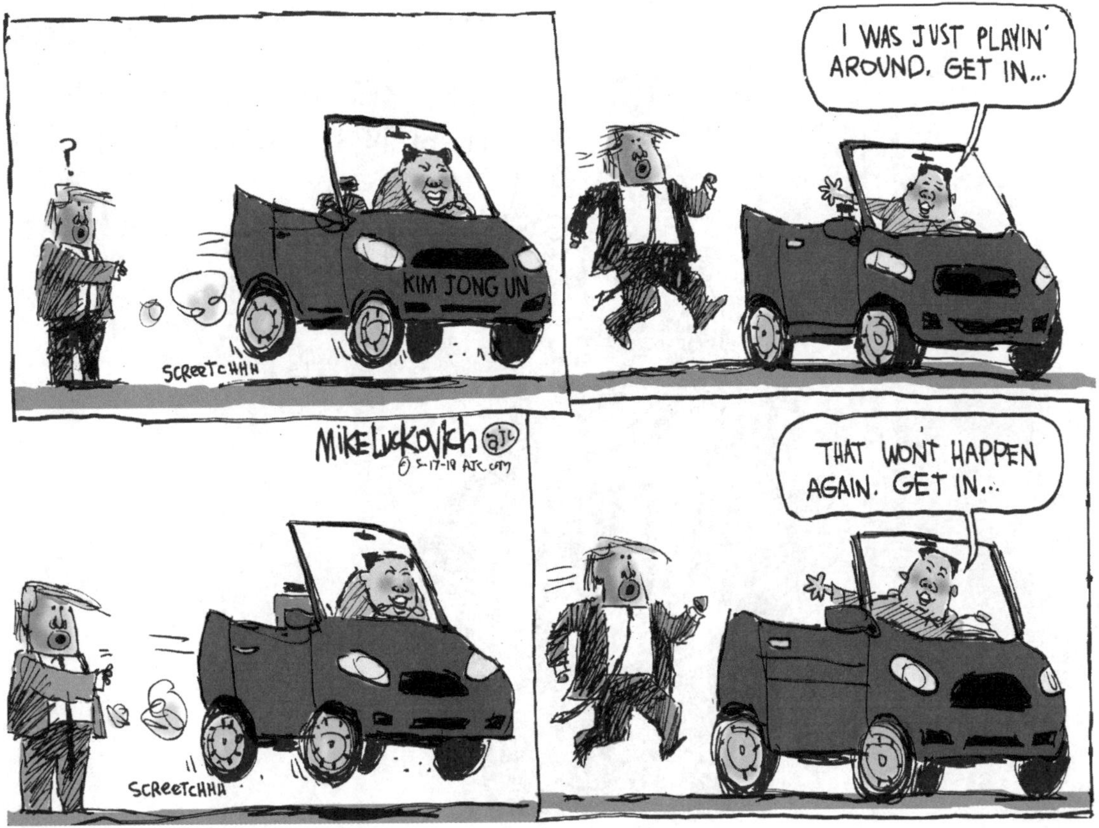
?
KIM JONG UN
SCREETCHHH
I WAS JUST PLAYIN' AROUND. GET IN...
MIKE LUCKOVICH
SCREETCHHH
THAT WON'T HAPPEN AGAIN. GET IN...

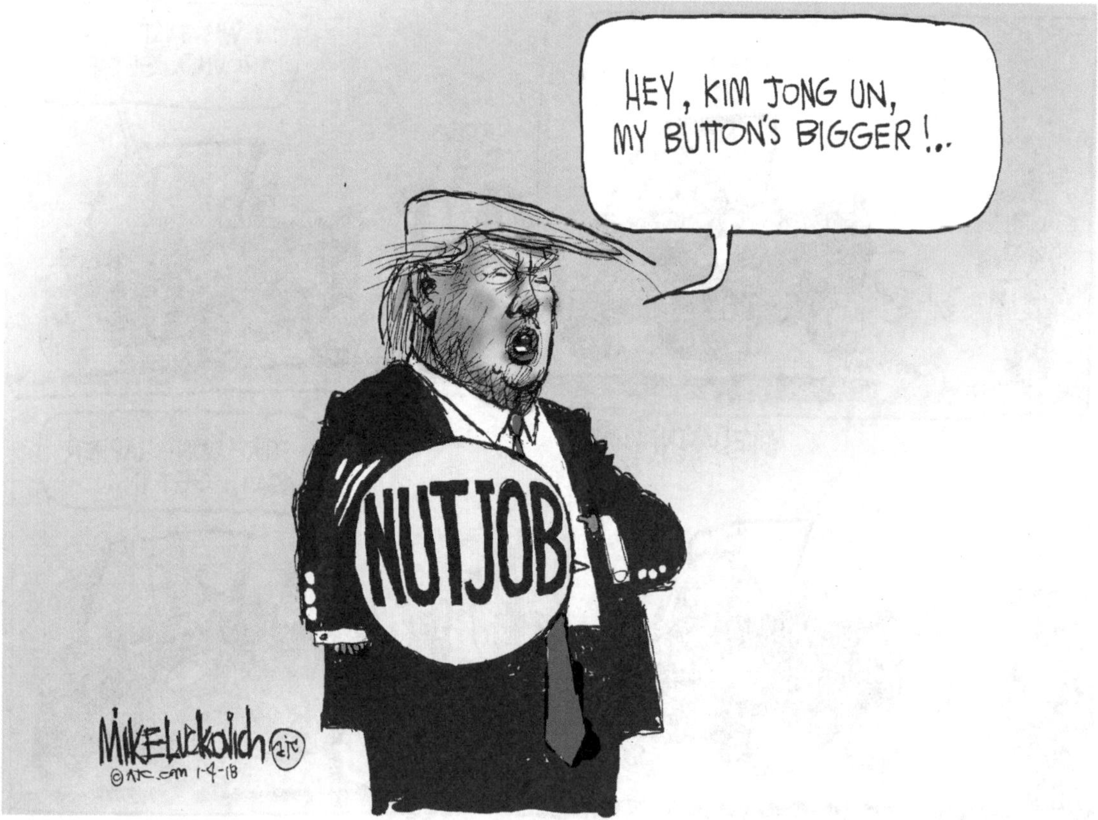
HEY, KIM JONG UN,
MY BUTTON'S BIGGER!..
NUTJOB
MIKELUCKOVICH
©AJC.com 1-4-18

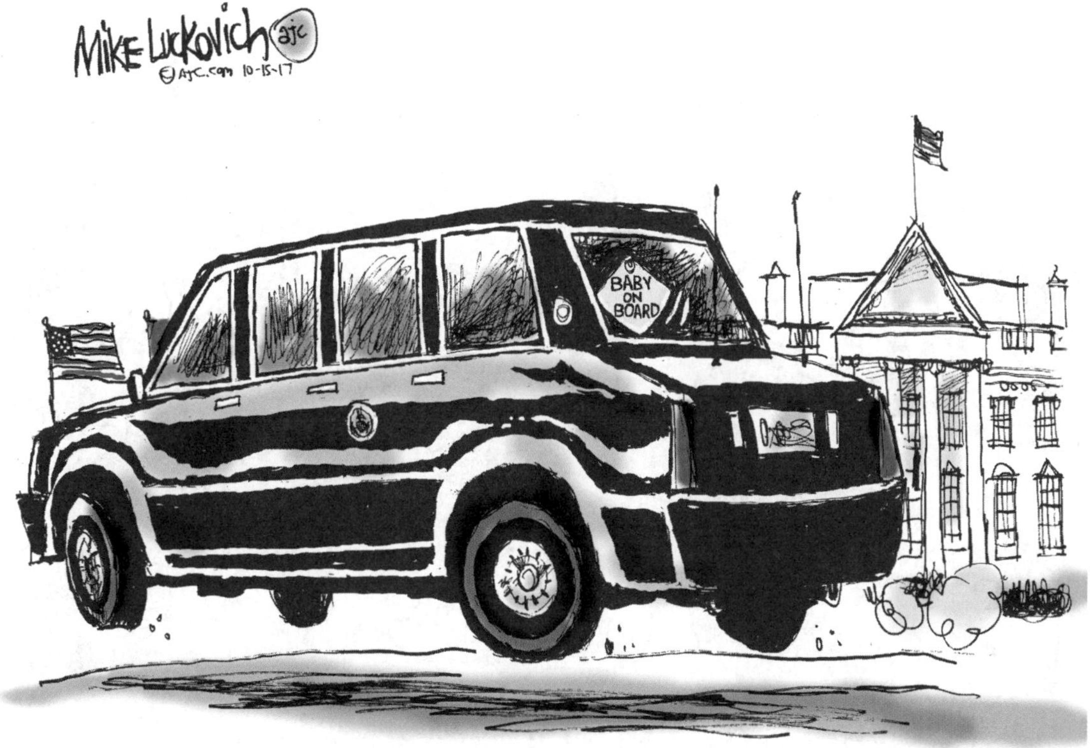
MIKE LUCKOVICH ajc
© AJC.com 10-15-17
BABY ON BOARD

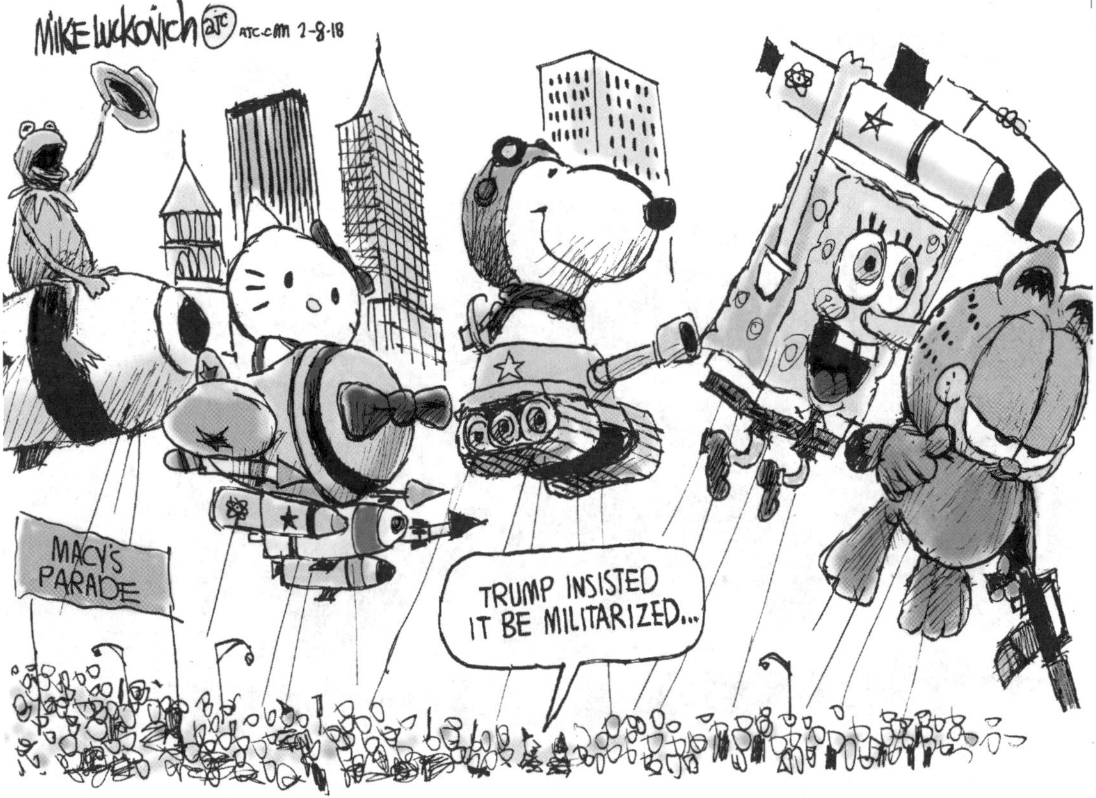
MIKE LUCKOVICH AJC AJC.COM 2-8-18
MACY'S PARADE
TRUMP INSISTED IT BE MILITARIZED...

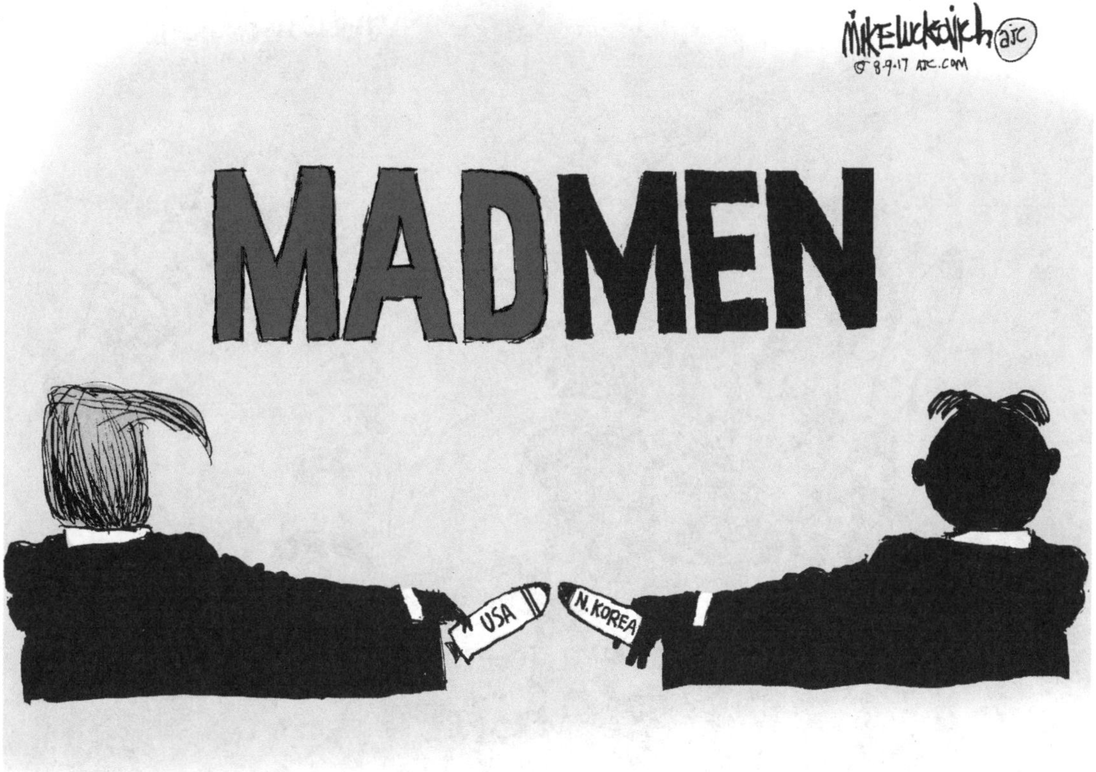
MIKE LUCKOVICH AJC
© 8-9-17 AJC.COM
MADMEN
USA
N. KOREA

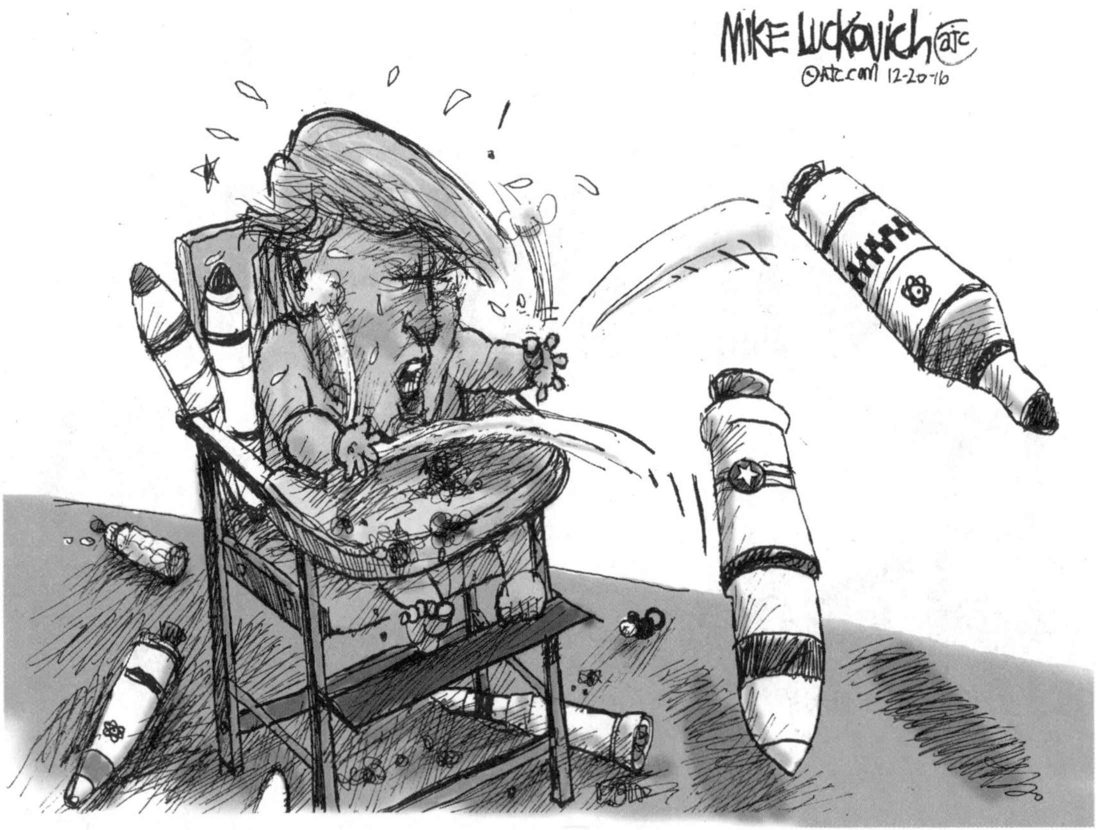
MIKE LUCKOVICH @AJC
©AJC.COM 12-20-16

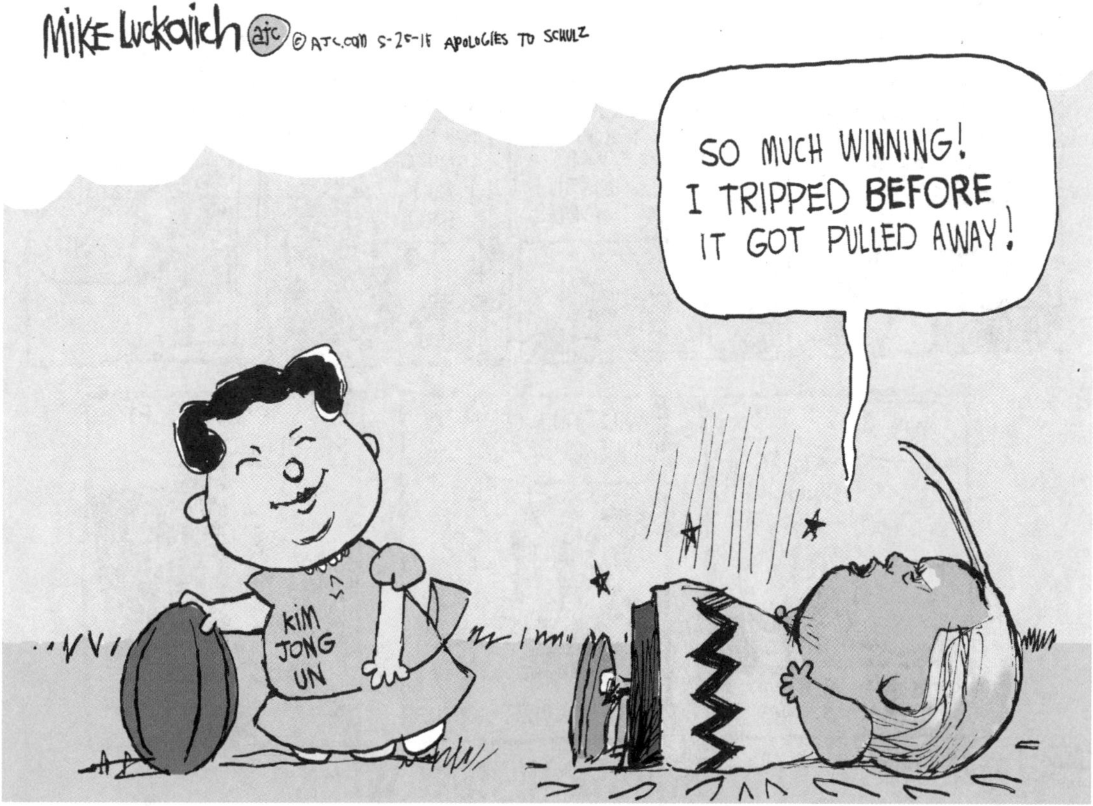
MIKE LUCKOVICH ajc © AJC.COM 5-25-18 APOLOGIES TO SCHULZ
SO MUCH WINNING! I TRIPPED **BEFORE** IT GOT PULLED AWAY!
KIM JONG UN

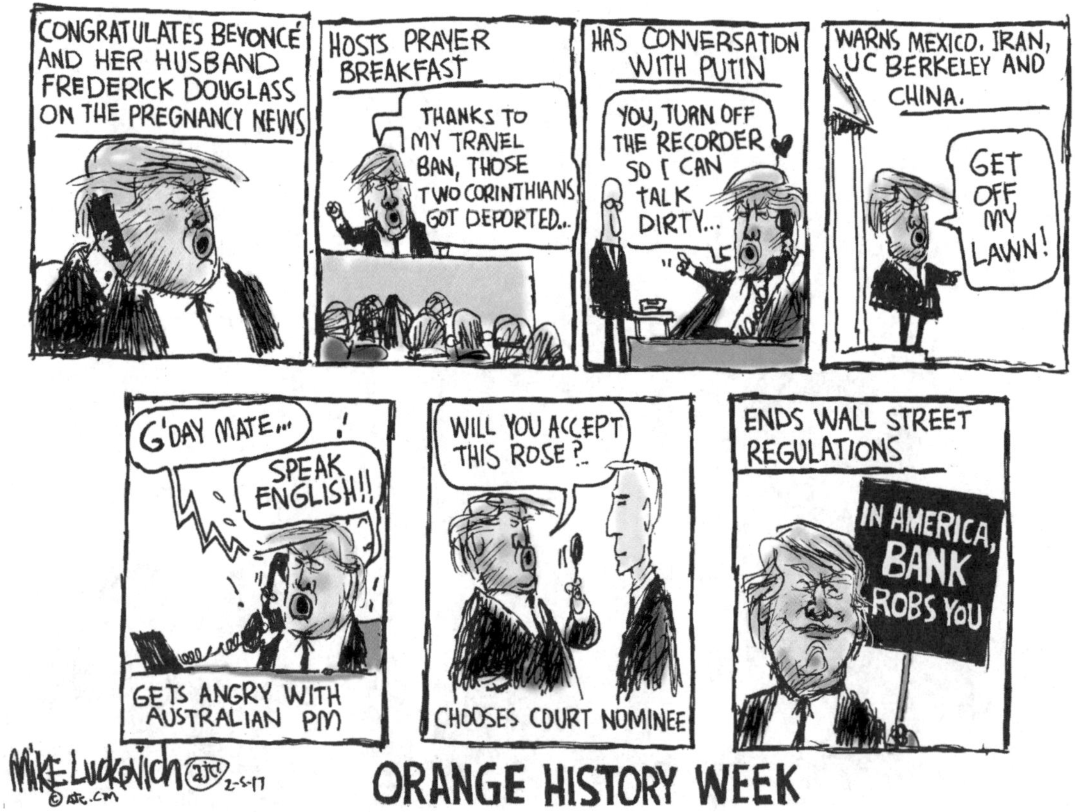
CONGRATULATES BEYONCÉ AND HER HUSBAND FREDERICK DOUGLASS ON THE PREGNANCY NEWS
HOSTS PRAYER BREAKFAST
THANKS TO MY TRAVEL BAN, THOSE TWO CORINTHIANS GOT DEPORTED...
HAS CONVERSATION WITH PUTIN
YOU, TURN OFF THE RECORDER SO I CAN TALK DIRTY...
WARNS MEXICO, IRAN, UC BERKELEY AND CHINA.
GET OFF MY LAWN!
G'DAY MATE...
SPEAK ENGLISH!!
GETS ANGRY WITH AUSTRALIAN PM
WILL YOU ACCEPT THIS ROSE?
CHOOSES COURT NOMINEE
ENDS WALL STREET REGULATIONS
IN AMERICA, BANK ROBS YOU
MIKE LUCKOVICH AJC 2-5-17
© AJC.COM
ORANGE HISTORY WEEK

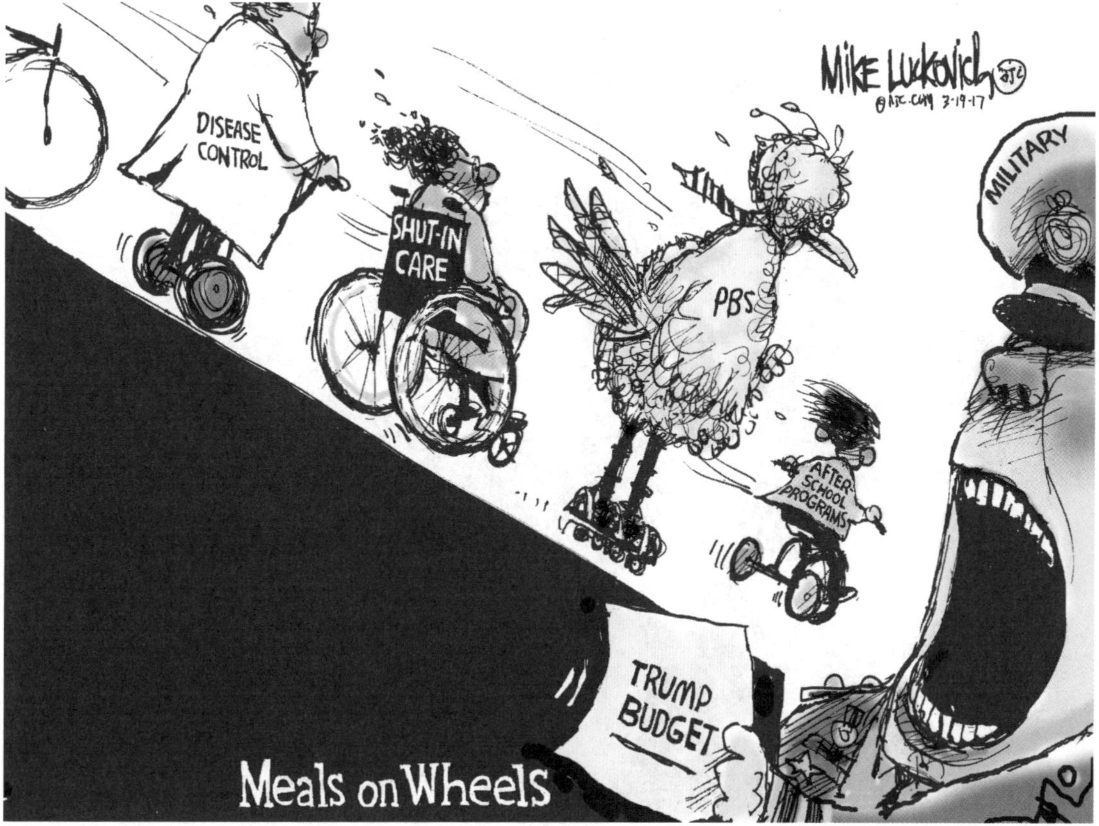
MIKE LUCKOVICH AJC
©AJC.COM 3-19-17
DISEASE CONTROL
SHUT-IN CARE
PBS
AFTER-SCHOOL PROGRAMS
MILITARY
TRUMP BUDGET
Meals on Wheels

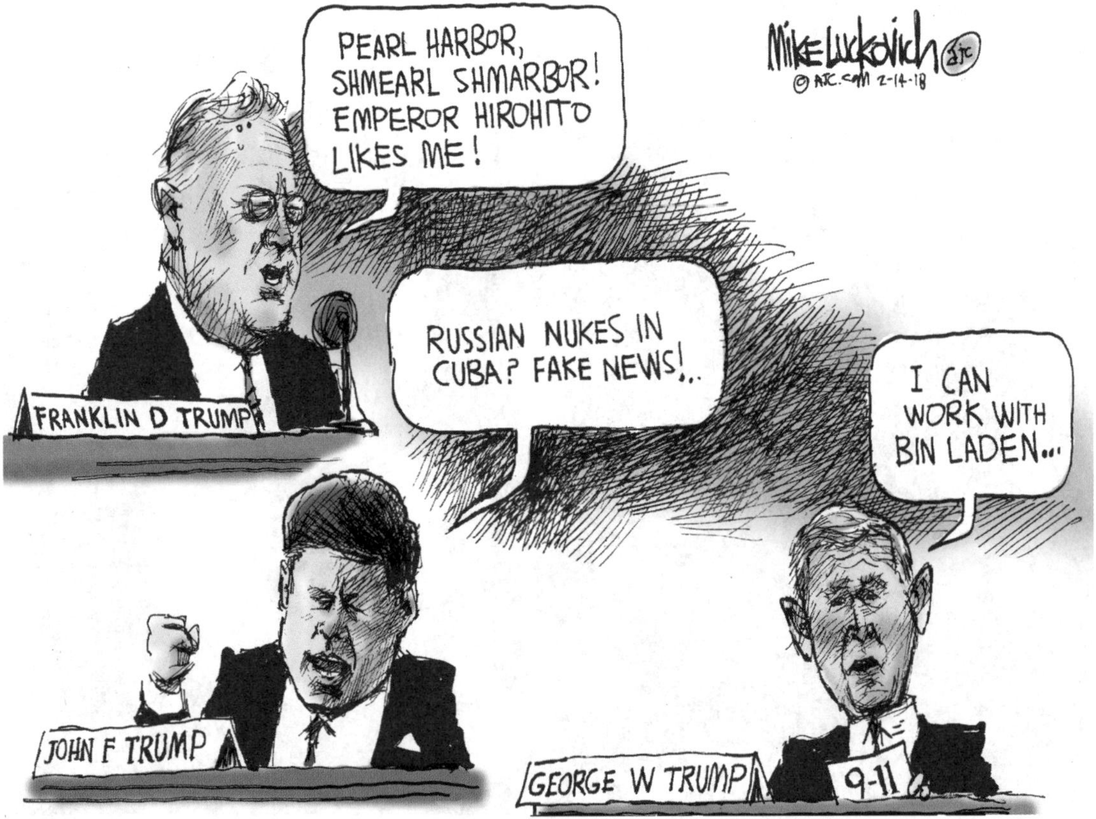
PEARL HARBOR, SHMEARL SHMARBOR! EMPEROR HIROHITO LIKES ME!
FRANKLIN D TRUMP
RUSSIAN NUKES IN CUBA? FAKE NEWS!..
JOHN F TRUMP
I CAN WORK WITH BIN LADEN...
GEORGE W TRUMP
9-11
MIKE LUCKOVICH
ajc
© AJC.com 2-14-18

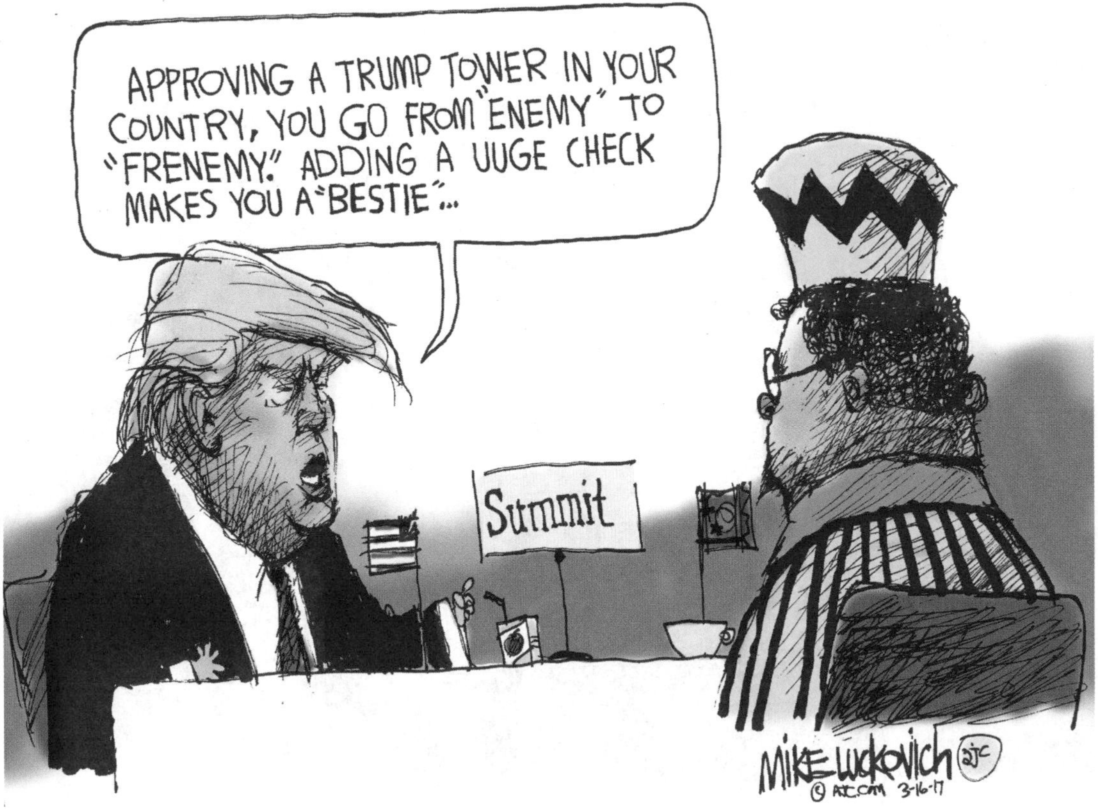
APPROVING A TRUMP TOWER IN YOUR COUNTRY, YOU GO FROM "ENEMY" TO "FRENEMY." ADDING A UUGE CHECK MAKES YOU A "BESTIE"...
Summit
MIKE LUCKOVICH
AJC
© AJC.COM 3-16-17

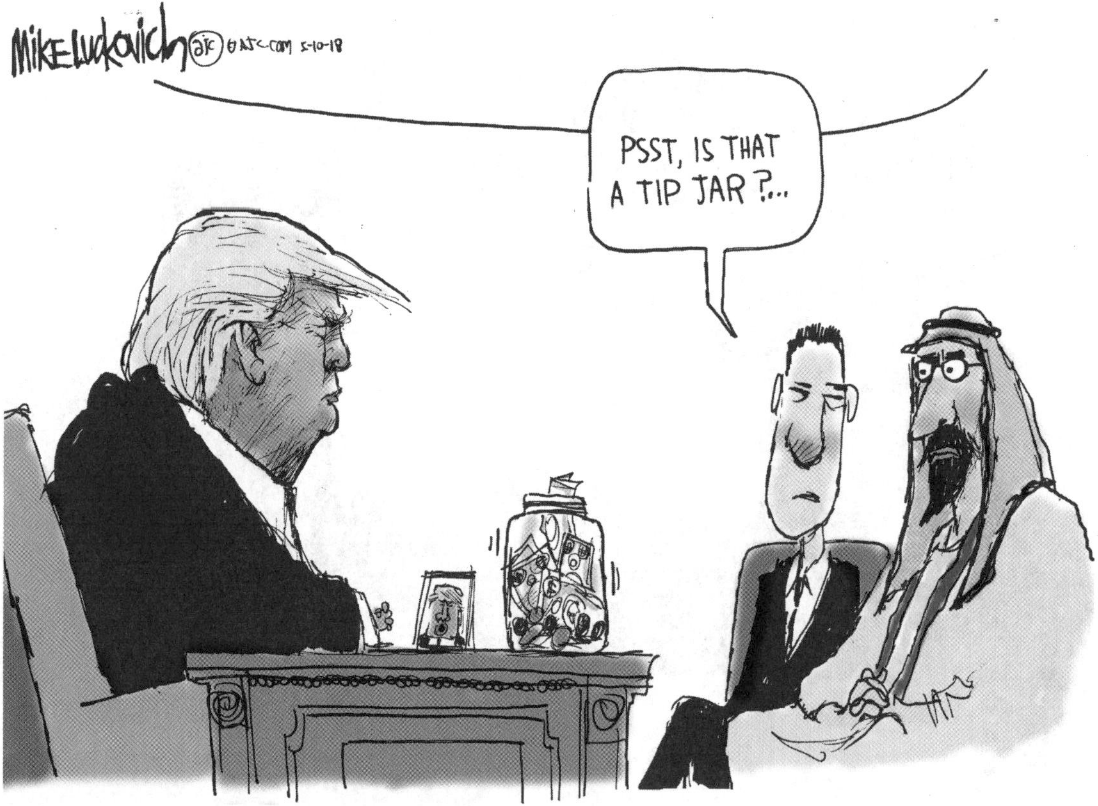
MIKELUCKOVICH
AJC ©AJC.COM 5-10-18
PSST, IS THAT A TIP JAR ?...

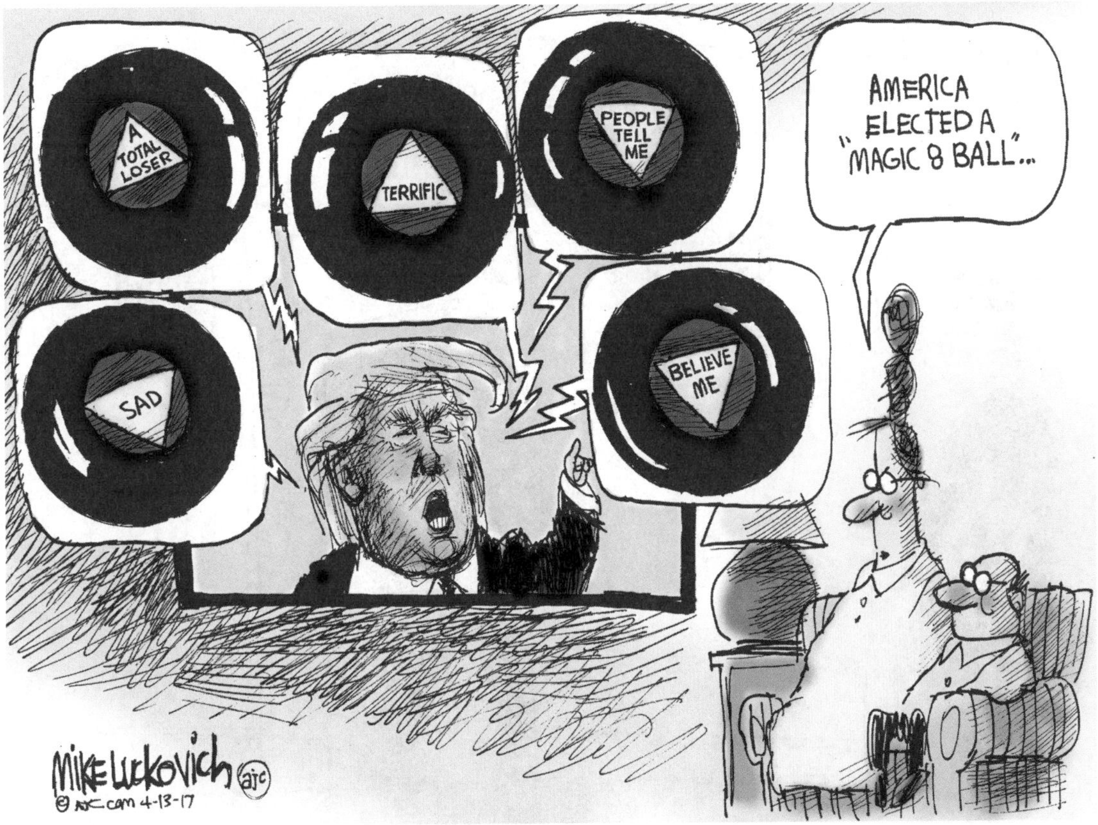
A TOTAL LOSER
TERRIFIC
PEOPLE TELL ME
SAD
BELIEVE ME
AMERICA ELECTED A "MAGIC 8 BALL"...
MIKE LUCKOVICH
ajc
© AJC.com 4-13-17

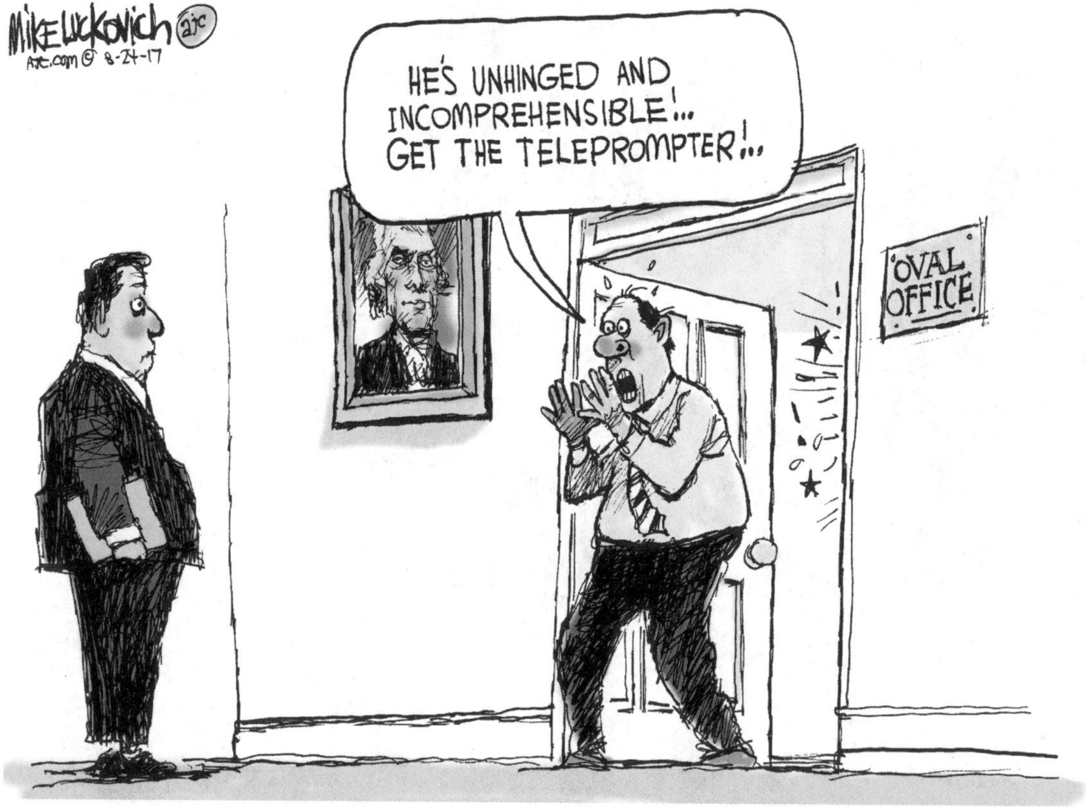
MIKE LUCKOVICH ajc
AJC.com © 8-24-17
HE'S UNHINGED AND INCOMPREHENSIBLE!... GET THE TELEPROMPTER!...
OVAL OFFICE

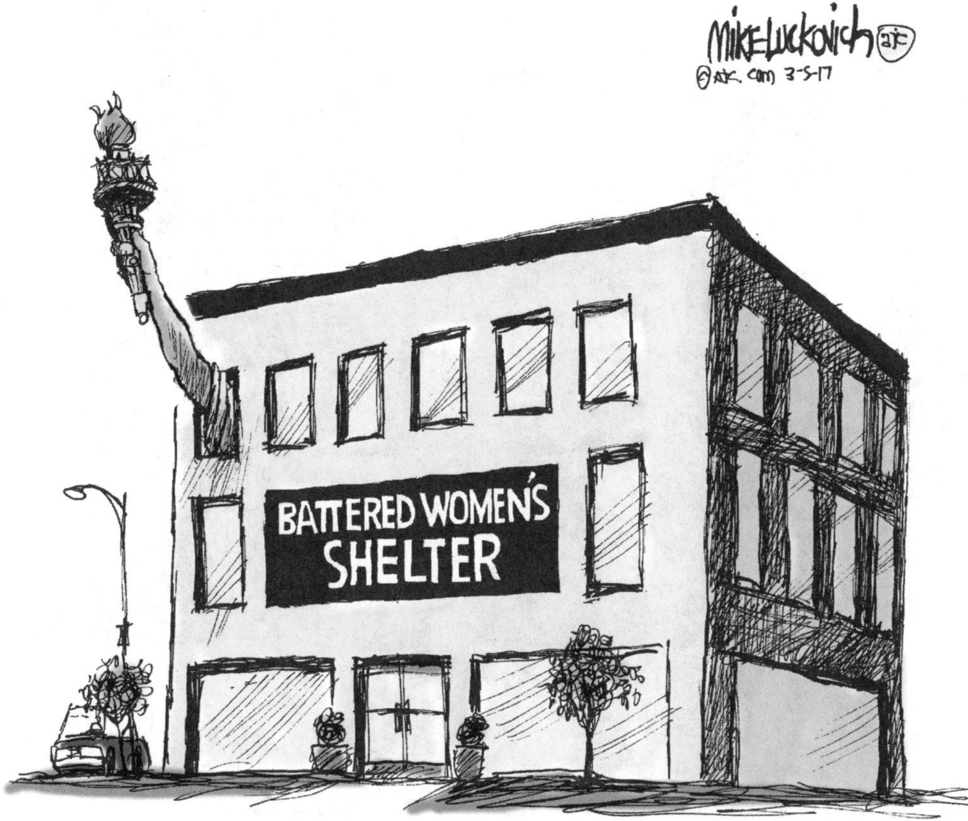
MIKE LUCKOVICH
©AJC.com 3-5-17
BATTERED WOMEN'S
SHELTER

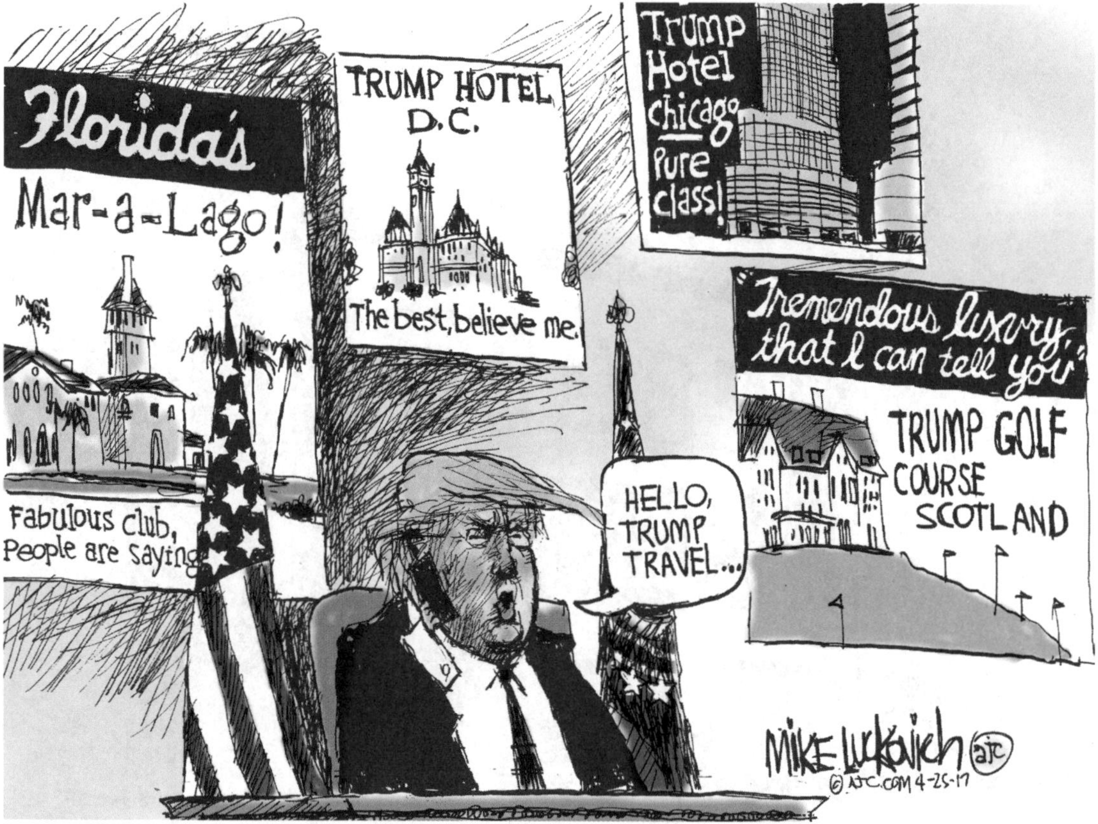
Florida's
Mar-a-Lago!
Fabulous club, People are saying
TRUMP HOTEL D.C.
The best, believe me.
Trump Hotel Chicago Pure class!
"Tremendous luxury, that I can tell you"
TRUMP GOLF COURSE SCOTLAND
HELLO, TRUMP TRAVEL...
MIKE LUCKOVICH ajc
© AJC.COM 4-25-17

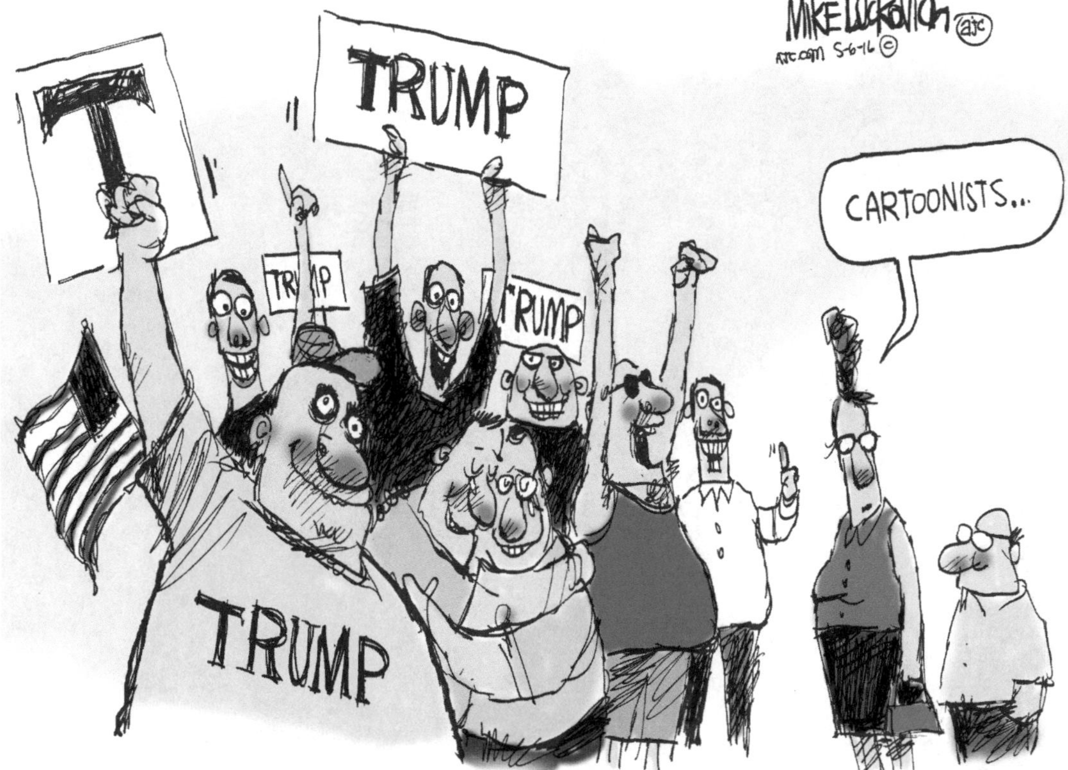
MIKE LUCKOVICH
ajc
ajc.com 5-6-16 ©
T
TRUMP
TRUMP
TRUMP
TRUMP
CARTOONISTS...

 Donald J. Trump
@realDonaldTrump

# THE GOP ENABLERS

RETWEETS    LIKES
3,582       9,935

↑ 1.7K    ⇄ 3.6K    ♥ 99K  ...

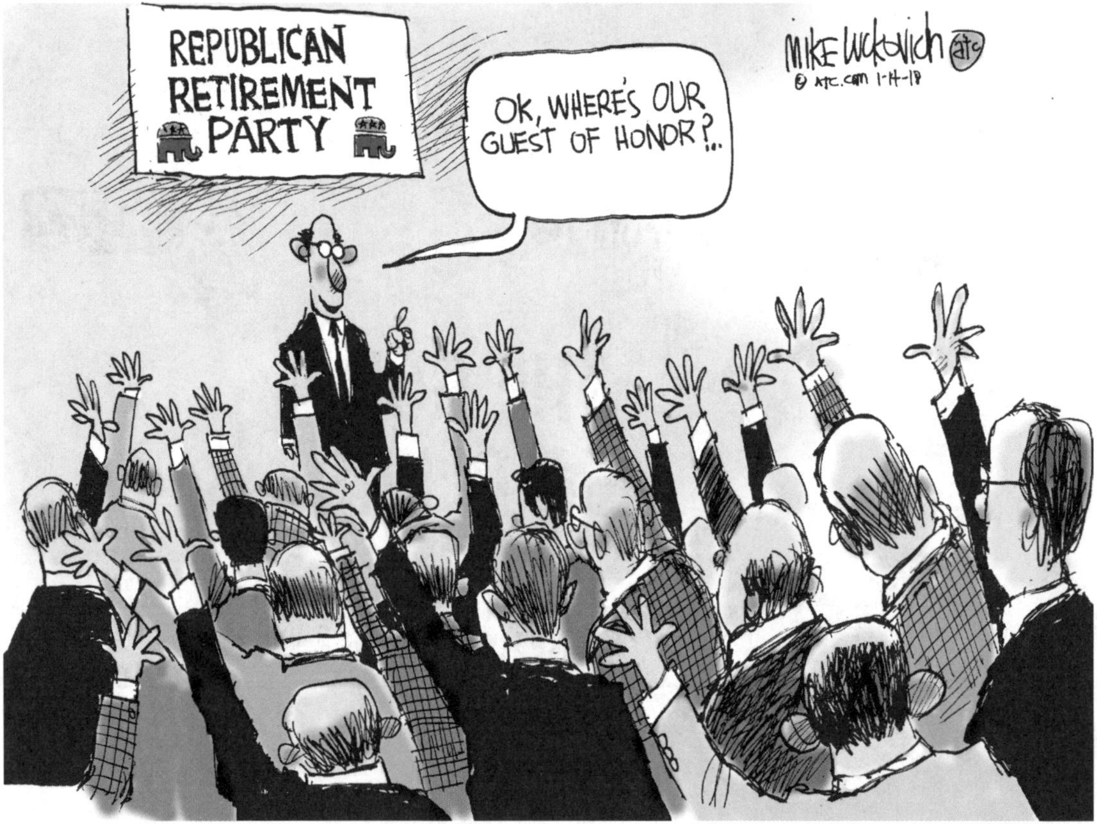
REPUBLICAN RETIREMENT PARTY
OK, WHERE'S OUR GUEST OF HONOR?..
MIKE LUCKOVICH
© AJC.com 1-14-18

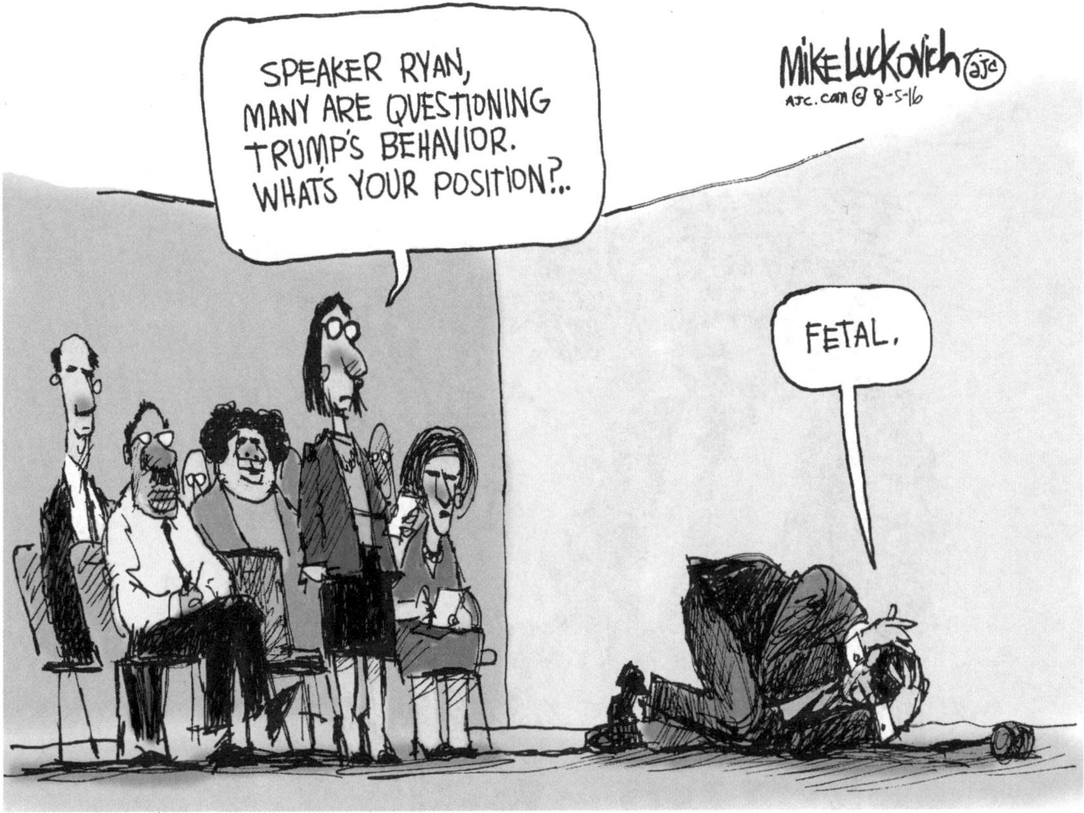
MIKE LUCKOVICH ajc
AJC.com © 8-5-16
SPEAKER RYAN, MANY ARE QUESTIONING TRUMP'S BEHAVIOR. WHAT'S YOUR POSITION?..
FETAL.

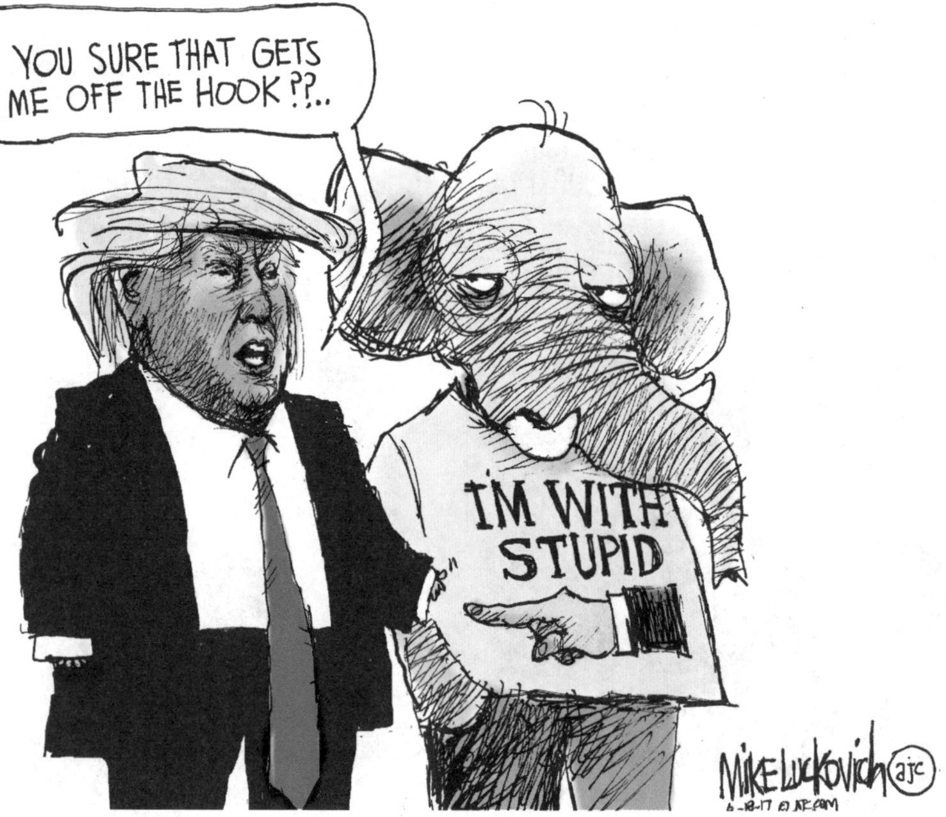
YOU SURE THAT GETS ME OFF THE HOOK ??..
I'M WITH STUPID
MIKE LUCKOVICH ajc

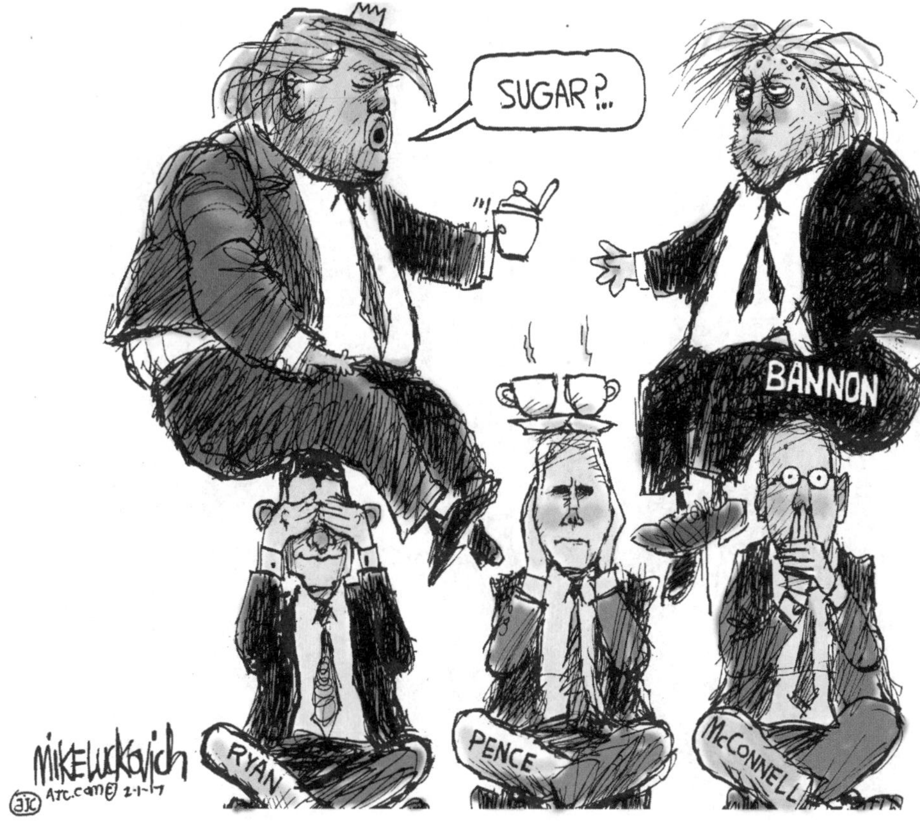
SUGAR?...
BANNON
RYAN
PENCE
McCONNELL
MIKELUCKOVICH

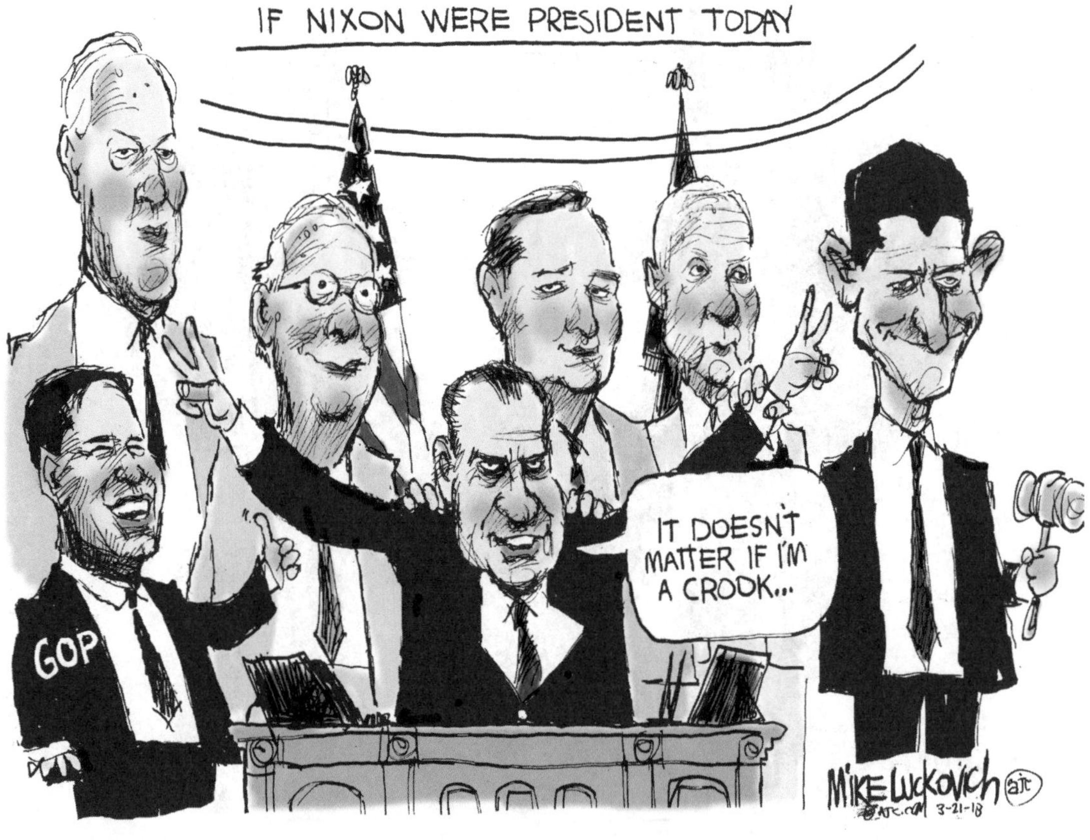
IF NIXON WERE PRESIDENT TODAY
GOP
IT DOESN'T MATTER IF I'M A CROOK...
MIKE LUCKOVICH
3-21-18

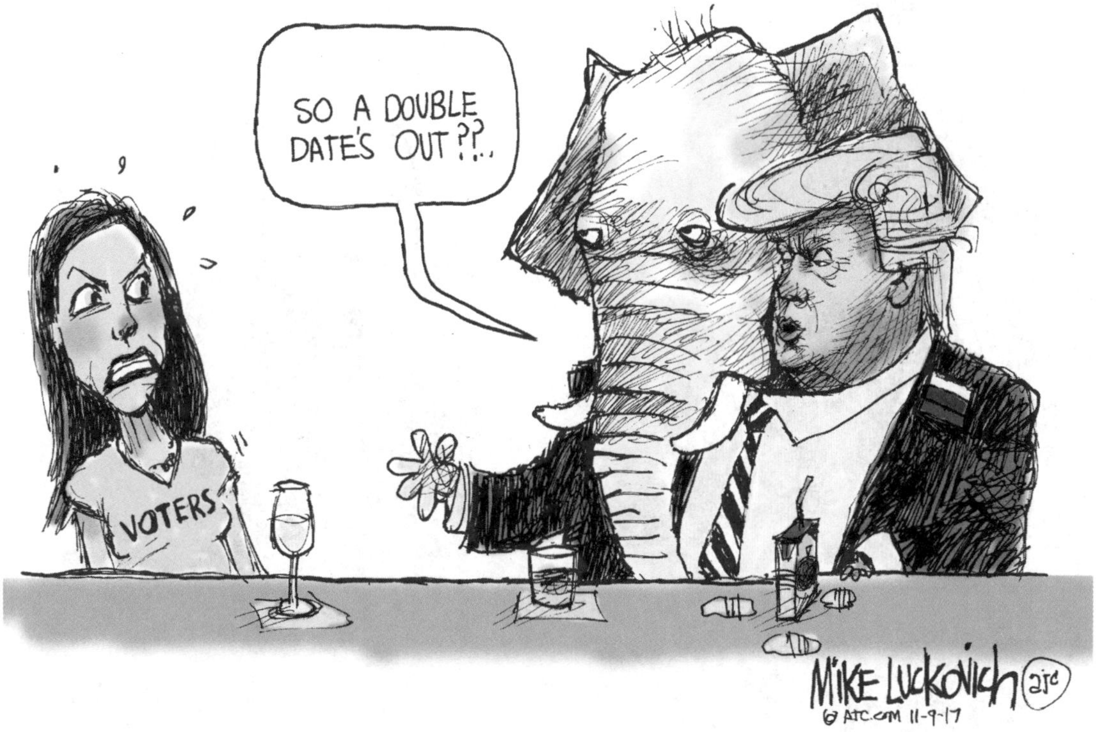
SO A DOUBLE DATE'S OUT??...
VOTERS
MIKE LUCKOVICH
ajc
© AJC.COM 11-9-17

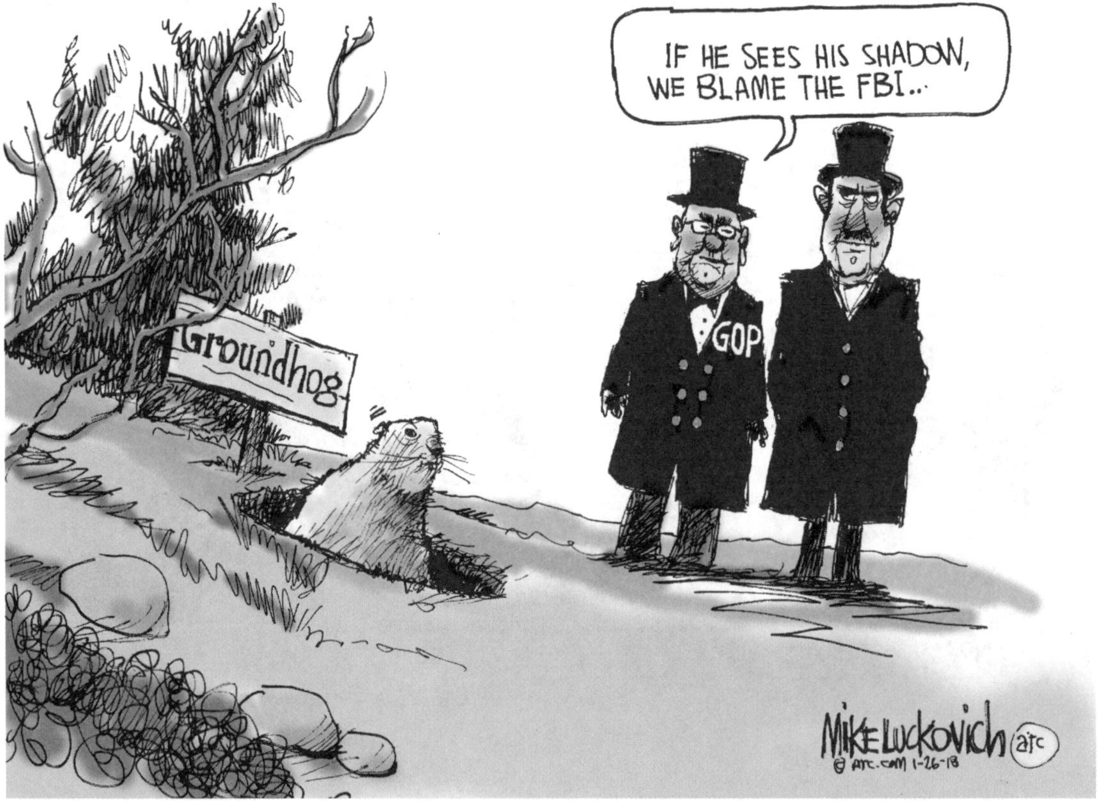
IF HE SEES HIS SHADOW, WE BLAME THE FBI...
Groundhog
GOP
MIKE LUCKOVICH ajc
© ajc.com 1-26-18

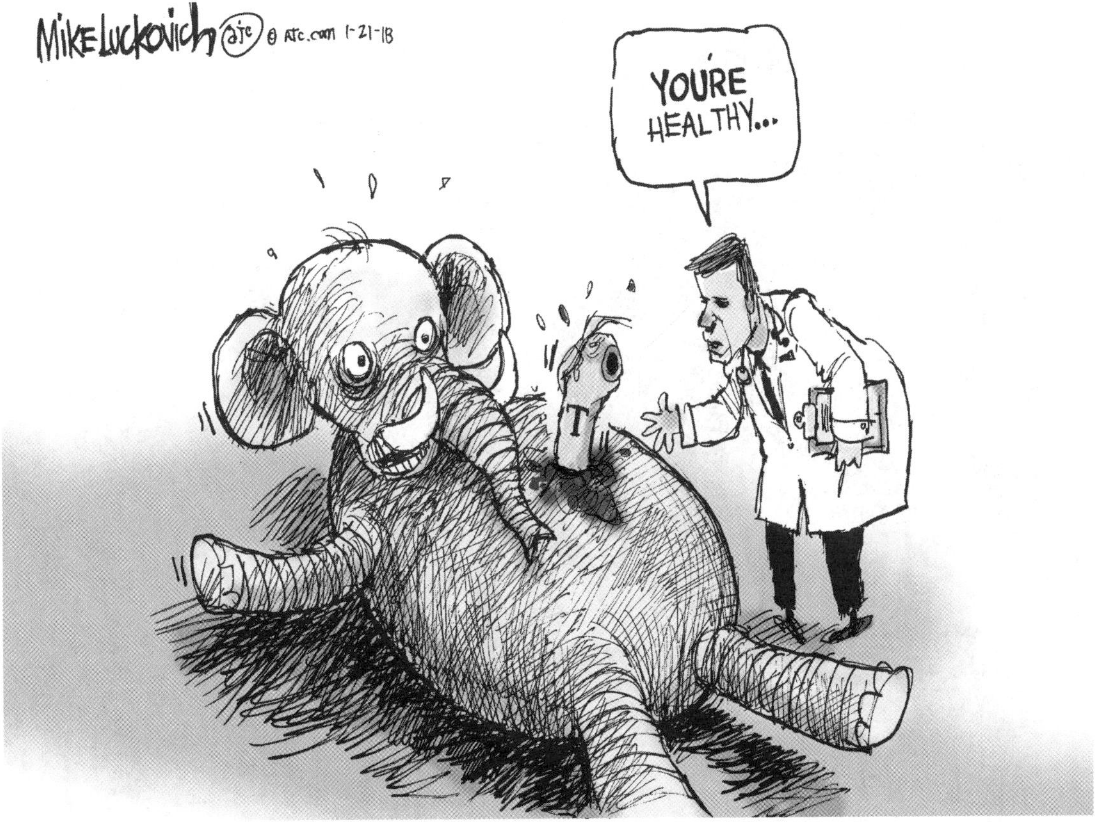
MIKE LUCKOVICH ajc © AJC.com 1-21-18
YOU'RE HEALTHY...
T

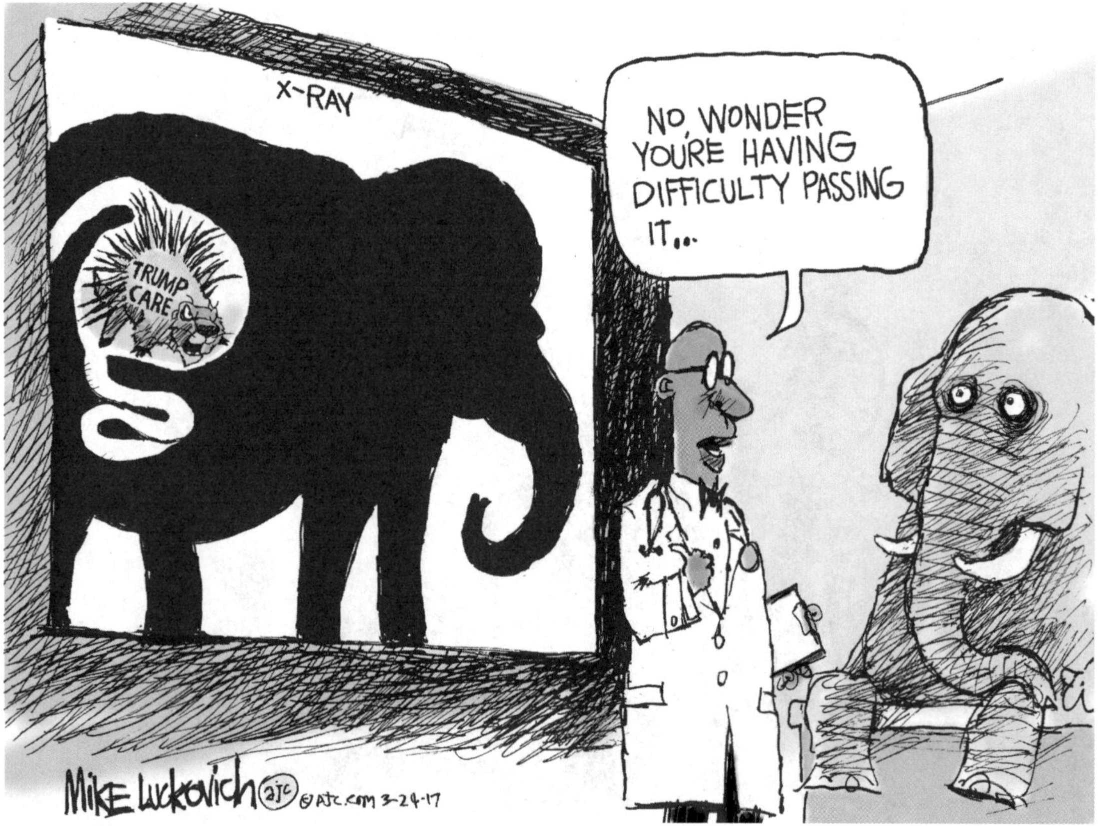
X-RAY
TRUMP CARE
NO, WONDER YOU'RE HAVING DIFFICULTY PASSING IT...
MIKE LUCKOVICH
©AJC.COM 3-24-17

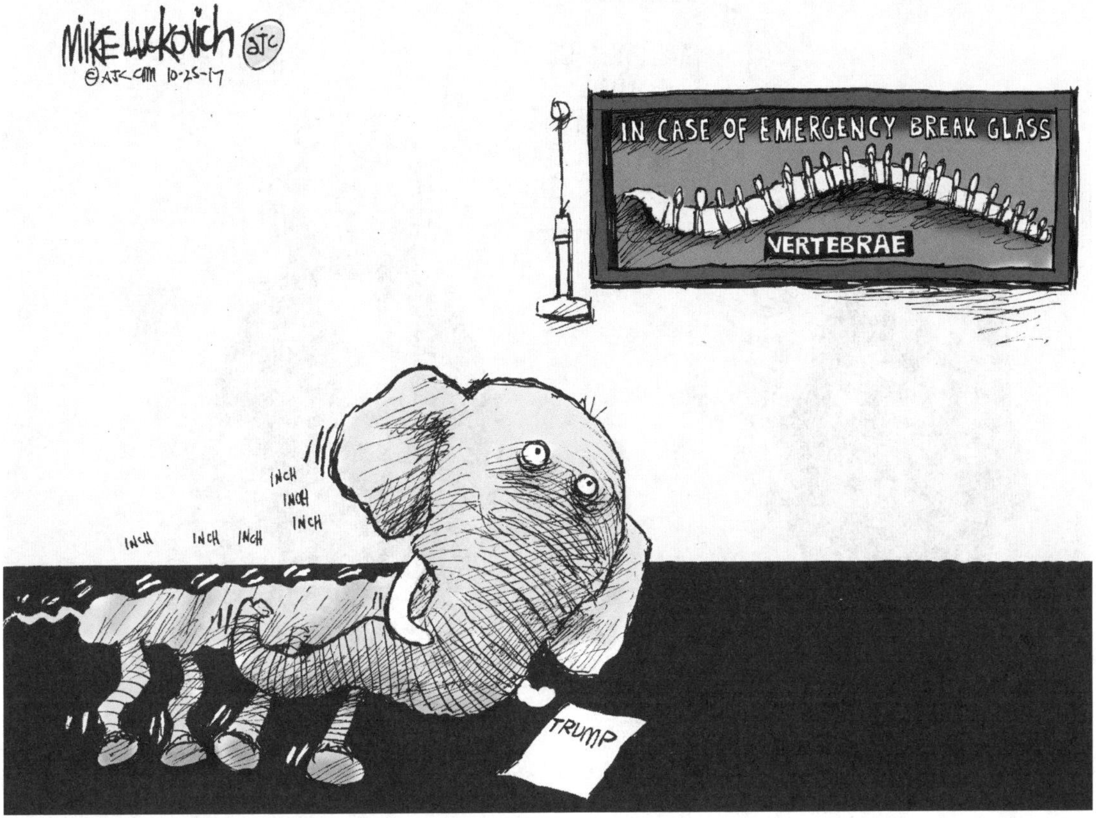
MIKE LUCKOVICH
AJC
©AJC.COM 10-25-17
IN CASE OF EMERGENCY BREAK GLASS
VERTEBRAE
INCH
INCH
INCH
INCH
INCH
INCH
TRUMP

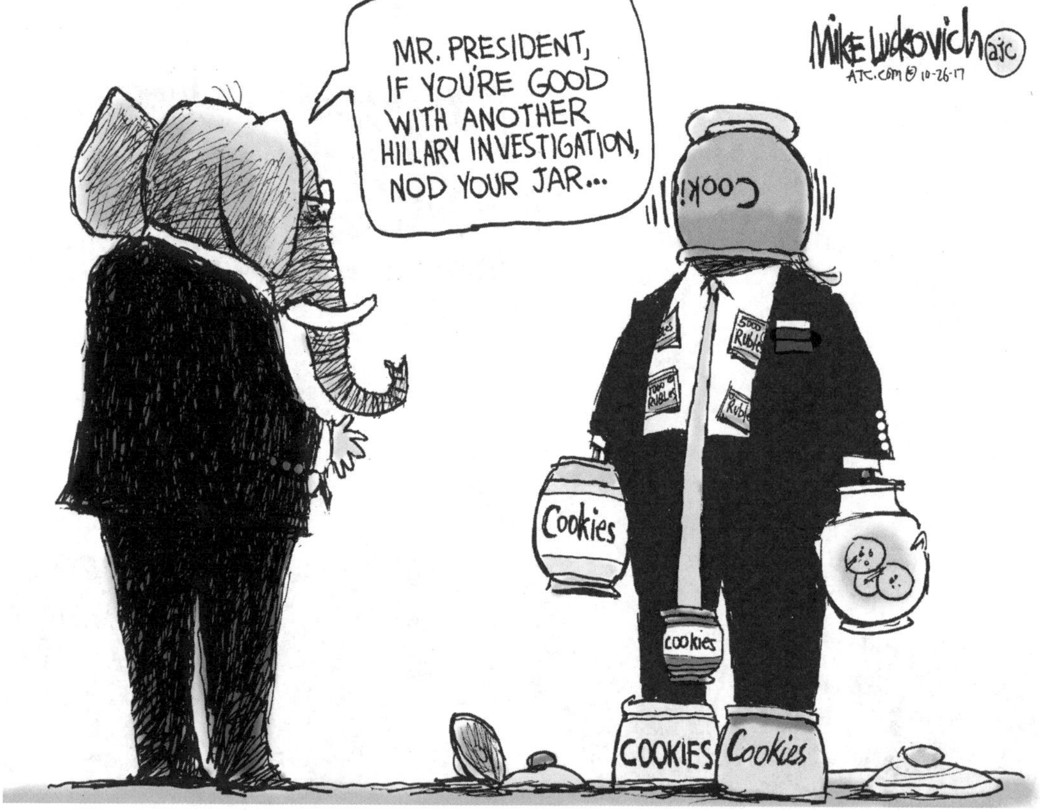
MR. PRESIDENT, IF YOU'RE GOOD WITH ANOTHER HILLARY INVESTIGATION, NOD YOUR JAR...
MIKE LUCKOVICH ajc
AJC.com © 10-26-17
Cookies
cookies
COOKIES
Cookies

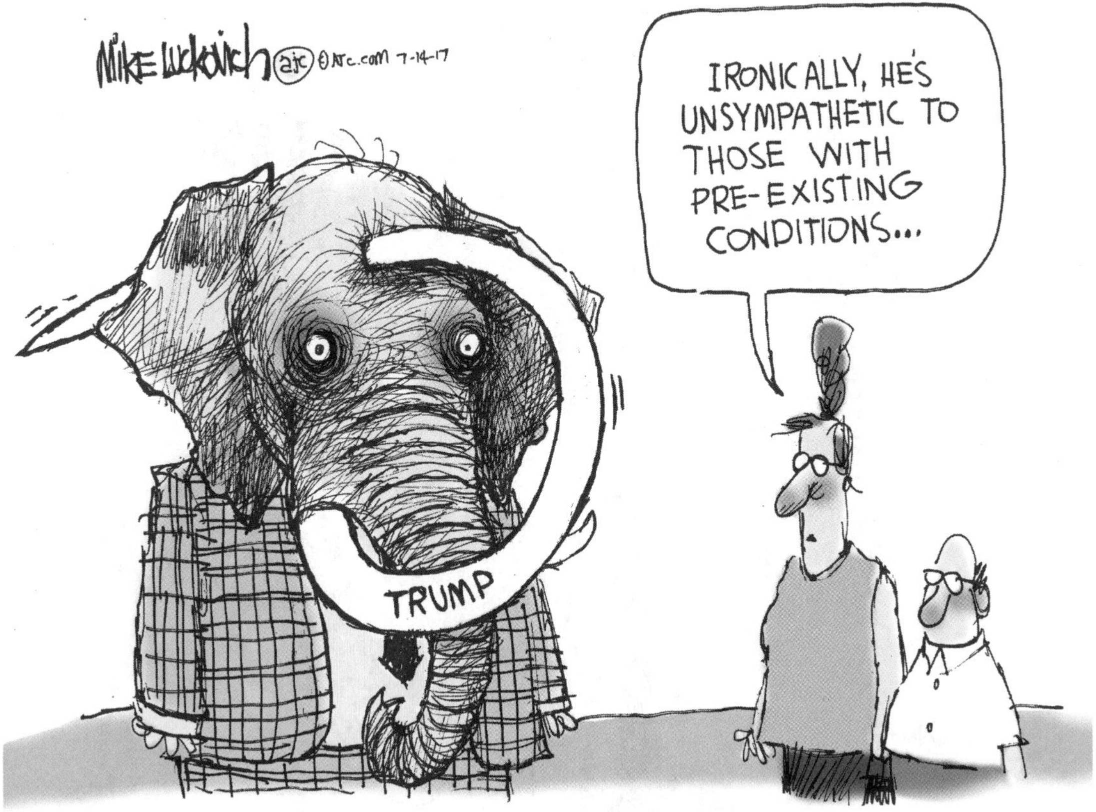

MIKE LUCKOVICH ajc ©AJC.com 7-14-17
IRONICALLY, HE'S UNSYMPATHETIC TO THOSE WITH PRE-EXISTING CONDITIONS...
TRUMP

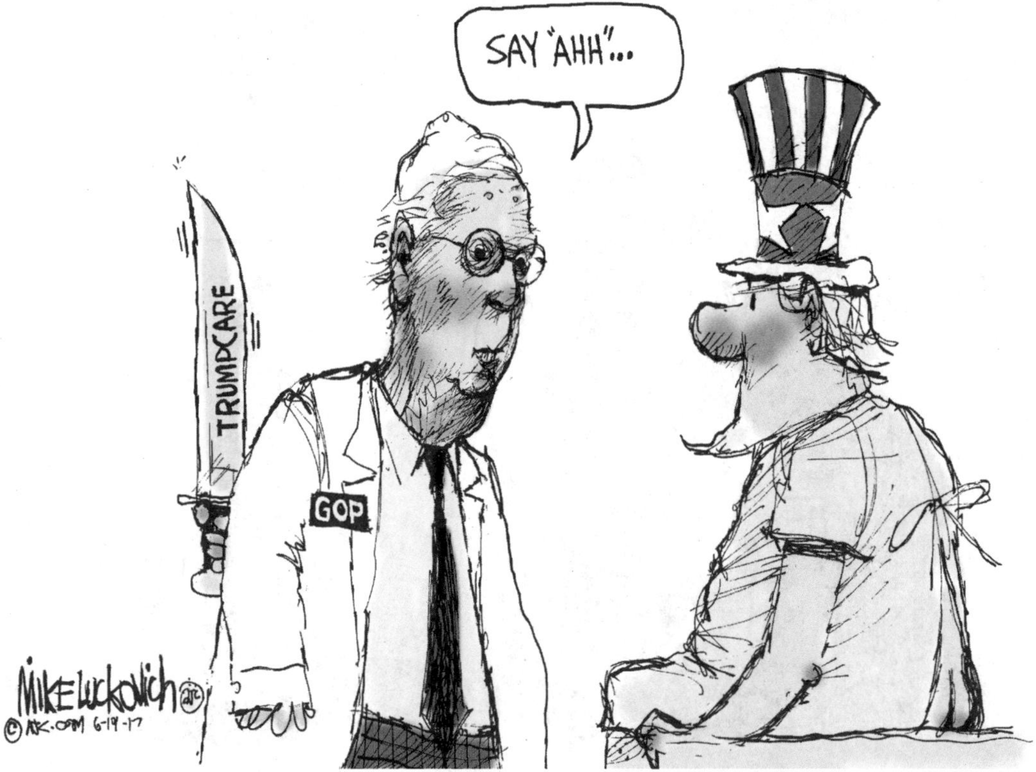
SAY "AHH"...
TRUMPCARE
GOP
MIKE LUCKOVICH
© AJC.COM 6-19-17

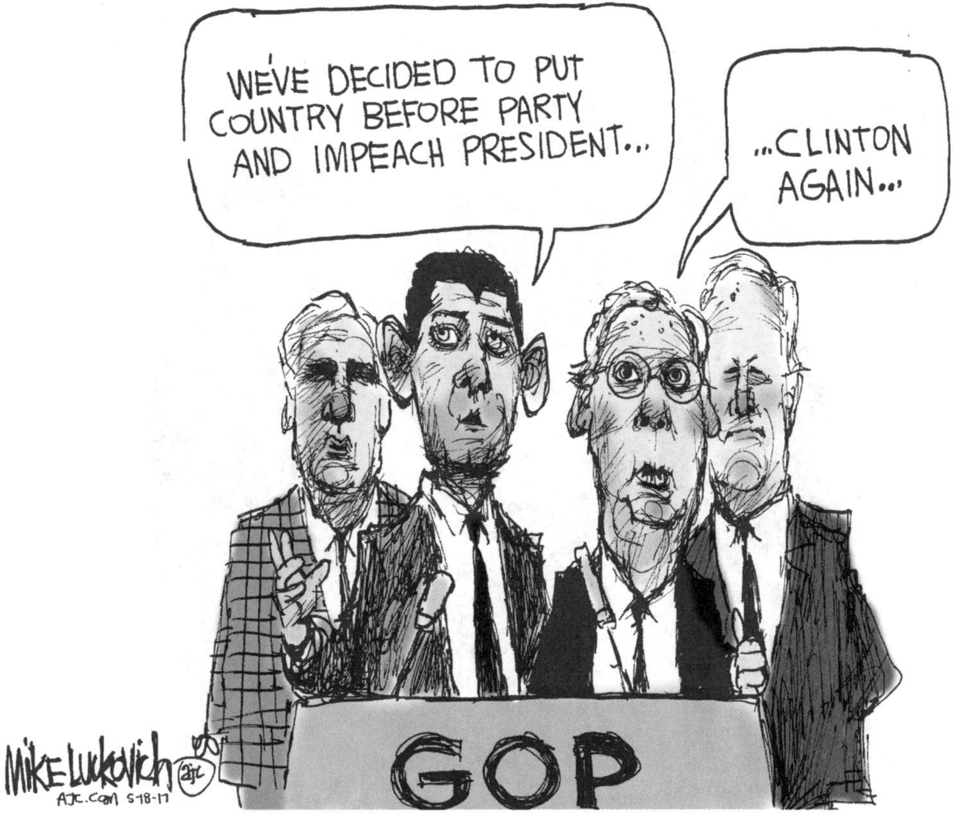
WE'VE DECIDED TO PUT COUNTRY BEFORE PARTY AND IMPEACH PRESIDENT...
...CLINTON AGAIN...
GOP
MIKE LUCKOVICH
AJC.COM 5-18-17

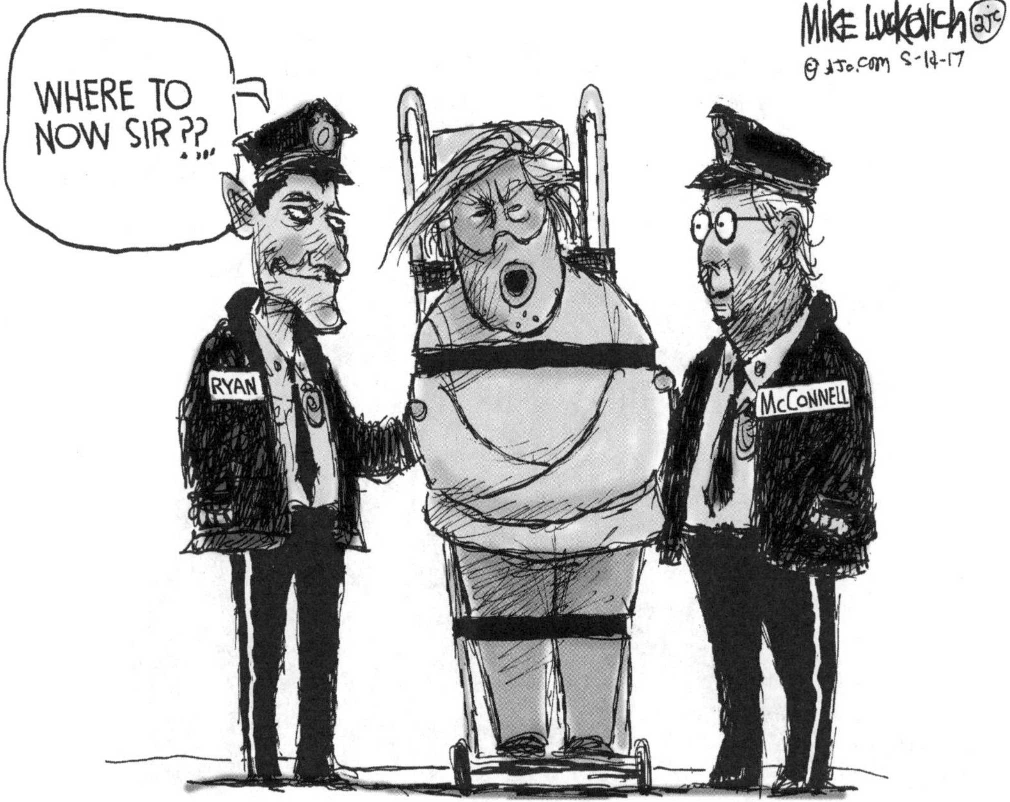
MIKE LUCKOVICH AJC
© AJC.com 5-14-17
WHERE TO NOW SIR ??
RYAN
McCONNELL

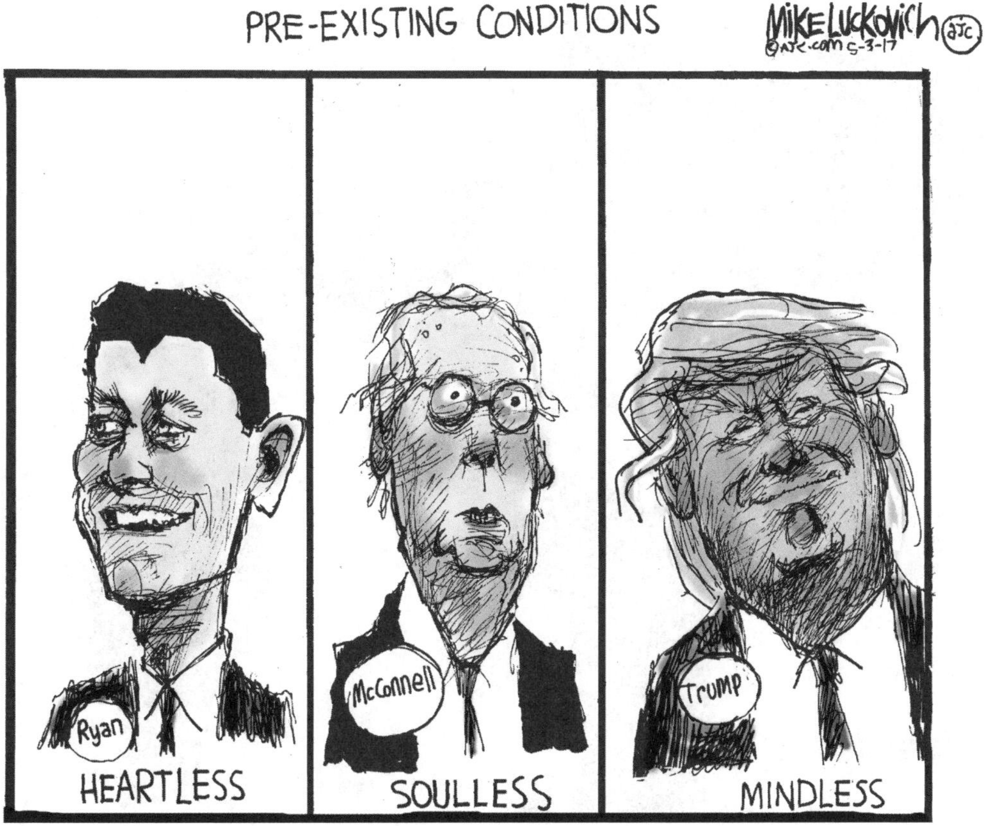
PRE-EXISTING CONDITIONS
MIKE LUCKOVICH ©ajc.com 5-3-17 ajc
Ryan
HEARTLESS
McConnell
SOULLESS
Trump
MINDLESS

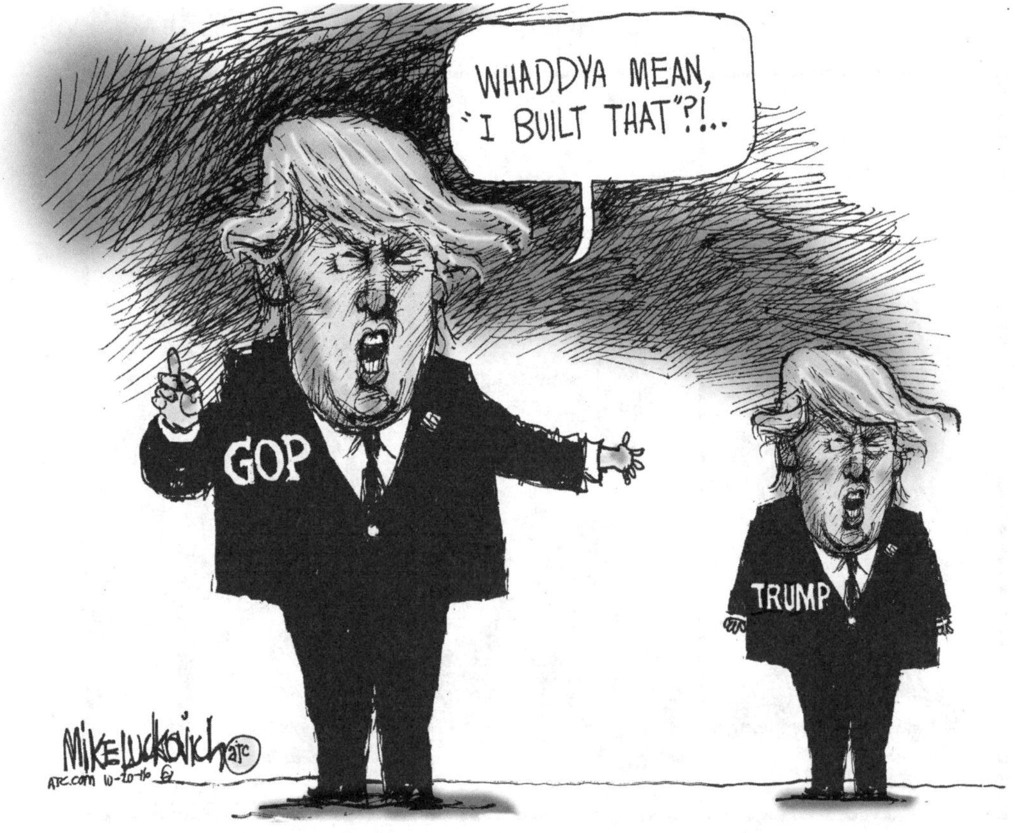
WHADDYA MEAN, "I BUILT THAT"?!...
GOP
TRUMP
MIKELUCKOVICH

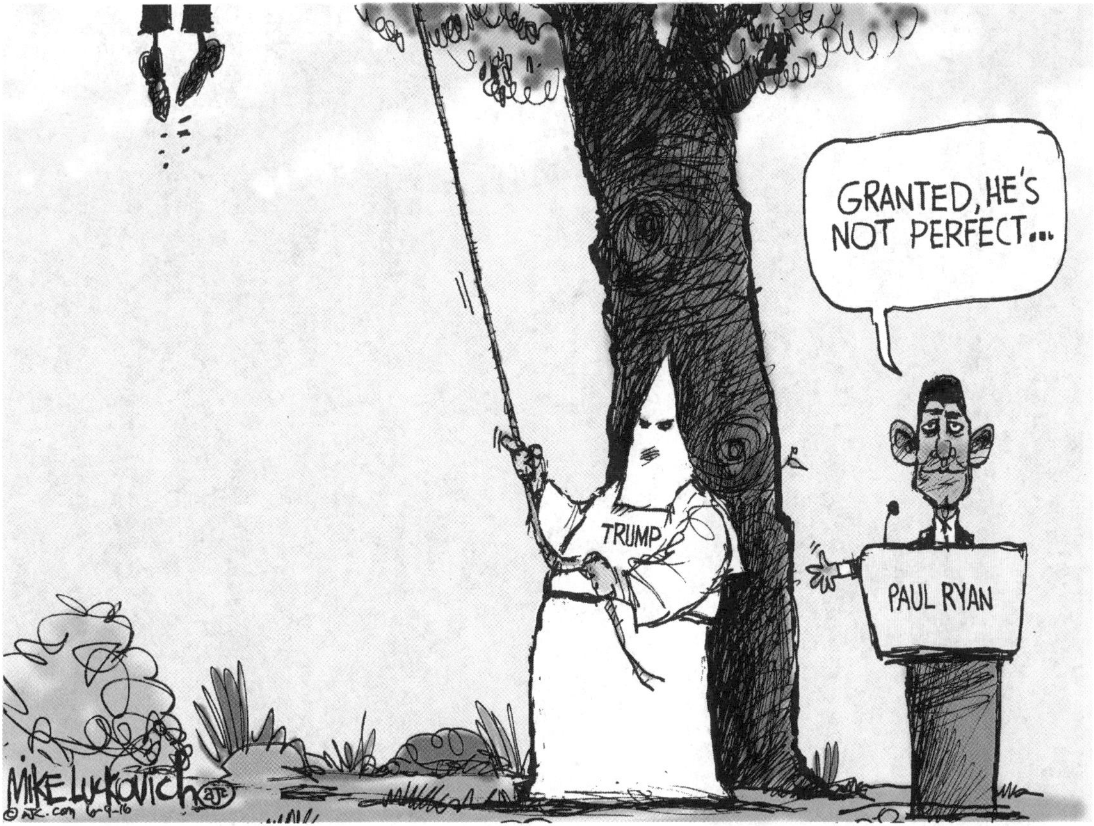
GRANTED, HE'S NOT PERFECT...
TRUMP
PAUL RYAN
MIKE LUCKOVICH

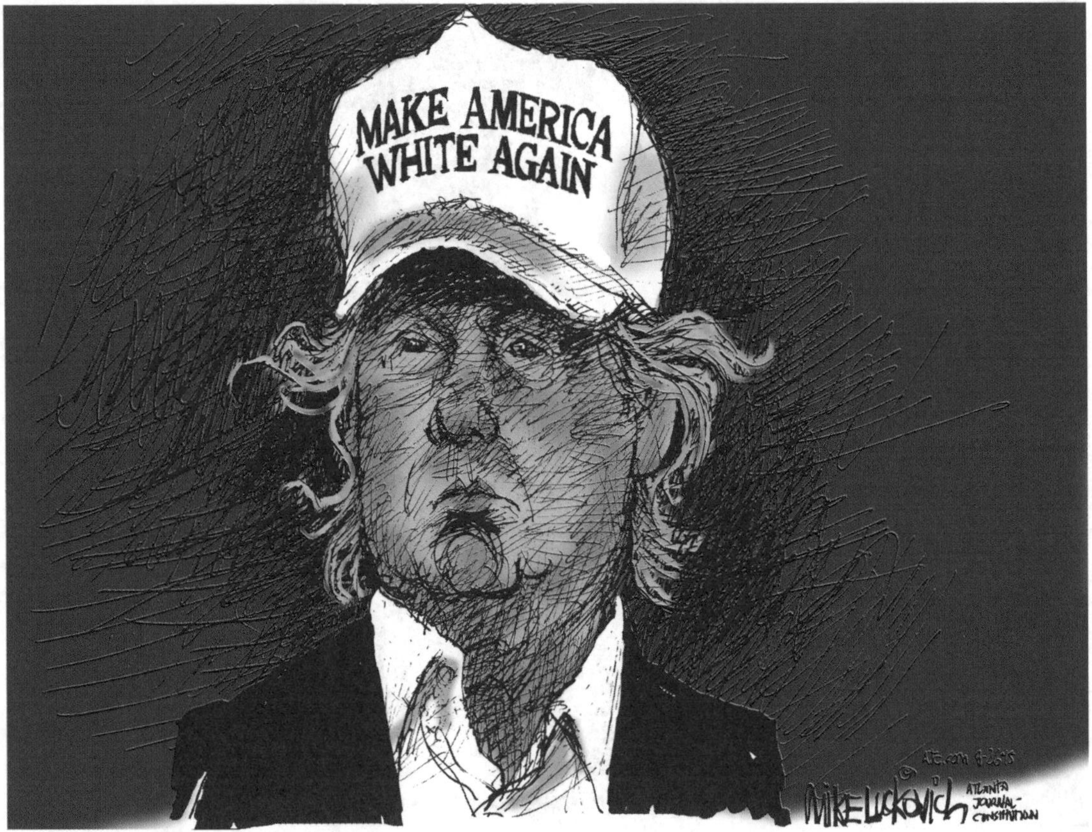
MAKE AMERICA
WHITE AGAIN
MIKE LUCKOVICH
ATLANTA JOURNAL-CONSTITUTION

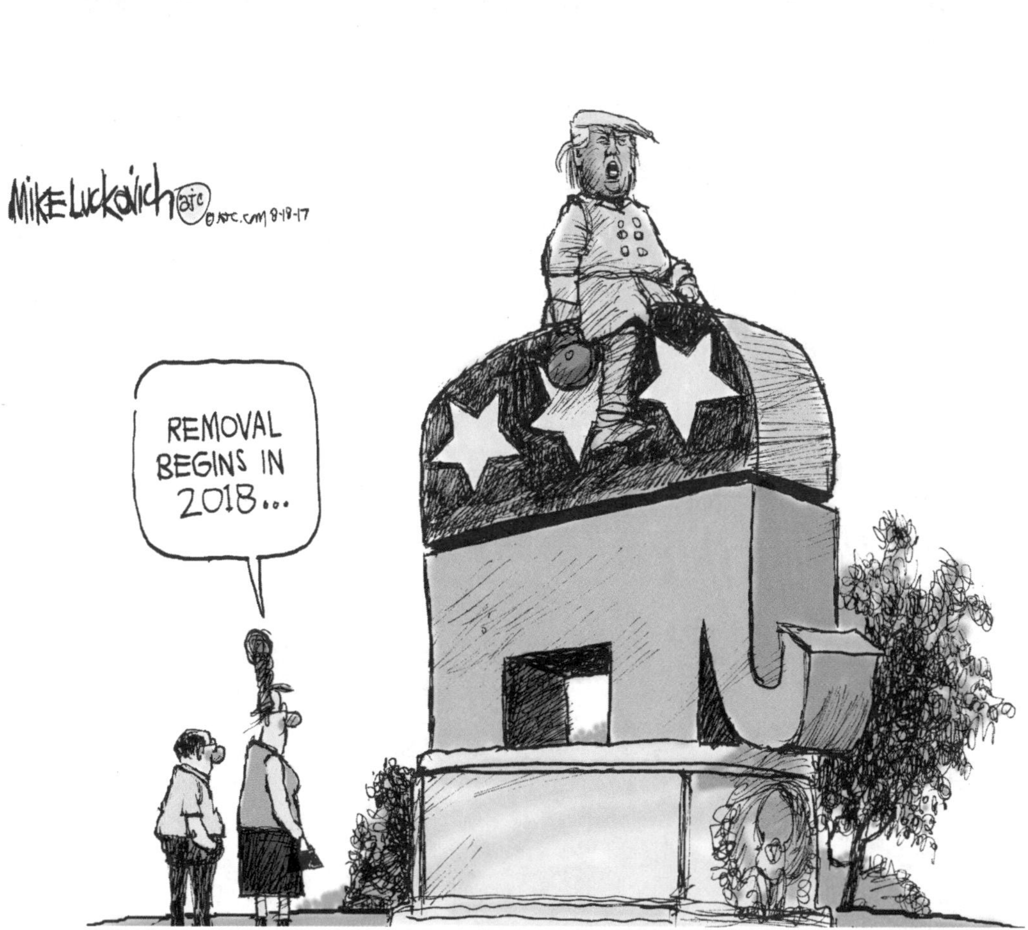
MIKE LUCKOVICH
REMOVAL BEGINS IN 2018...

 Donald J. Trump
@realDonaldTrump

 Following

# FREE MELANIA!
# THE TRUMP FAMILY

RETWEETS   LIKES
3,582      9,935

1.7K   3.6K   99K ...

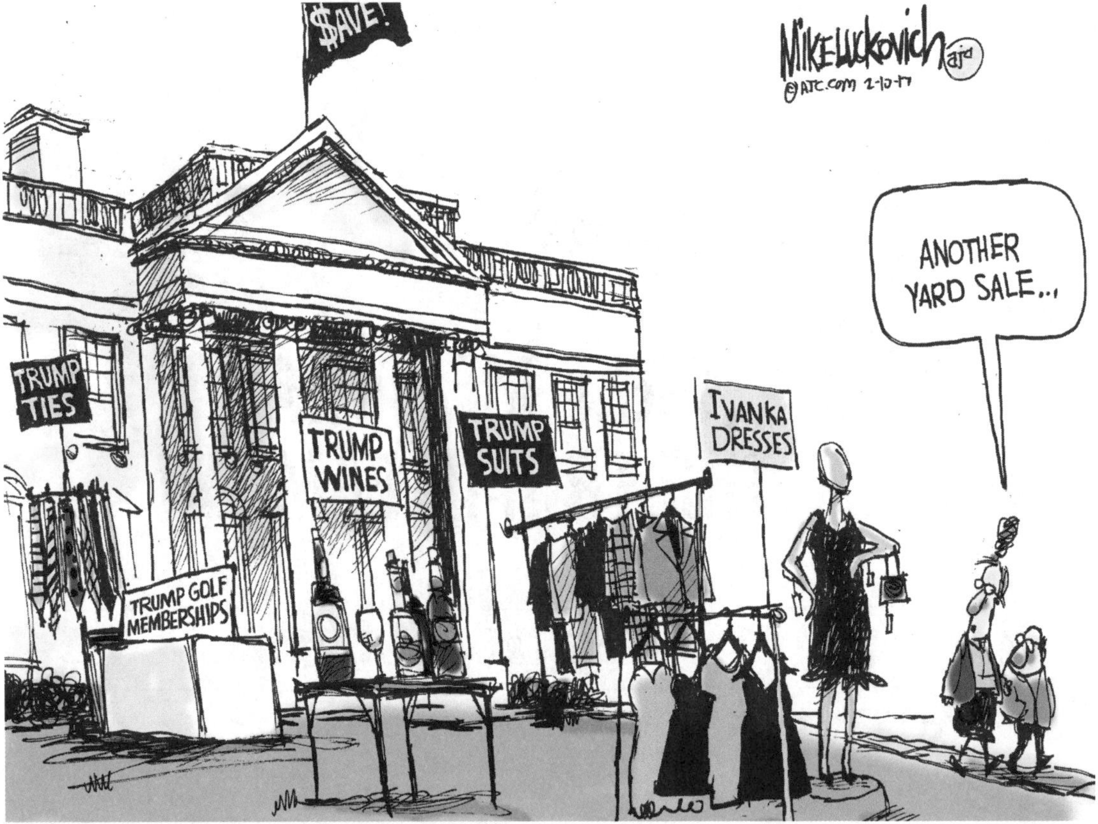
$AVE!
MIKE LUCKOVICH AJC
©AJC.com 2-10-17
TRUMP TIES
TRUMP GOLF MEMBERSHIPS
TRUMP WINES
TRUMP SUITS
IVANKA DRESSES
ANOTHER YARD SALE...

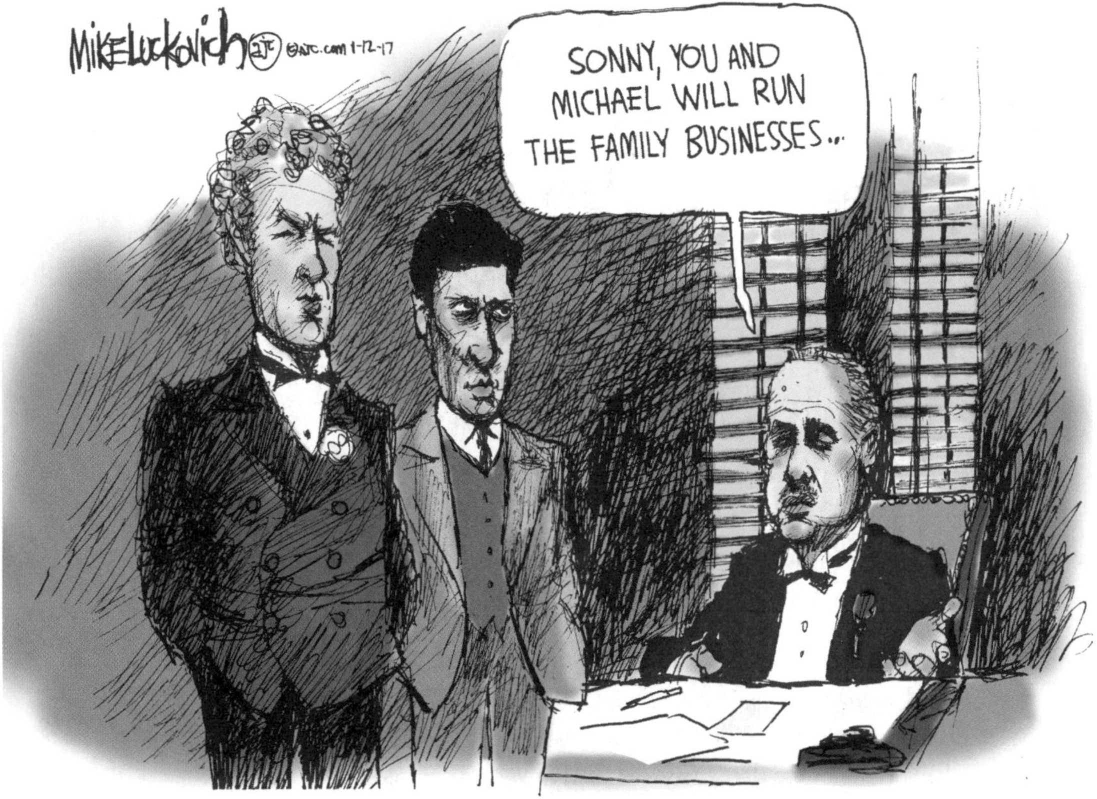
MIKELUCKOVICH AJC ©AJC.com 1-12-17
SONNY, YOU AND MICHAEL WILL RUN THE FAMILY BUSINESSES...

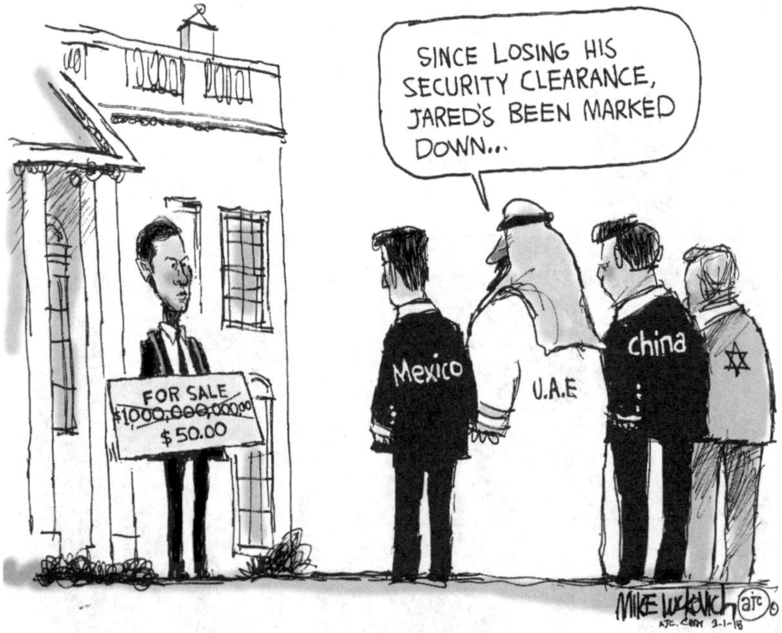
SINCE LOSING HIS SECURITY CLEARANCE, JARED'S BEEN MARKED DOWN...
FOR SALE
$1000,000,000.00
$50.00
Mexico
U.A.E
china
MIKE LUCKOVICH
AJC.COM

The chaos Trump produces almost makes you forget about the corruption. Jared, Ivanka's husband, is another shady operator. Drowning in debt, he's every bit the businessman his father-in-law is. Jared's eyes seem kind of dead to me, and he always looks like he's about to dart away. I recently tweeted a photo of Jared's head next to a photo of a deer's head; they looked like they were separated at birth.

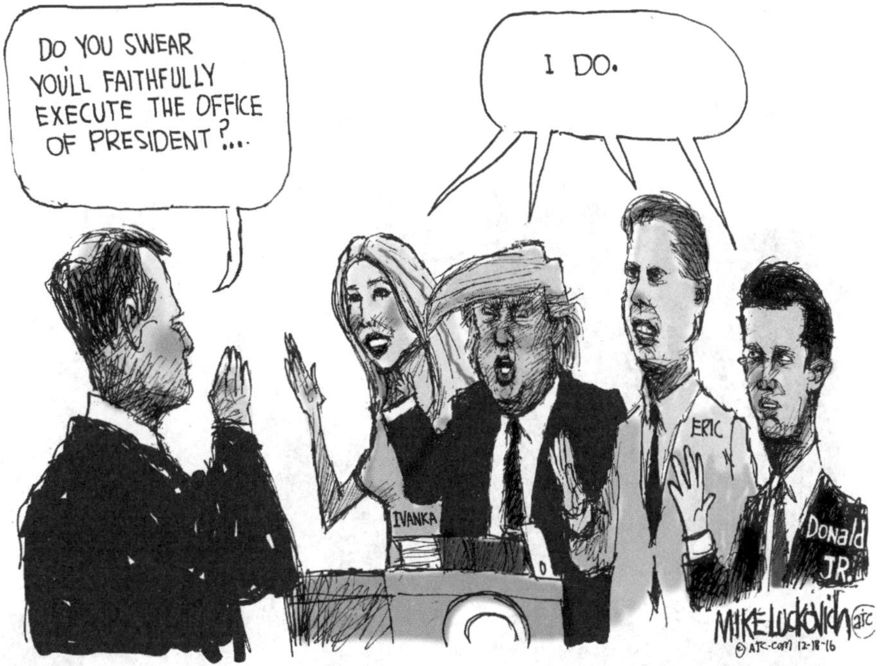
DO YOU SWEAR YOU'LL FAITHFULLY EXECUTE THE OFFICE OF PRESIDENT?...
I DO.
IVANKA
ERIC
DONALD JR.
MIKE LUCKOVICH
© AJC.COM 12-18-16

If I had to choose my favorite Trump family members, they'd be the sons, Don Jr. and Eric. They're funny looking, both having a chin that kind of blends into their necks — plus they're stupid. Beavis and Butthead come to life. Other than Trump's youngest son, Barron, the entire lot of them are grifters.

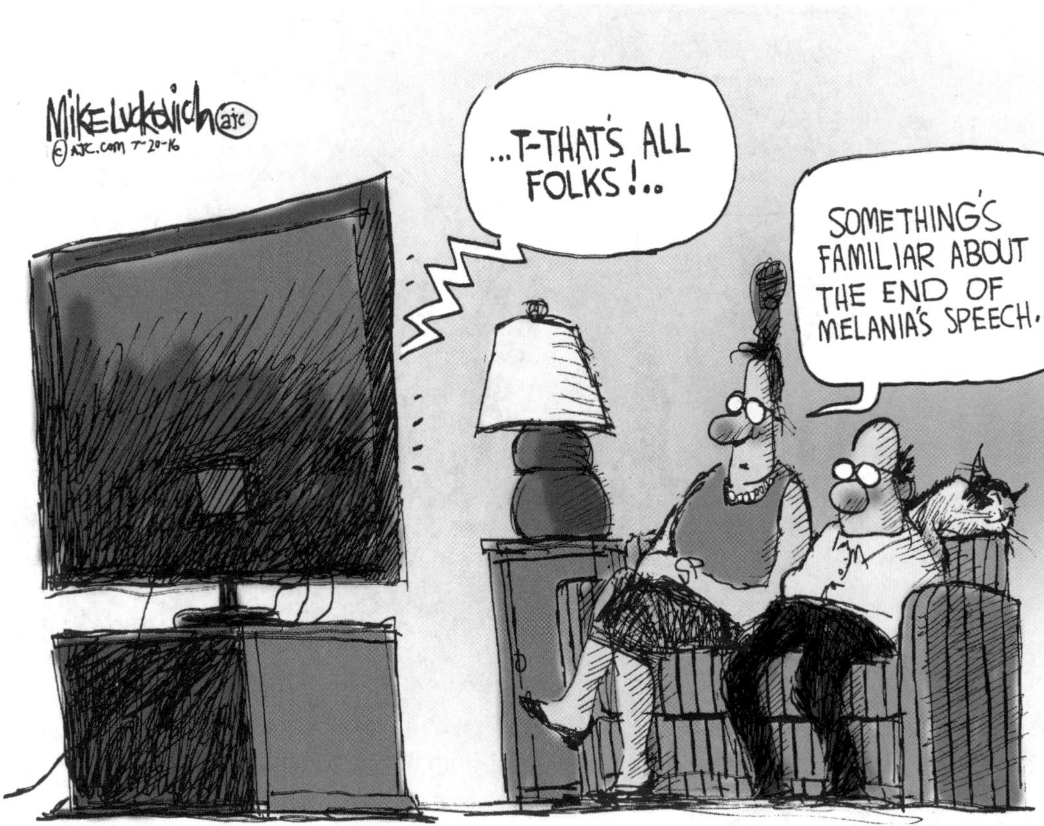
MIKE LUCKOVICH AJC
© AJC.com 7-20-16
...T-THAT'S ALL FOLKS!..
SOMETHING'S FAMILIAR ABOUT THE END OF MELANIA'S SPEECH...

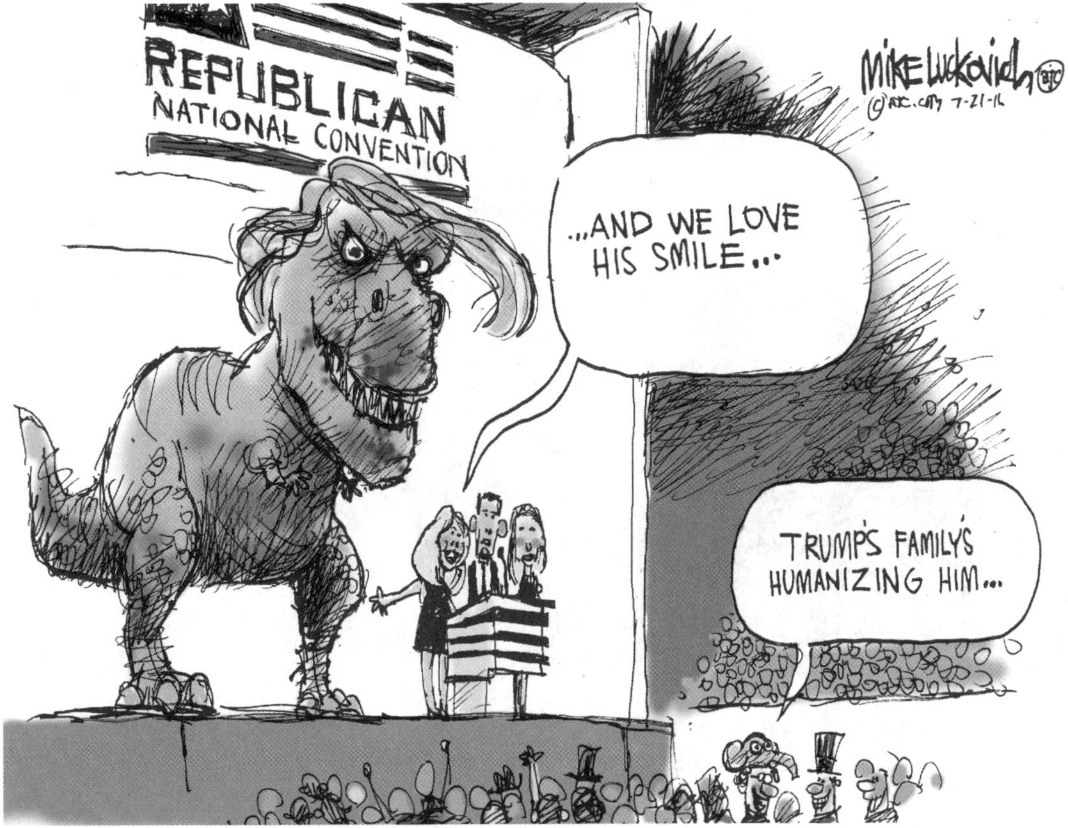
REPUBLICAN NATIONAL CONVENTION
MIKE LUCKOVICH
...AND WE LOVE HIS SMILE...
TRUMP'S FAMILY'S HUMANIZING HIM...

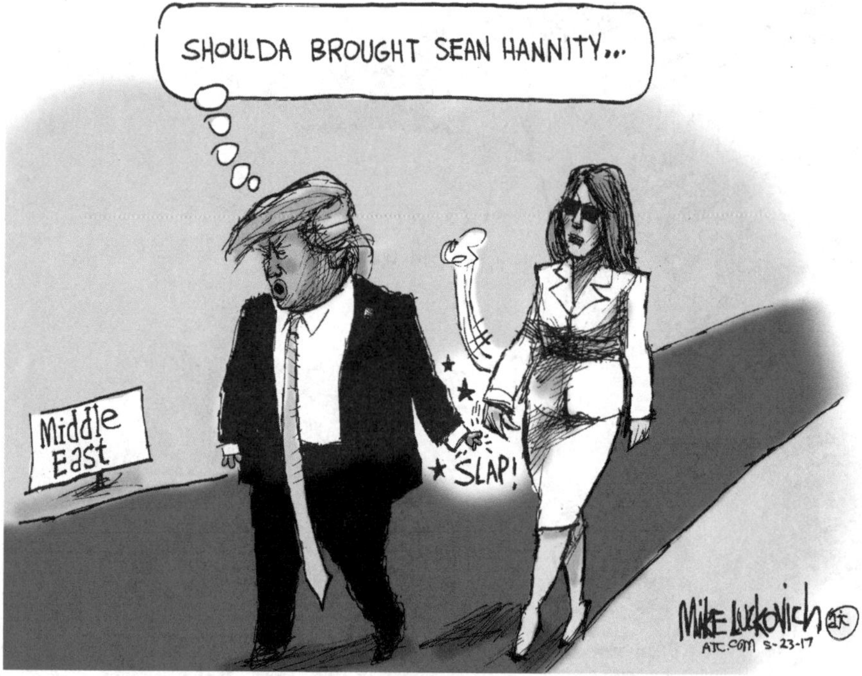
SHOULDA BROUGHT SEAN HANNITY...
Middle East
SLAP!
MIKE LUCKOVICH
AJC.com 5-23-17

My views on Melania are a little more nuanced. There are times I feel sorry for her having to put up with that orange cretin, but then I remind myself she signed up for this.

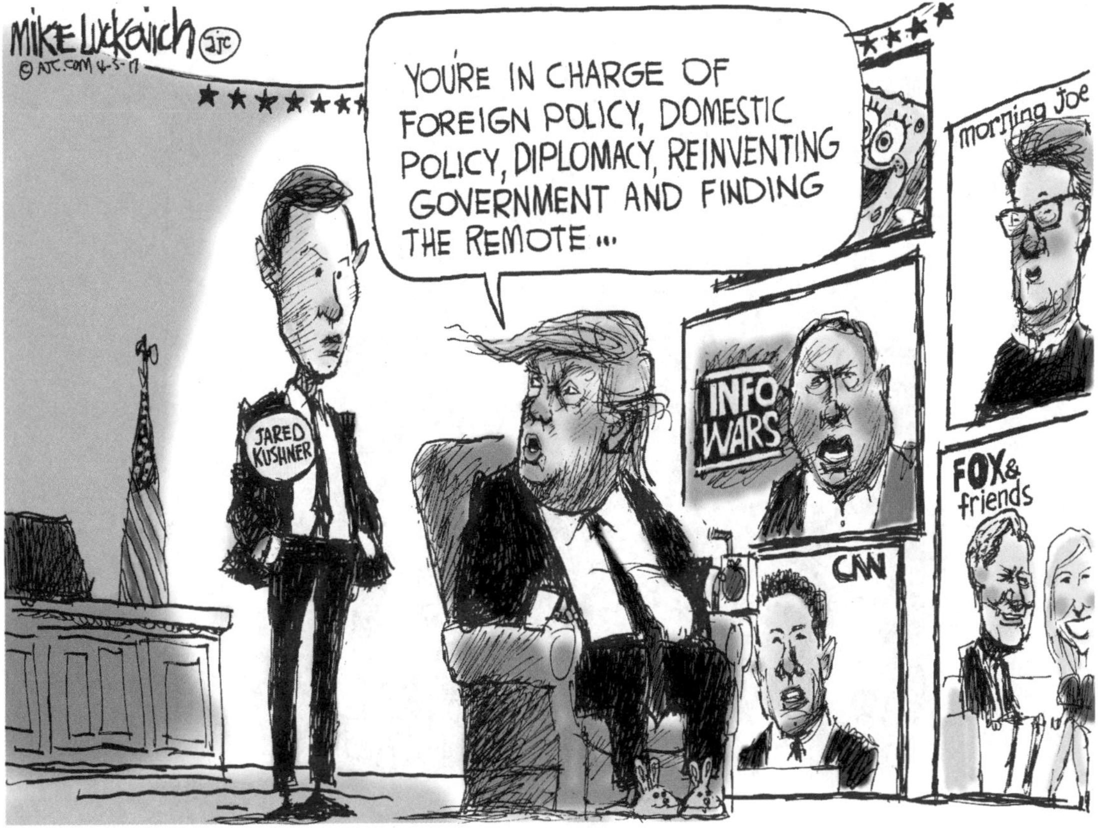
MIKE LUCKOVICH AJC
© AJC.COM 6-3-17
YOU'RE IN CHARGE OF FOREIGN POLICY, DOMESTIC POLICY, DIPLOMACY, REINVENTING GOVERNMENT AND FINDING THE REMOTE ...
morning Joe
INFO WARS
JARED KUSHNER
FOX & friends
CNN

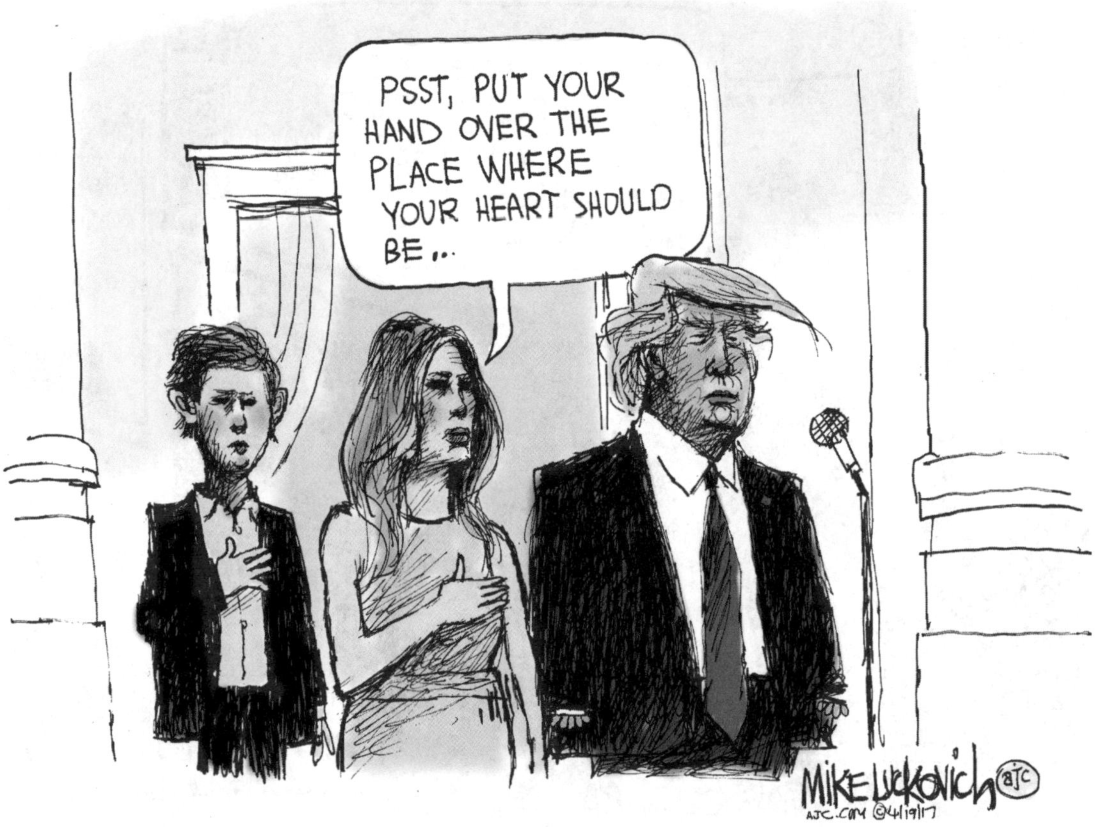
PSST, PUT YOUR HAND OVER THE PLACE WHERE YOUR HEART SHOULD BE...
MIKE LUCKOVICH
AJC.COM ©4/19/17

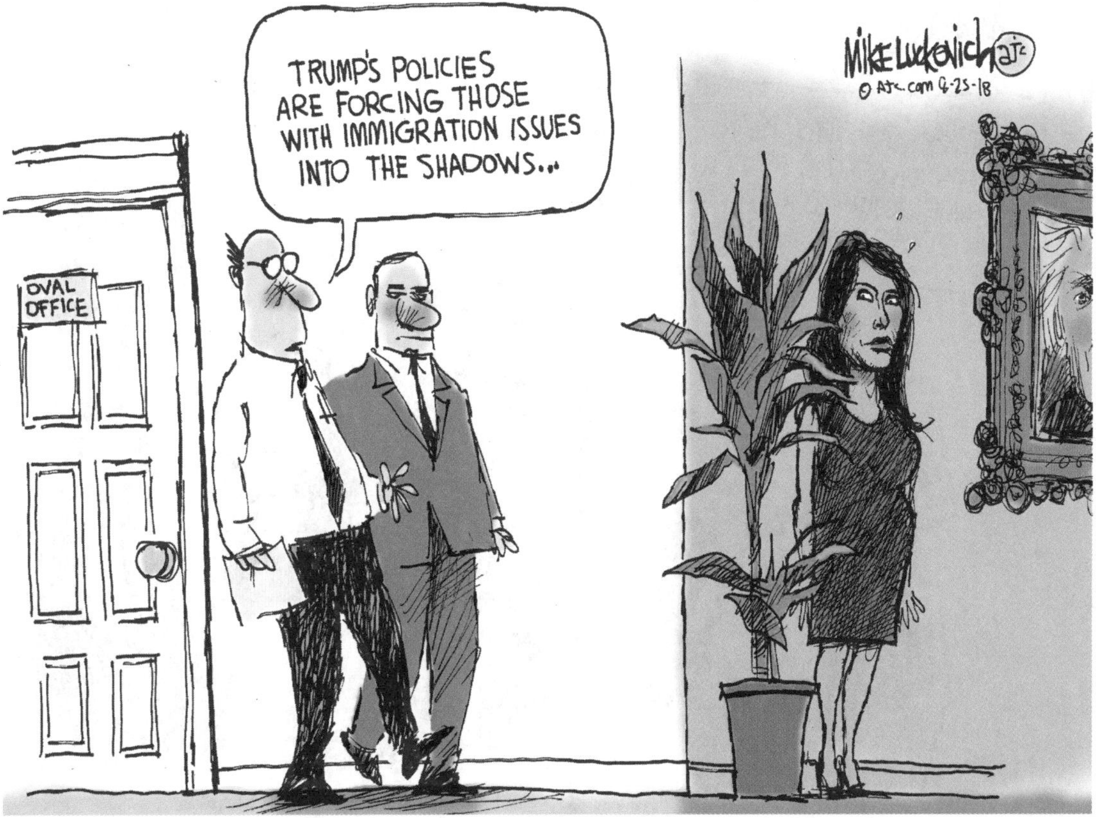
TRUMP'S POLICIES ARE FORCING THOSE WITH IMMIGRATION ISSUES INTO THE SHADOWS...
OVAL OFFICE
MIKE LUCKOVICH
© AJC.com 6-25-18

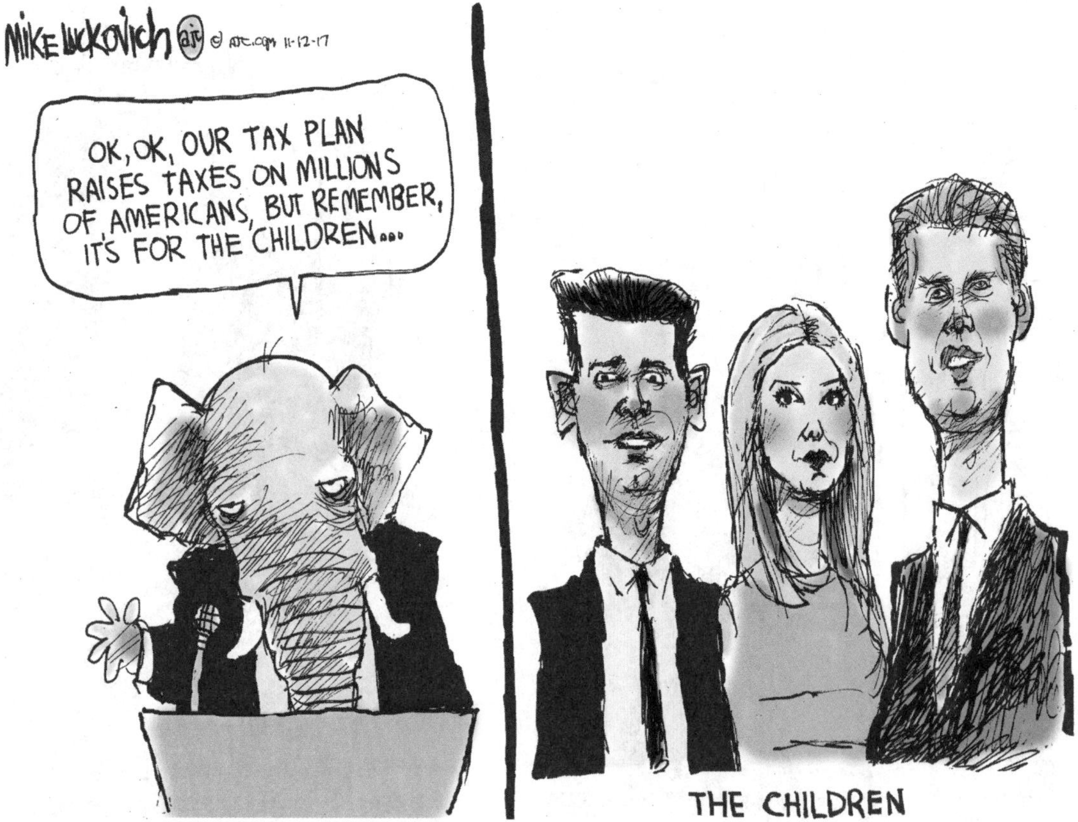
MIKE LUCKOVICH ajc © ajc.com 11-12-17
OK, OK, OUR TAX PLAN RAISES TAXES ON MILLIONS OF AMERICANS, BUT REMEMBER, IT'S FOR THE CHILDREN...
THE CHILDREN

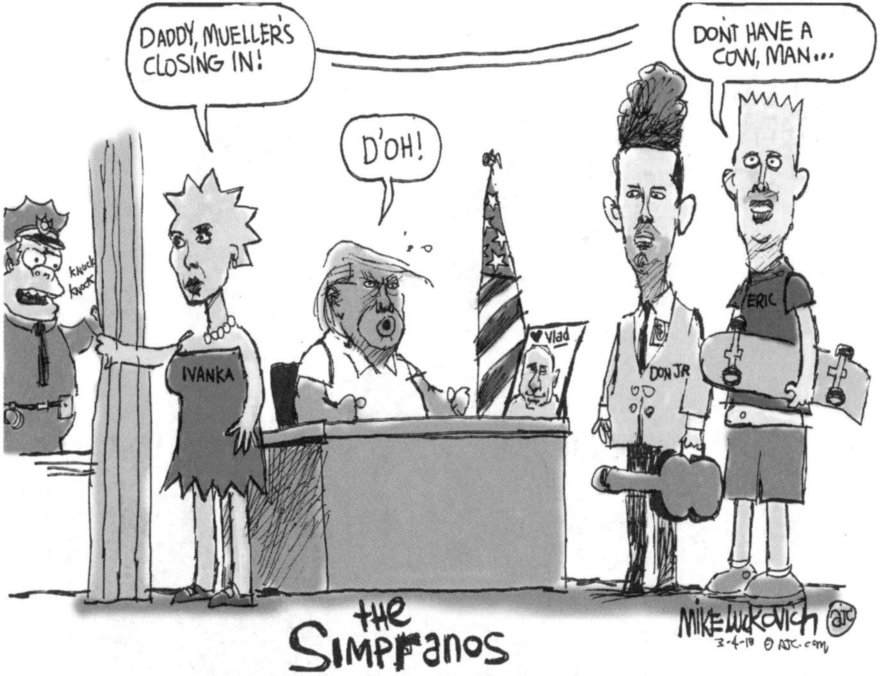
DADDY, MUELLER'S CLOSING IN!
D'OH!
DON'T HAVE A COW, MAN...
knock knock
IVANKA
Vlad
DON JR
ERIC
the SIMPRANOS
MIKE LUCKOVICH
3-4-18 © AJC.com

I like this cartoon primarily because it reflects my view of Trump and his associates and relatives. They're a dysfunctional, incompetent, corrupt crime family. I hope Trump's presidential portrait is an oil painting of his mug shot.

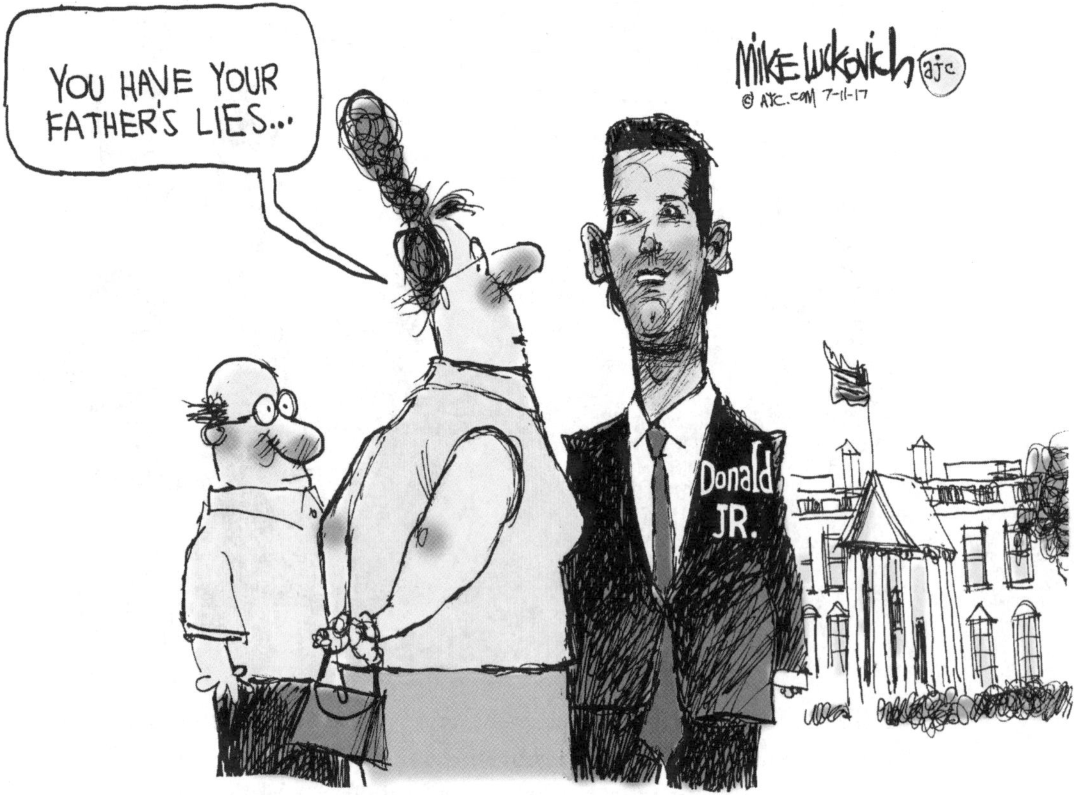
YOU HAVE YOUR FATHER'S LIES...
MIKE LUCKOVICH
ajc
© AJC.com 7-11-17
Donald JR.

 Donald J. Trump
@realDonaldTrump

 Following

# THE TRUMP ADMINISTRATION:
# ONLY THE BEST PEOPLE

RETWEETS    LIKES
3,582       9.935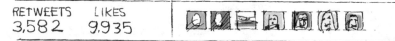

1.7K    3.6K    99K ...

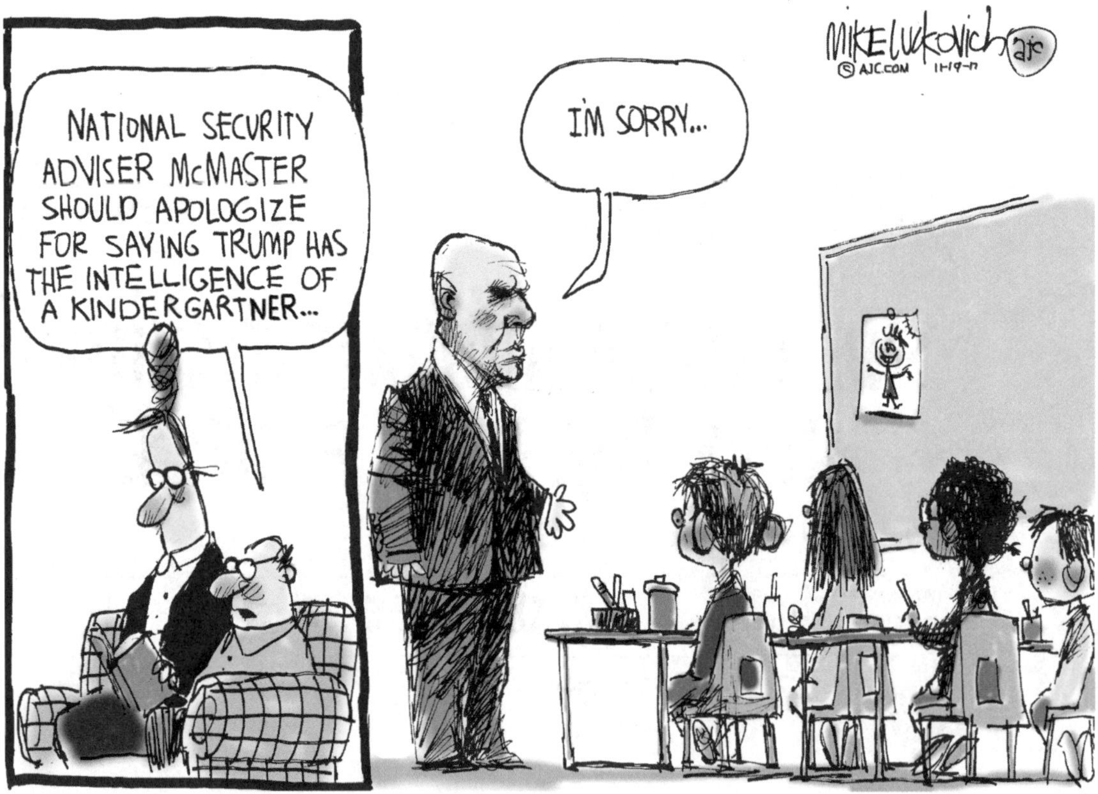

NATIONAL SECURITY ADVISER McMASTER SHOULD APOLOGIZE FOR SAYING TRUMP HAS THE INTELLIGENCE OF A KINDERGARTNER...
I'M SORRY...
MIKELUCKOVICH
© AJC.COM 11-19-17

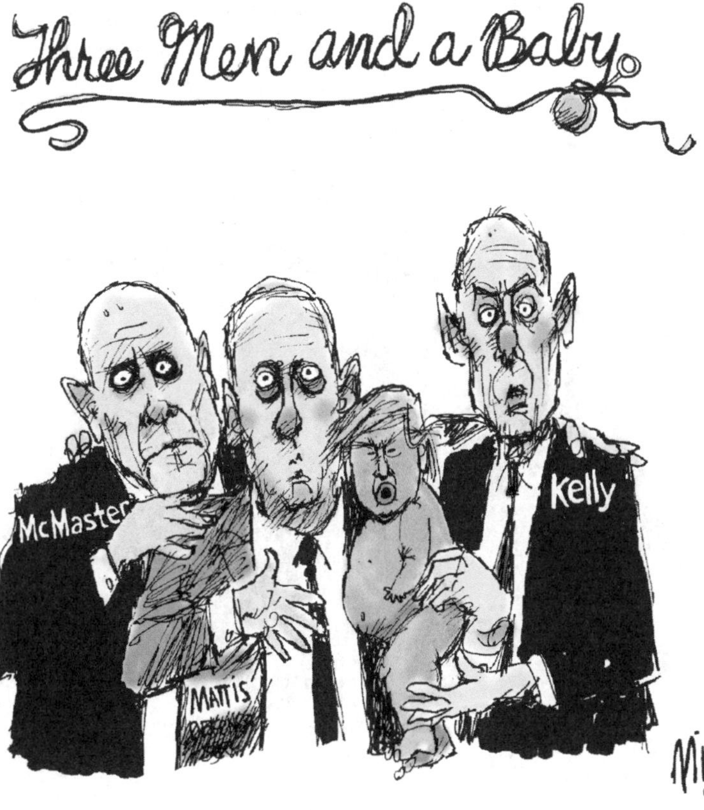
Three Men and a Baby
McMaster
MATTIS
Kelly
Mike Luckovich
ajc
©AJC.com 8-6-17

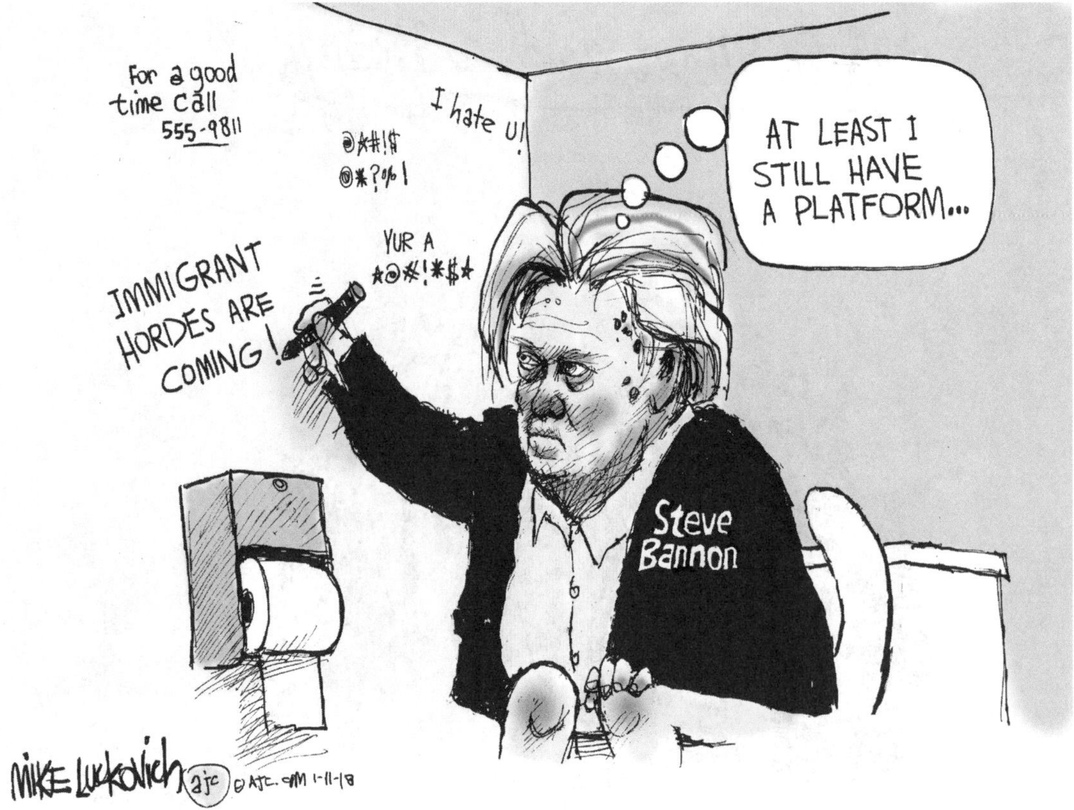
For a good time call 555-9811
I hate U!
@*#!$
@*?%!
YUR A *@#!*$*
IMMIGRANT HORDES ARE COMING!
AT LEAST I STILL HAVE A PLATFORM...
Steve Bannon
MIKE LUCKOVICH
ajc
© AJC.COM 1-11-18

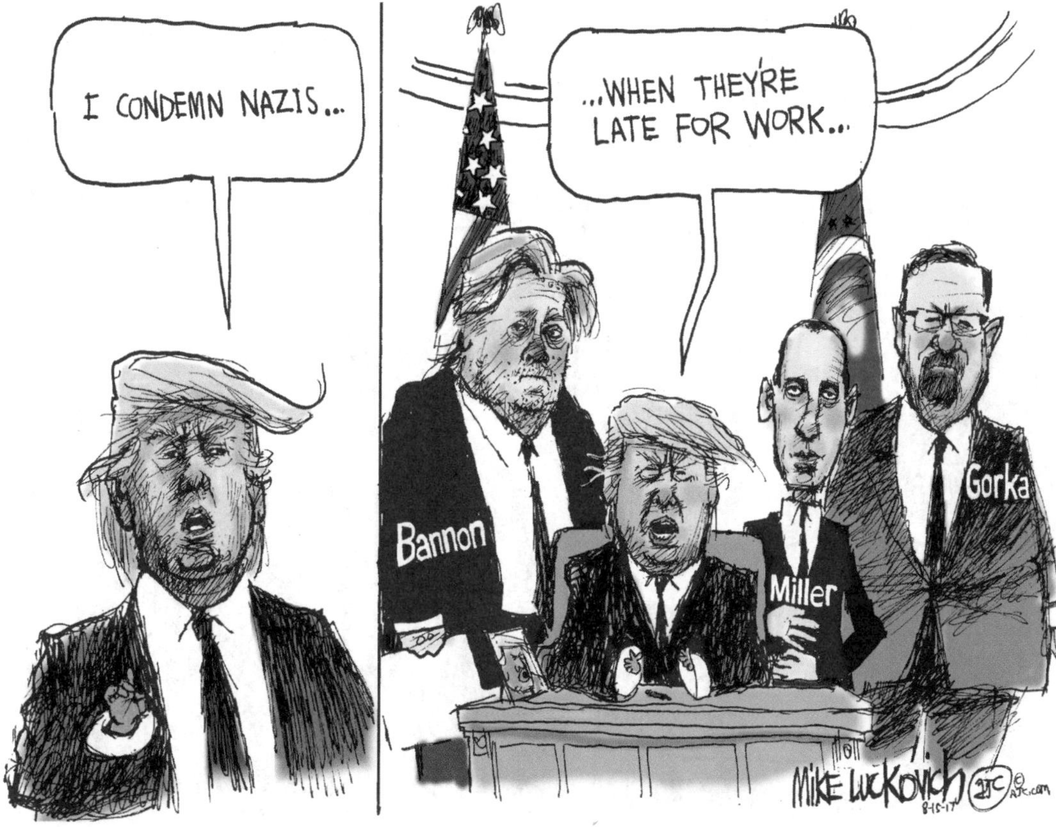
I CONDEMN NAZIS...
...WHEN THEY'RE LATE FOR WORK...
Bannon
Miller
Gorka
MIKE LUCKOVICH

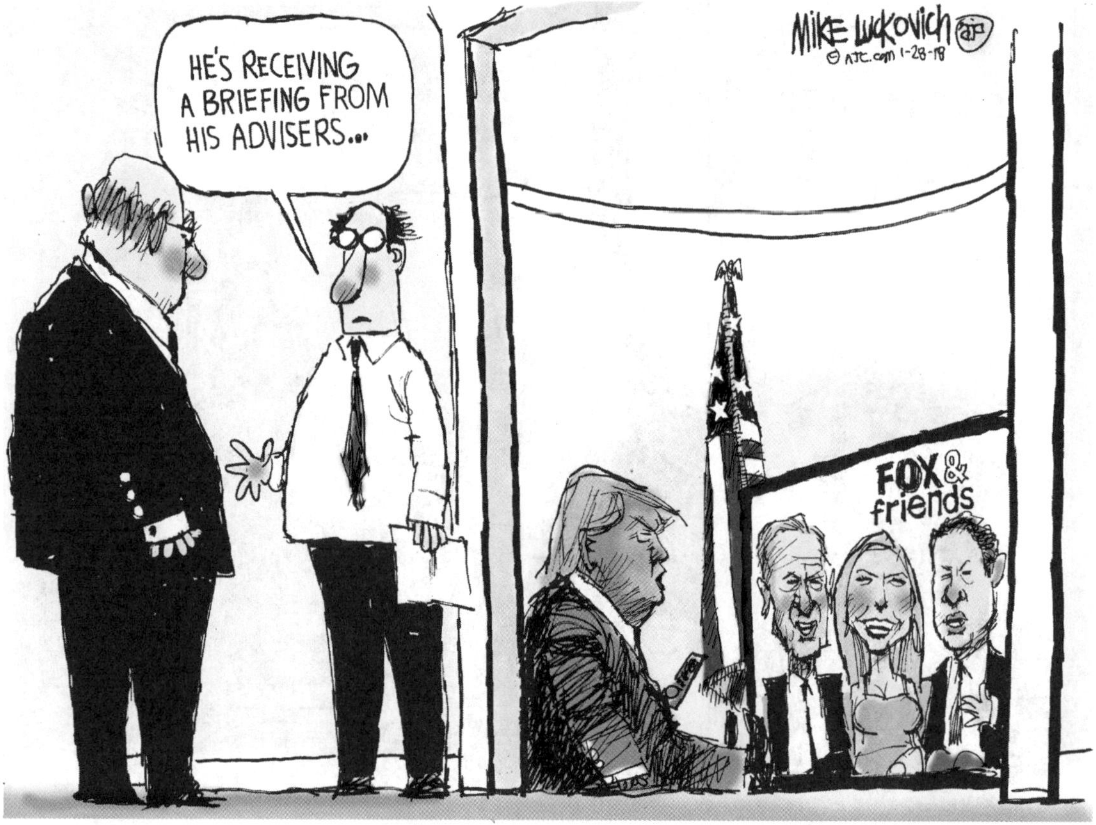
HE'S RECEIVING A BRIEFING FROM HIS ADVISERS...
MIKE LUCKOVICH
© AJC.com 1-28-18
FOX & friends

I have a friend who's smart and successful but who watches Fox News. He emails me regularly to expound on his worldview. He was convinced Obama was trying to drive America "off a cliff," though he could never articulate how or why Obama wanted to do such a thing. He just knew it was true. He hates Hillary with a passion. Same with Nancy Pelosi. Again, without concrete reasons why. What's interesting is he agrees with me on most issues. He believes climate change is occurring and that we should fight it. He supports a living wage and women's reproductive freedom. If he didn't watch Sean Hannity, he'd be a Democrat.

Even now, he has no idea what a crappy president Trump is. He recently sent me an email where he referred to Obama as "Air Force One Obama" because apparently he thought Obama spent too much time flying around. He also criticized him for golfing too much. I wrote back, "Do you have any idea how much Trump has golfed since becoming president and how he's on Air Force One almost every weekend jetting to Mar-a-Lago to play on his own course?" He replied he'd check with his "sources" and get back to me, which he never did.

It's actually kind of depressing to correspond with him because he's so far into the Fox News bubble, he doesn't know basic facts, and at least thirty percent of Americans are happily stuck in that bubble with him.

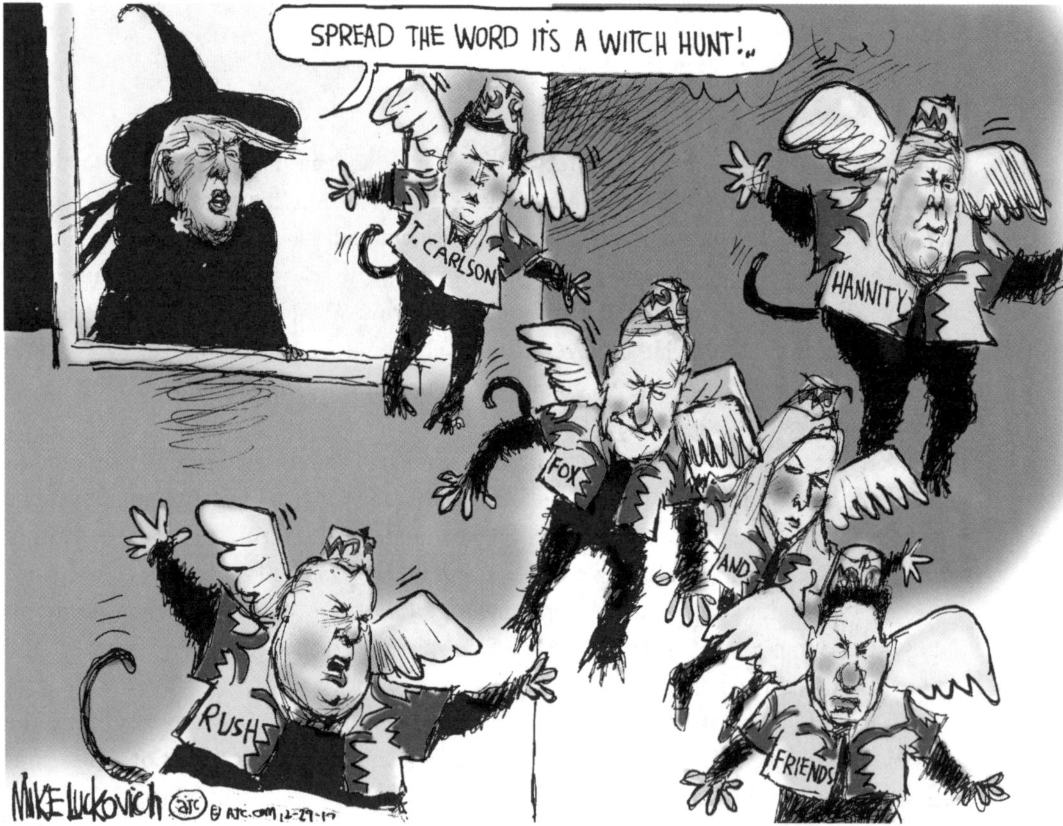
SPREAD THE WORD IT'S A WITCH HUNT!..
T. CARLSON
HANNITY
FOX
AND
FRIENDS
RUSH
MIKE LUCKOVICH

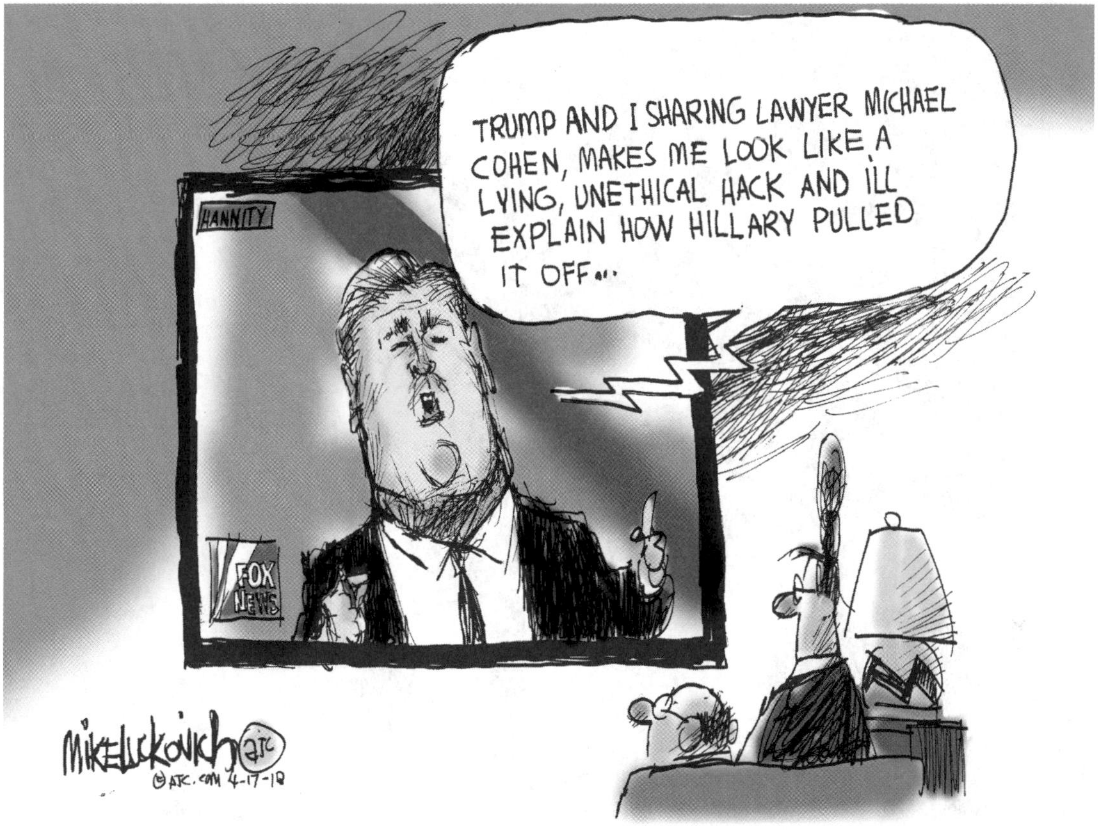
TRUMP AND I SHARING LAWYER MICHAEL COHEN, MAKES ME LOOK LIKE A LYING, UNETHICAL HACK AND I'LL EXPLAIN HOW HILLARY PULLED IT OFF...
HANNITY
FOX NEWS
MIKELUCKOVICH AJC
©AJC.com 4-17-18

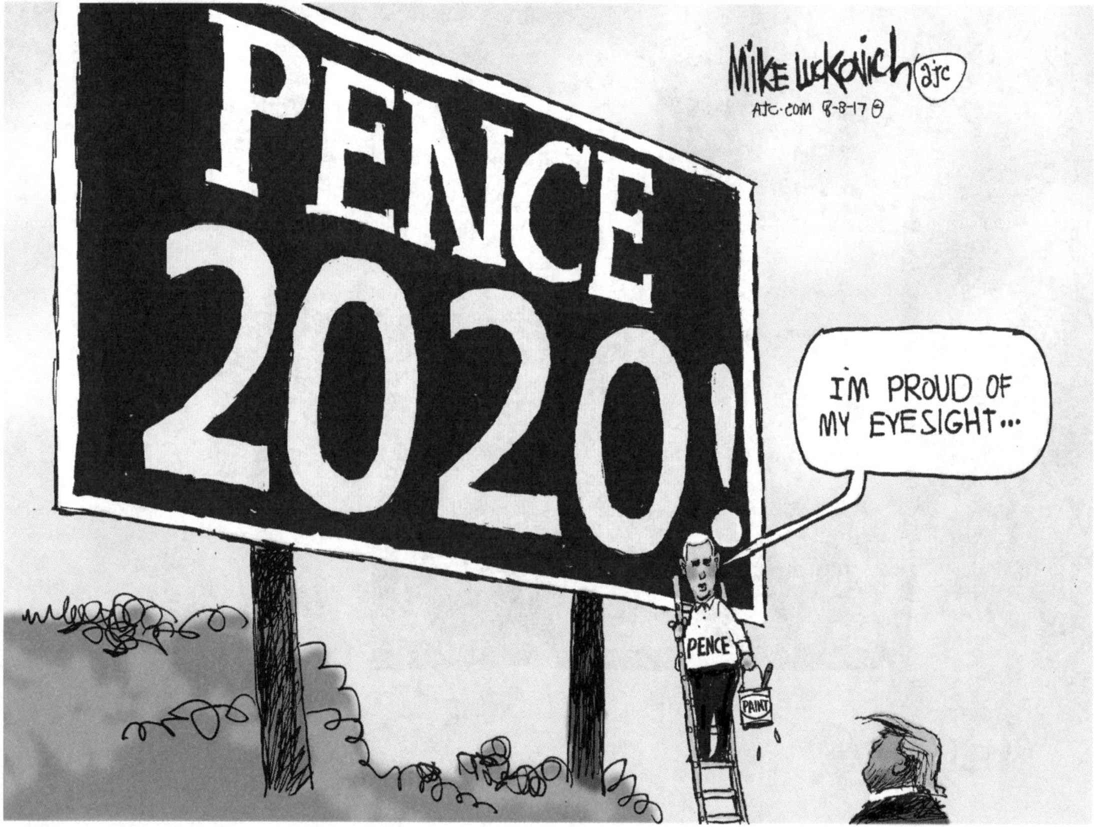
PENCE 2020!
I'M PROUD OF MY EYESIGHT...
PENCE
PAINT
MIKE LUCKOVICH ajc
AJC.COM 8-8-17

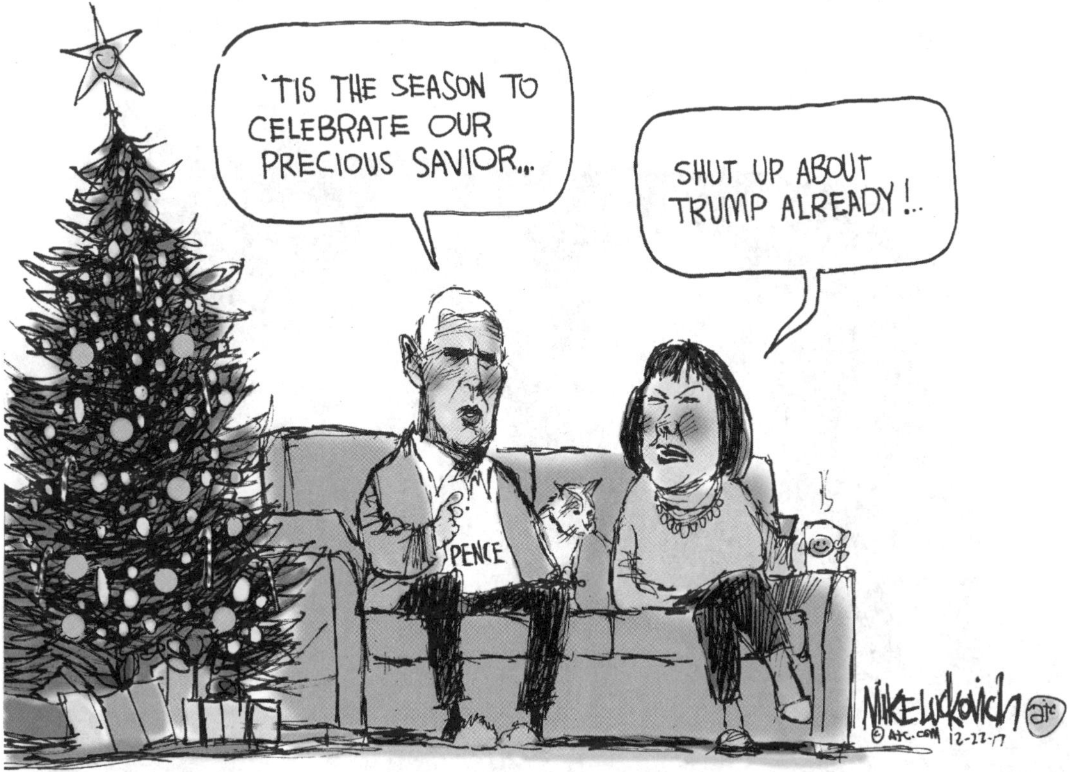
`TIS THE SEASON TO CELEBRATE OUR PRECIOUS SAVIOR...
SHUT UP ABOUT TRUMP ALREADY!..
PENCE
MIKE LUCKOVICH
© AJC.COM 12-22-17

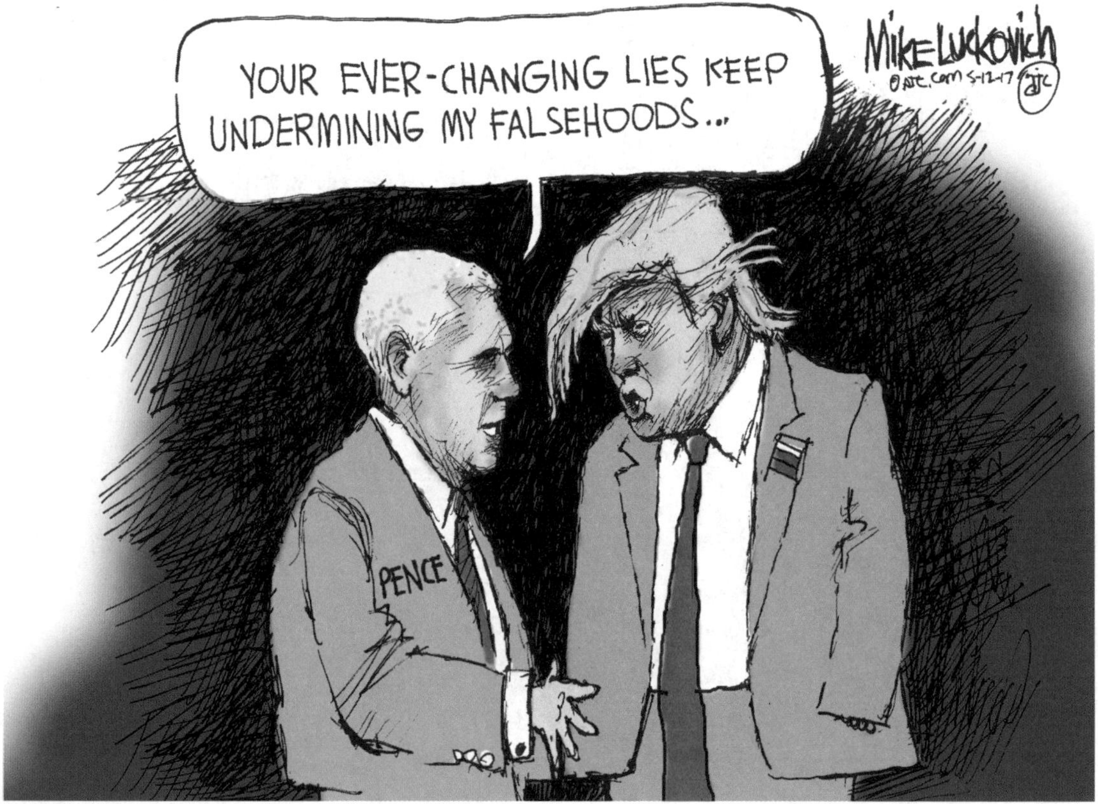
YOUR EVER-CHANGING LIES KEEP UNDERMINING MY FALSEHOODS...
MikeLuckovich
©ajc.com 5-12-17
PENCE

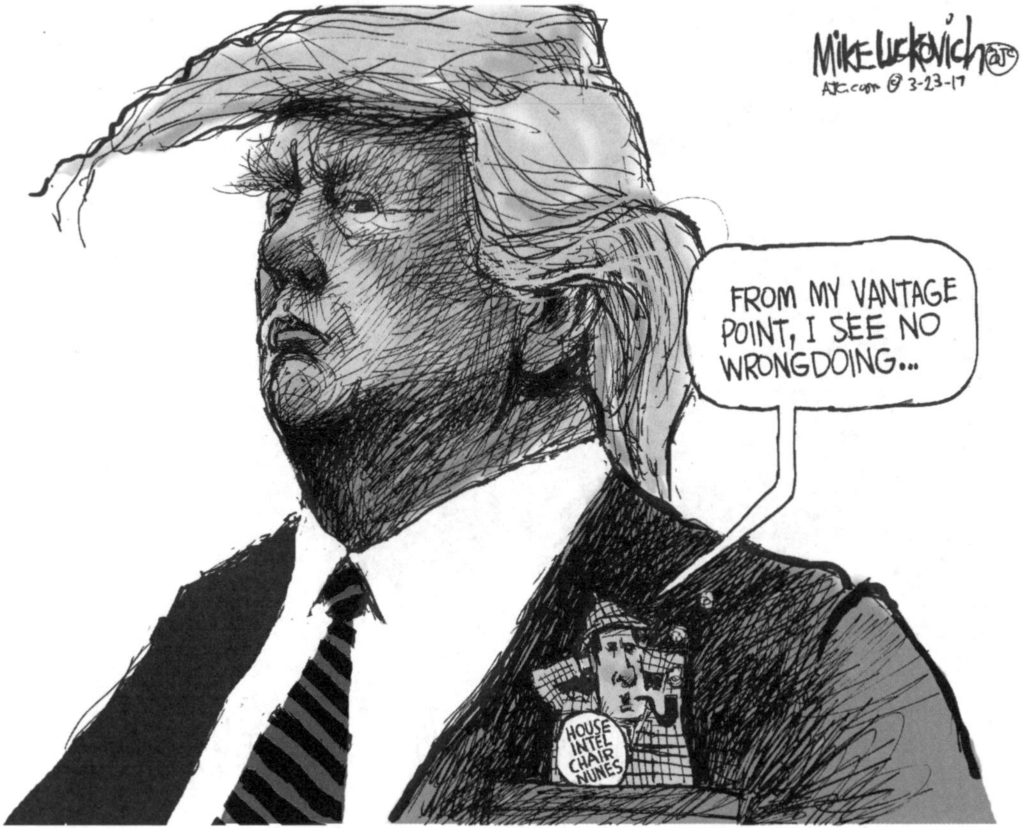
MIKE LUCKOVICH AJC
AJC.com © 3-23-17
FROM MY VANTAGE POINT, I SEE NO WRONGDOING...
HOUSE INTEL CHAIR NUNES

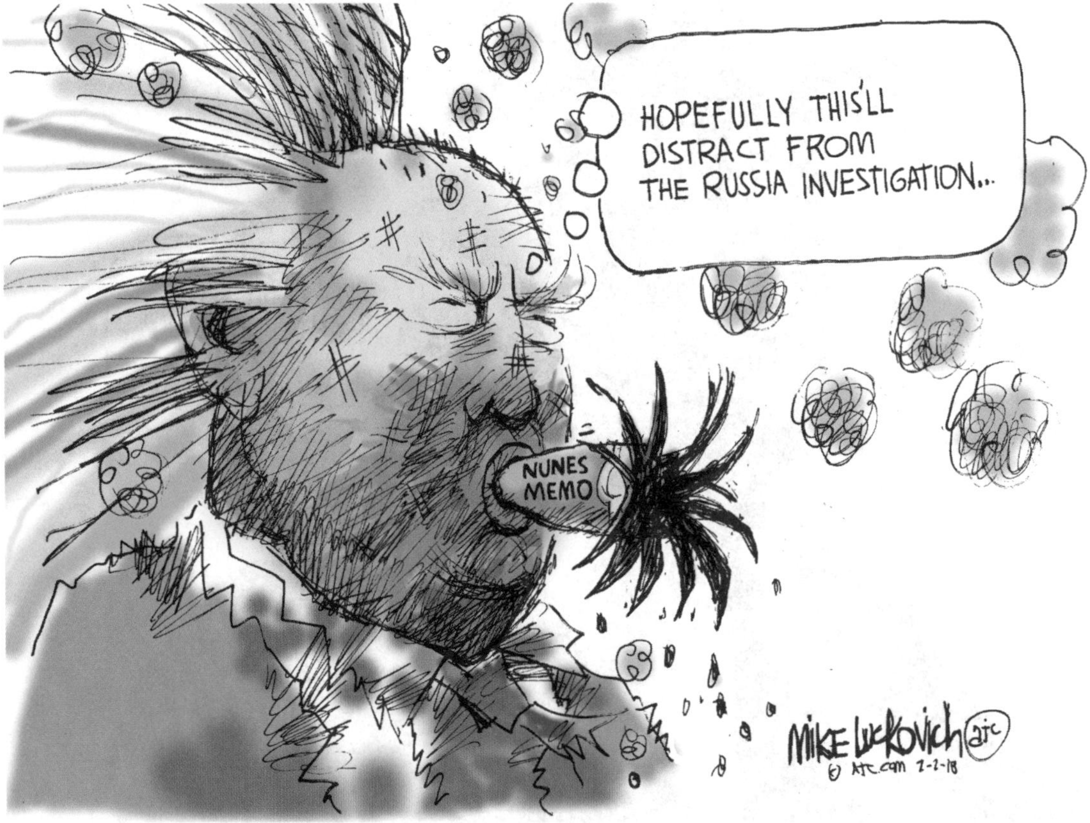
HOPEFULLY THIS'LL DISTRACT FROM THE RUSSIA INVESTIGATION...
NUNES MEMO
MIKE LUCKOVICH ajc
© AJC.com 2-2-18

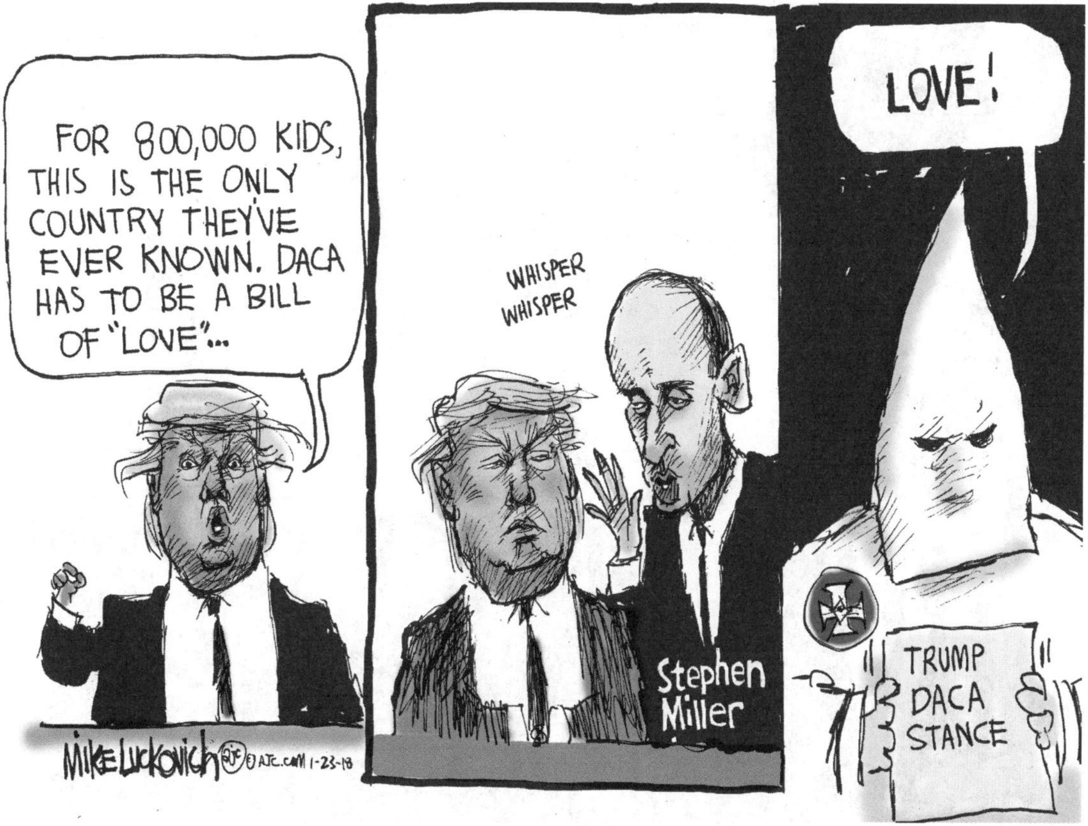
FOR 800,000 KIDS, THIS IS THE ONLY COUNTRY THEY'VE EVER KNOWN. DACA HAS TO BE A BILL OF "LOVE"...
MIKE LUCKOVICH ©AJC.COM 1-23-18
WHISPER WHISPER
Stephen Miller
LOVE!
TRUMP DACA STANCE

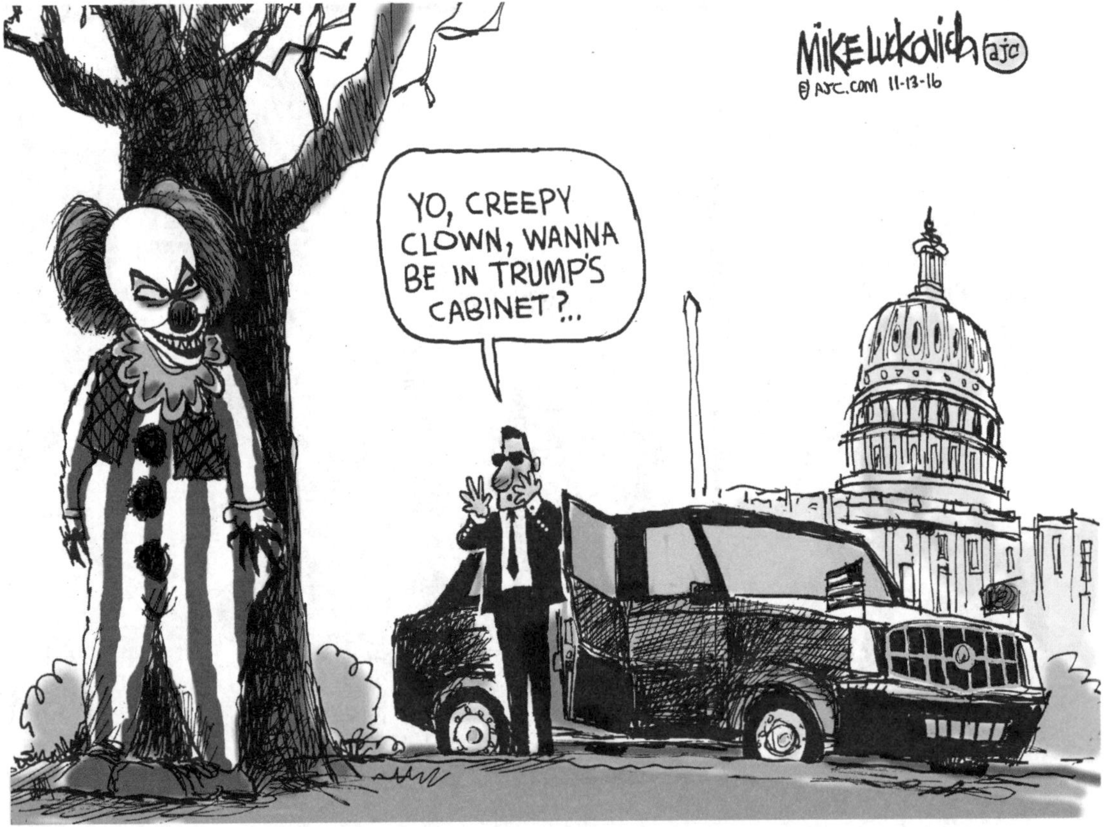
MIKE LUCKOVICH ajc
© AJC.COM 11-13-16
YO, CREEPY CLOWN, WANNA BE IN TRUMP'S CABINET?..

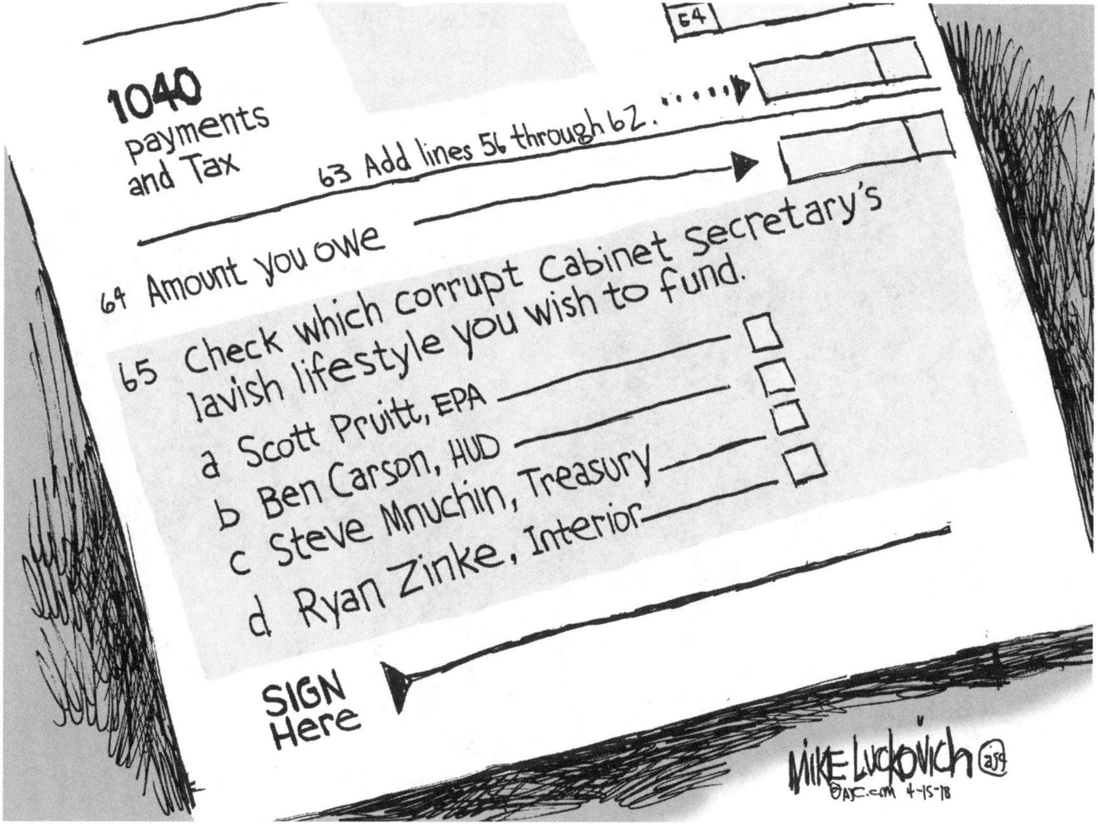

64
1040
payments and Tax
63 Add lines 56 through 62.
64 Amount you owe
65 Check which corrupt Cabinet Secretary's lavish lifestyle you wish to fund.
a Scott Pruitt, EPA
b Ben Carson, HUD
c Steve Mnuchin, Treasury
d Ryan Zinke, Interior
SIGN Here
MIKE LUCKOVICH
©AJC.com 4-15-18

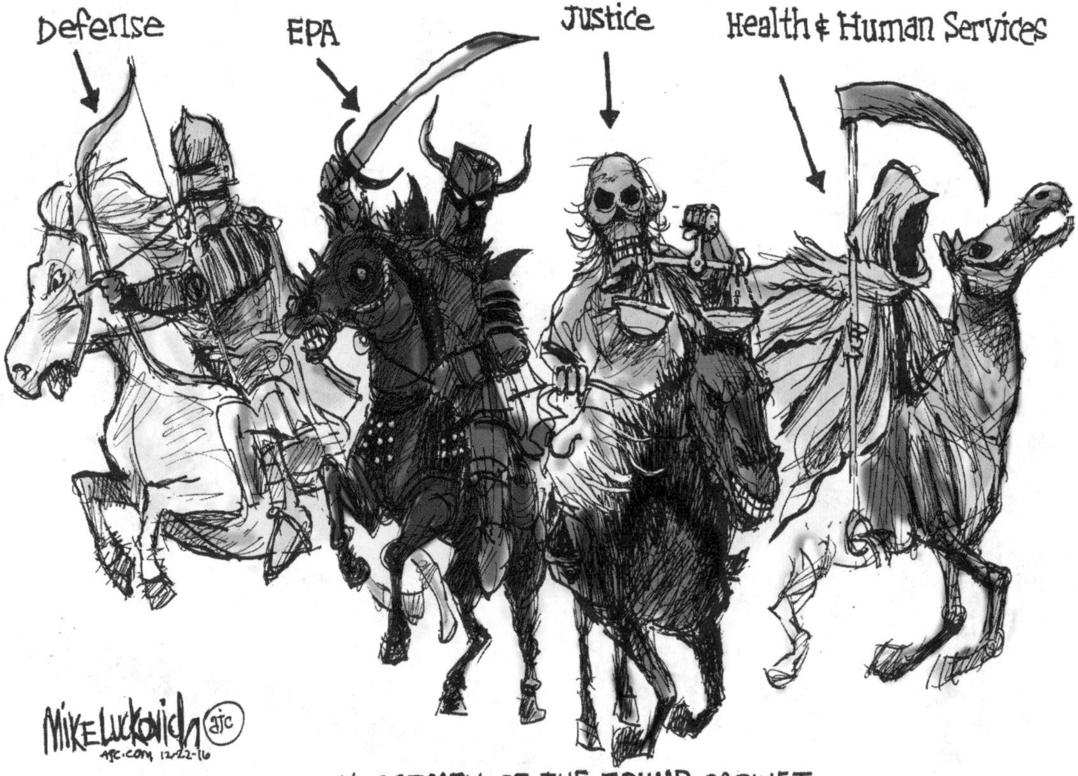
Defense
EPA
Justice
Health & Human Services
MIKE LUCKOVICH
ajc
ajc.com 12-22-16

HORSEMEN OF THE TRUMP CABINET

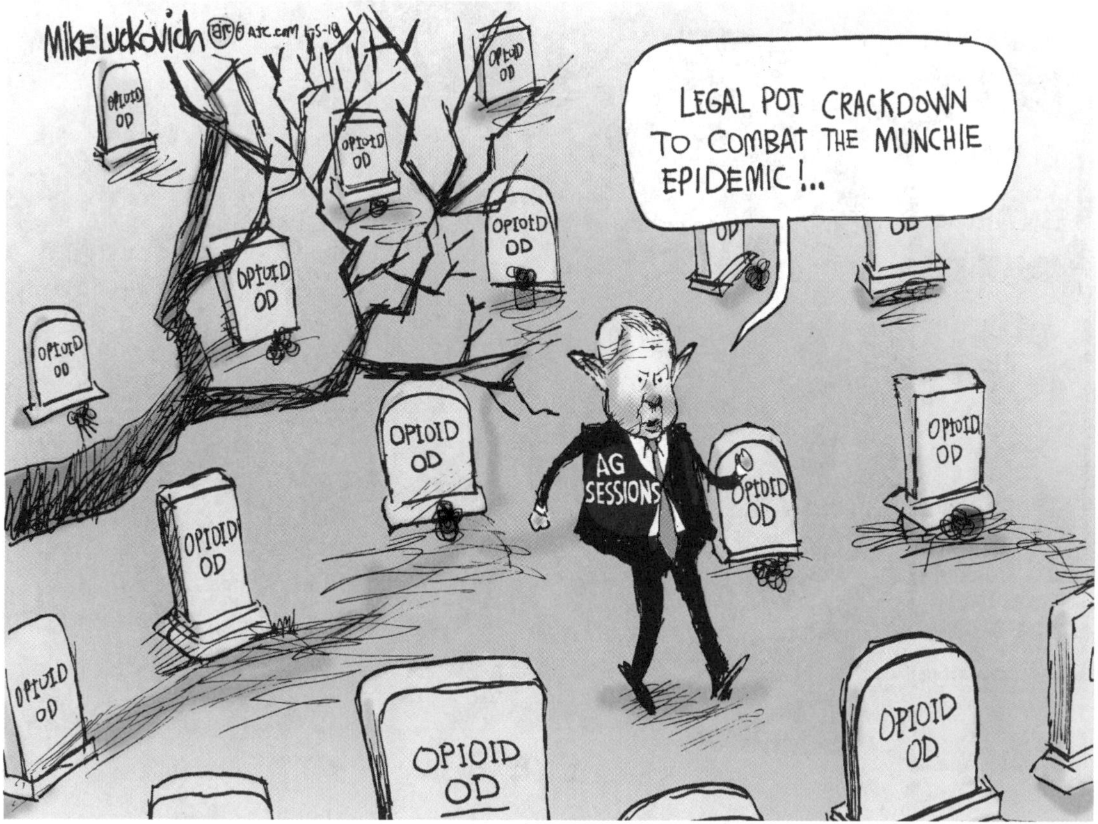
MIKE LUCKOVICH ©AJC.com
LEGAL POT CRACKDOWN TO COMBAT THE MUNCHIE EPIDEMIC!..
AG SESSIONS
OPIOID OD

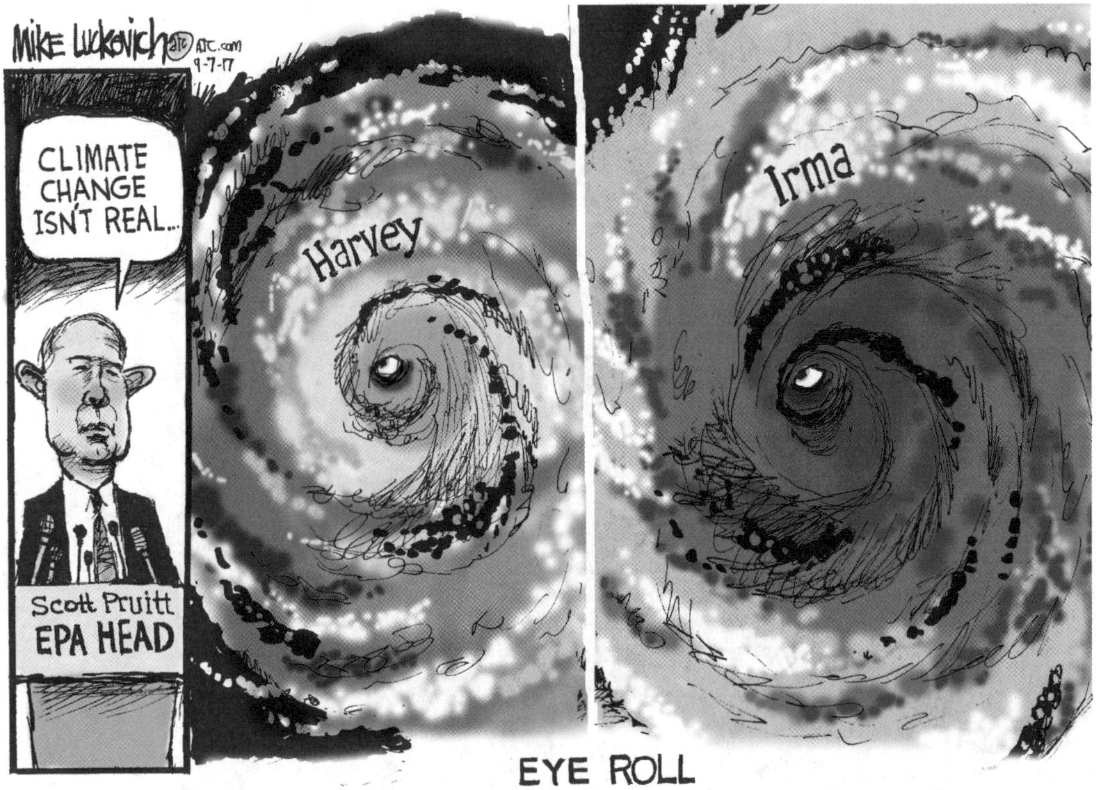
MIKE LUCKOVICH AJC AJC.com 9-7-17
CLIMATE CHANGE ISN'T REAL...
Scott Pruitt
EPA HEAD
Harvey
Irma
EYE ROLL

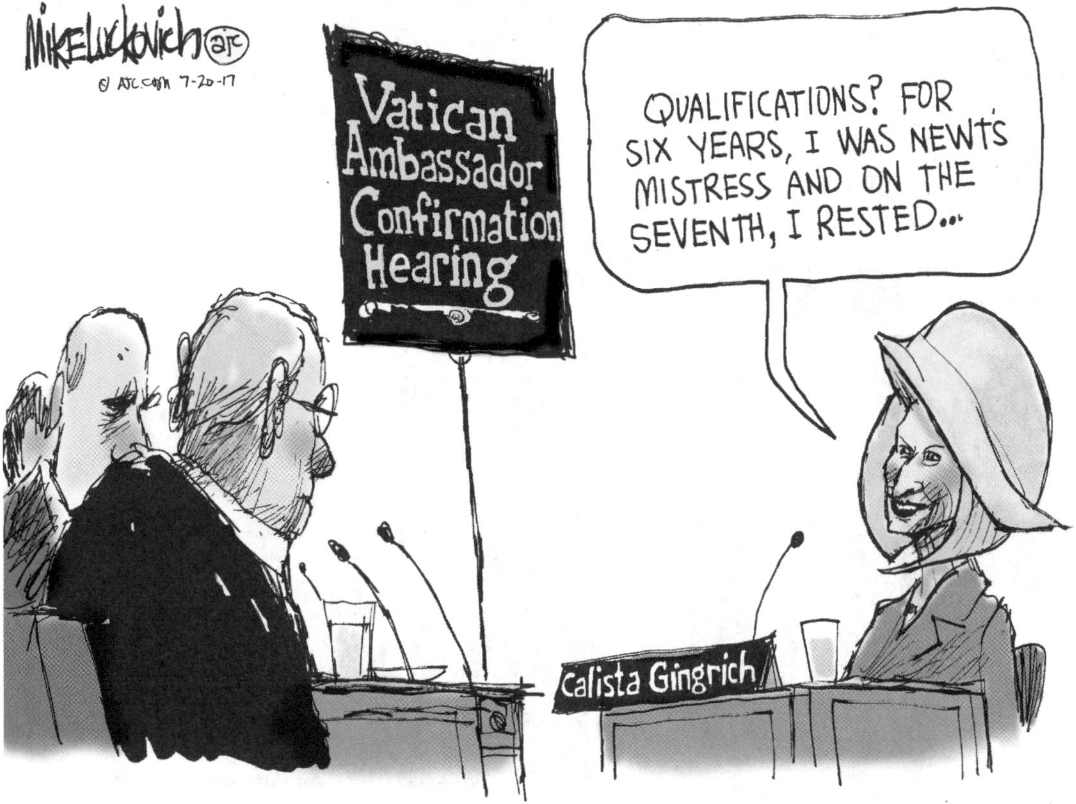
MIKELUCKOVICH ajc
© AJC.com 7-20-17
Vatican Ambassador Confirmation Hearing
QUALIFICATIONS? FOR SIX YEARS, I WAS NEWT'S MISTRESS AND ON THE SEVENTH, I RESTED...
Calista Gingrich

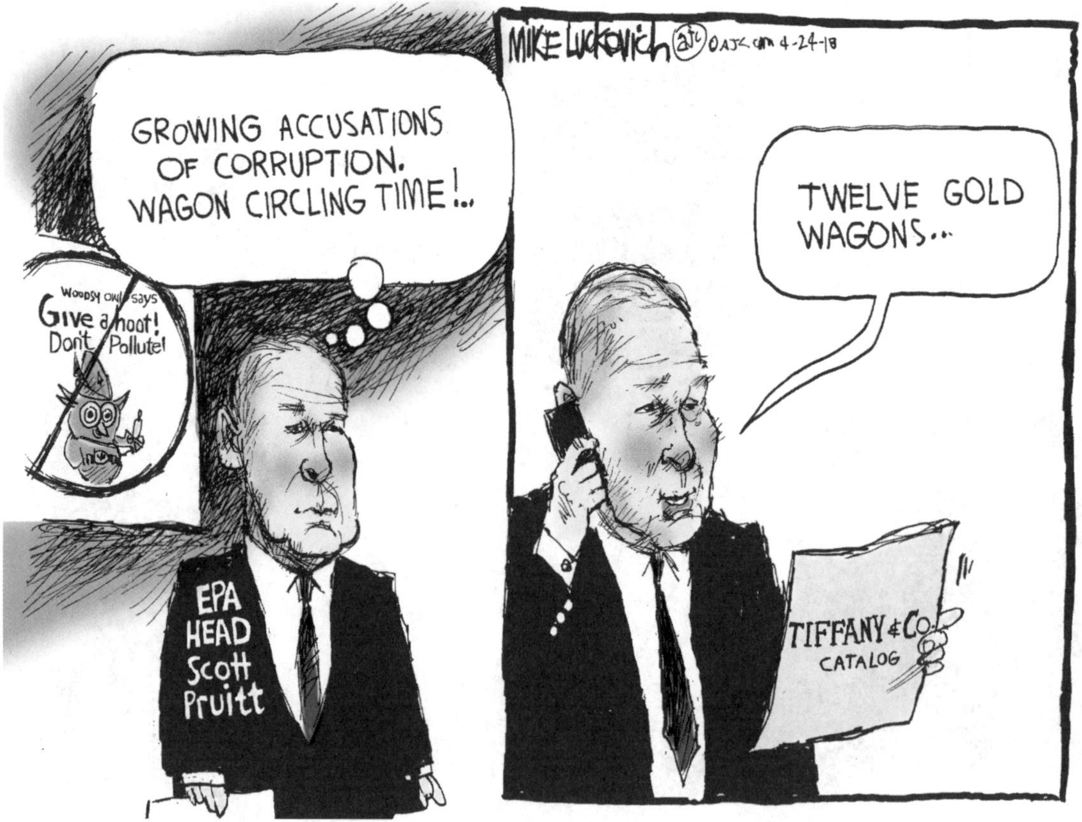
GROWING ACCUSATIONS OF CORRUPTION. WAGON CIRCLING TIME!..
Woodsy Owl says Give a hoot! Don't Pollute!
EPA HEAD Scott Pruitt
MIKE LUCKOVICH 4-24-18
TWELVE GOLD WAGONS...
TIFFANY & Co. CATALOG

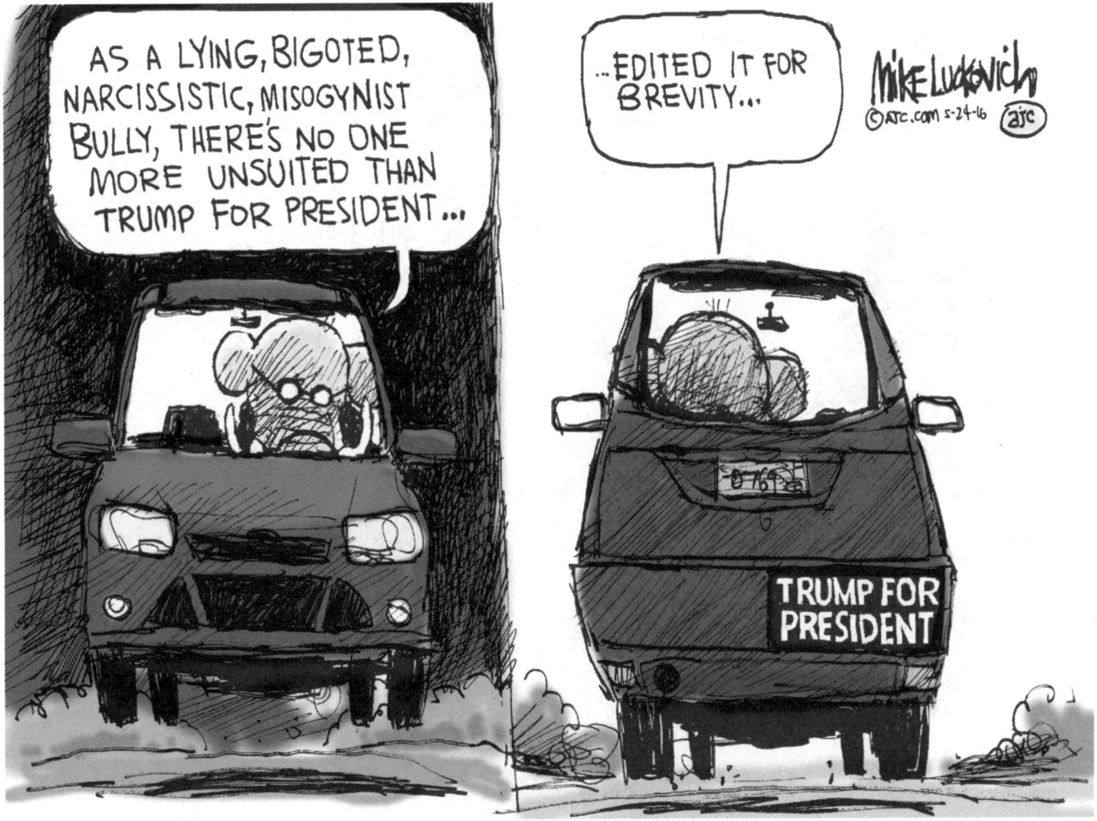
AS A LYING, BIGOTED, NARCISSISTIC, MISOGYNIST BULLY, THERE'S NO ONE MORE UNSUITED THAN TRUMP FOR PRESIDENT...
...EDITED IT FOR BREVITY...
TRUMP FOR PRESIDENT
Mike Luckovich
©AJC.com 5-24-16
ajc

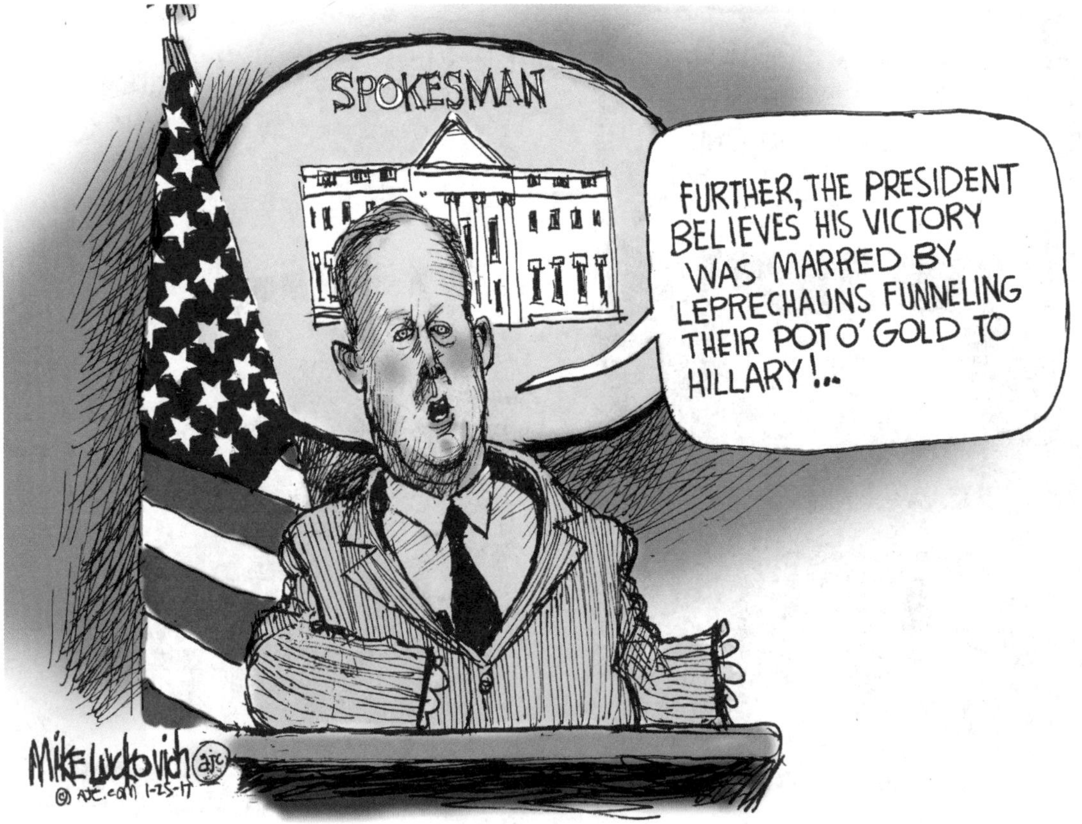
SPOKESMAN
FURTHER, THE PRESIDENT BELIEVES HIS VICTORY WAS MARRED BY LEPRECHAUNS FUNNELING THEIR POT O' GOLD TO HILLARY!..
MIKE LUCKOVICH ajc
© AJC.com 1-25-17

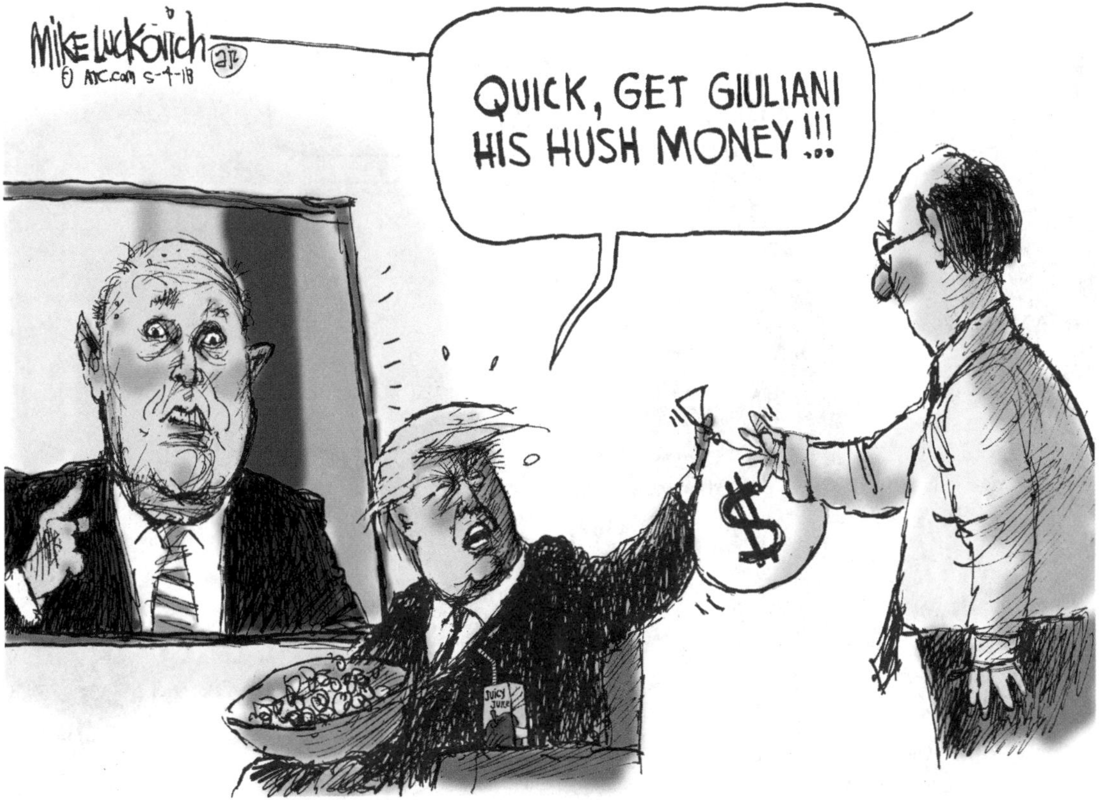
MIKE LUCKOVICH
© AJC.com 5-4-18
QUICK, GET GIULIANI HIS HUSH MONEY!!!
JUICY JUICE

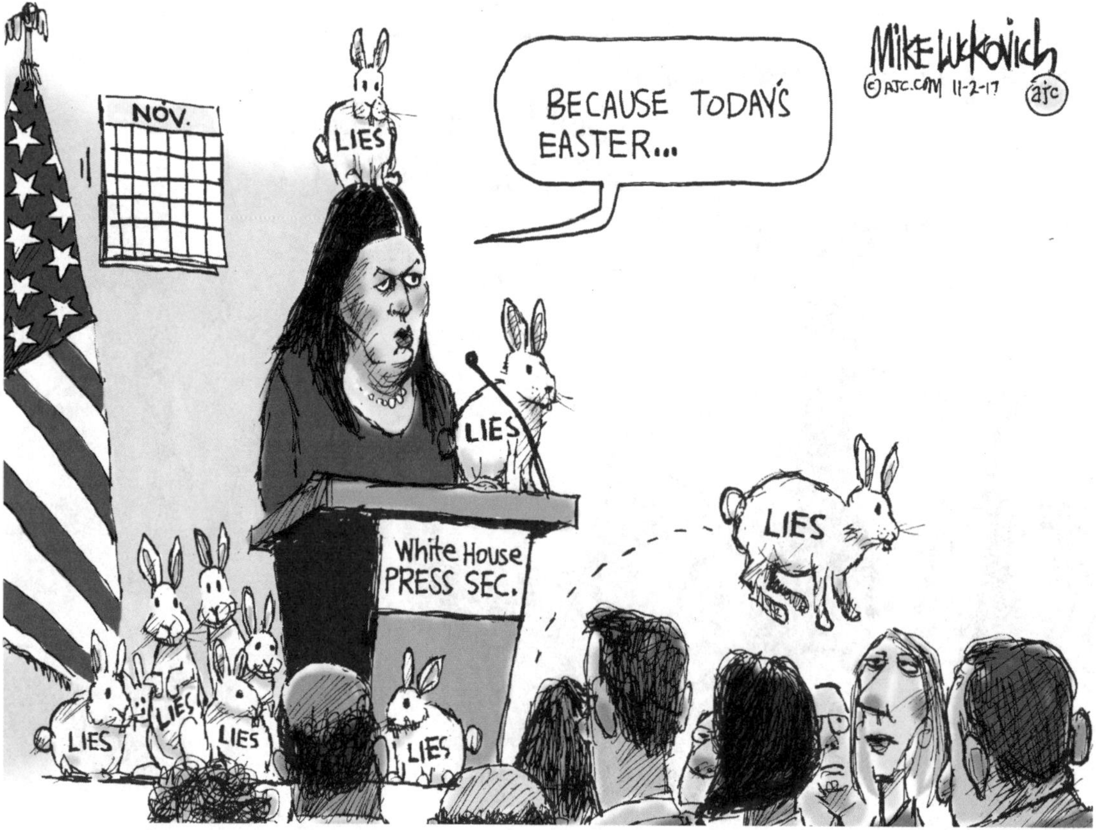
MIKE LUCKOVICH
©AJC.COM 11-2-17
ajc
NOV.
LIES
BECAUSE TODAY'S EASTER...
LIES
White House PRESS SEC.
LIES
LIES
LIES
LIES
LIES

 Donald J. Trump
@realDonaldTrump

# THE VOTERS:
# OMG, WHAT HAVE WE DONE?

RETWEETS    LIKES
3,582       9,935

↰ 1.7K   ⇄ 3.6K   ♥ 99K ···

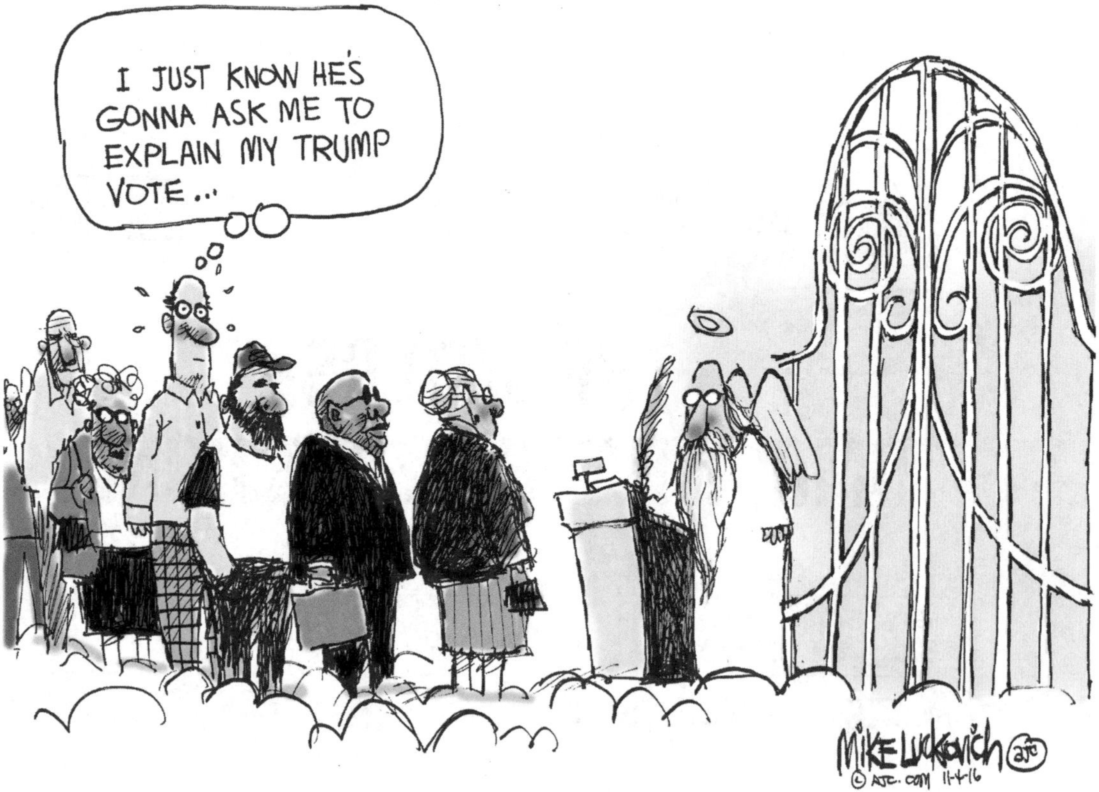
I JUST KNOW HE'S GONNA ASK ME TO EXPLAIN MY TRUMP VOTE...
MIKE LUCKOVICH
ajc
© AJC.COM 11-4-16

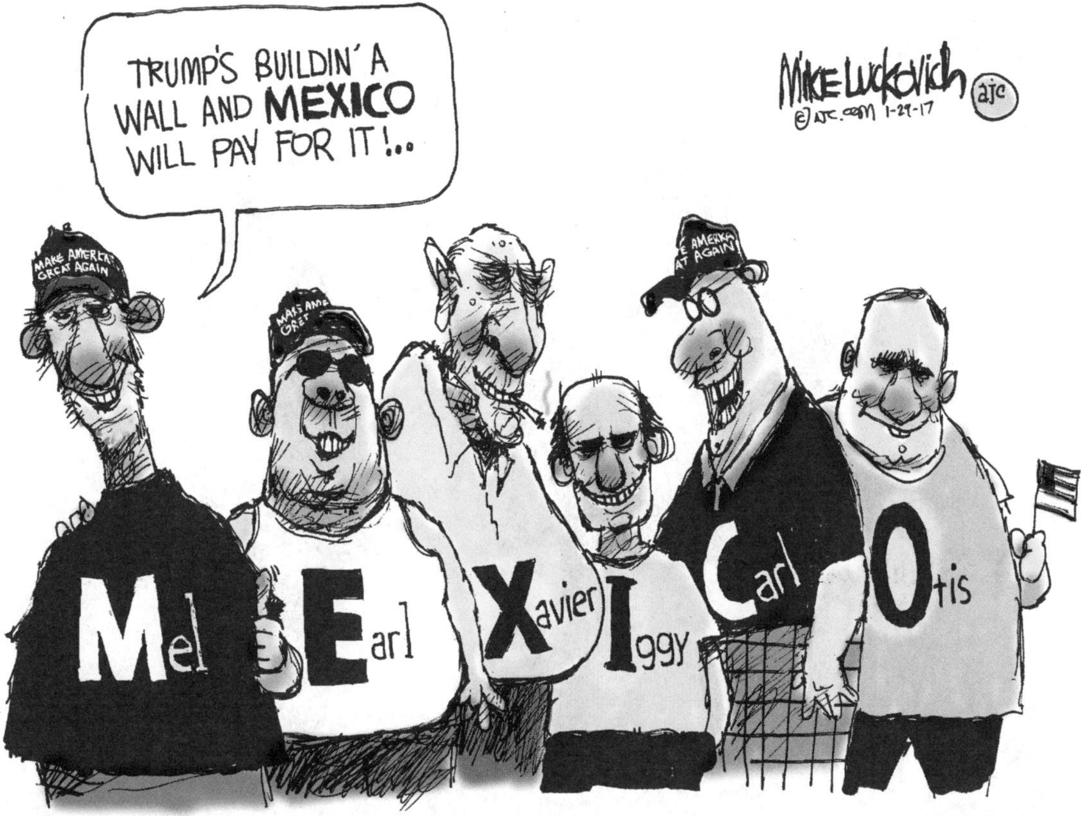
TRUMP'S BUILDIN' A WALL AND MEXICO WILL PAY FOR IT!...
MIKE LUCKOVICH
©ajc.com 1-29-17
ajc
MAKE AMERICA GREAT AGAIN
Mel
Earl
Xavier
Iggy
Carl
Otis

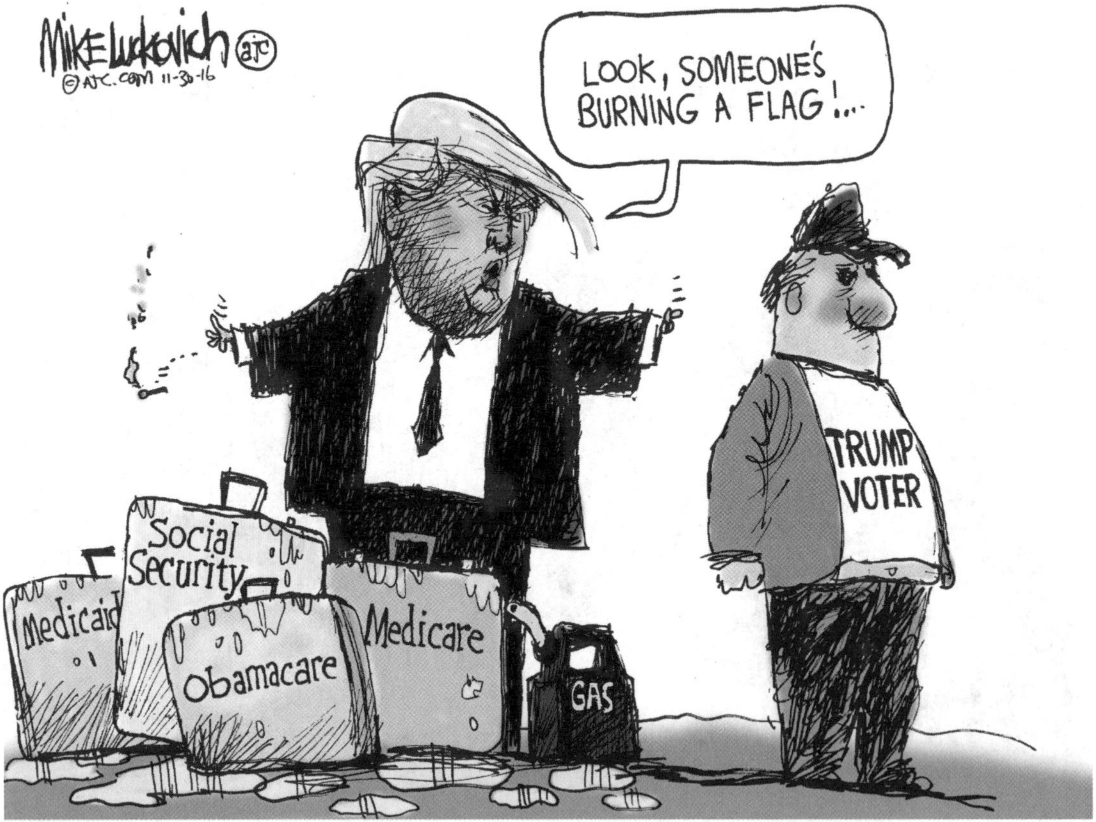
MIKE LUCKOVICH ajc
©AJC.COM 11-30-16
LOOK, SOMEONE'S BURNING A FLAG!...
Social Security
Medicaid
Obamacare
Medicare
GAS
TRUMP VOTER

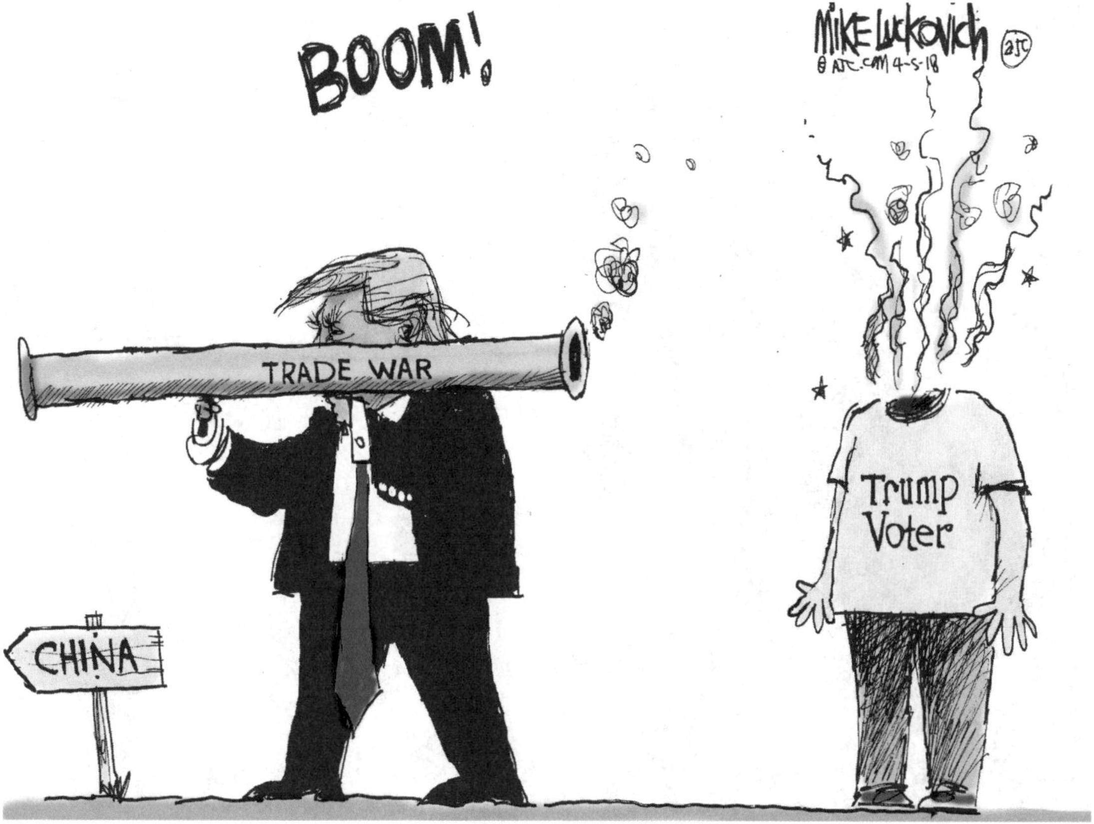
BOOM!
MIKE LUCKOVICH
© AJC.COM 4-5-18
TRADE WAR
CHINA
Trump Voter

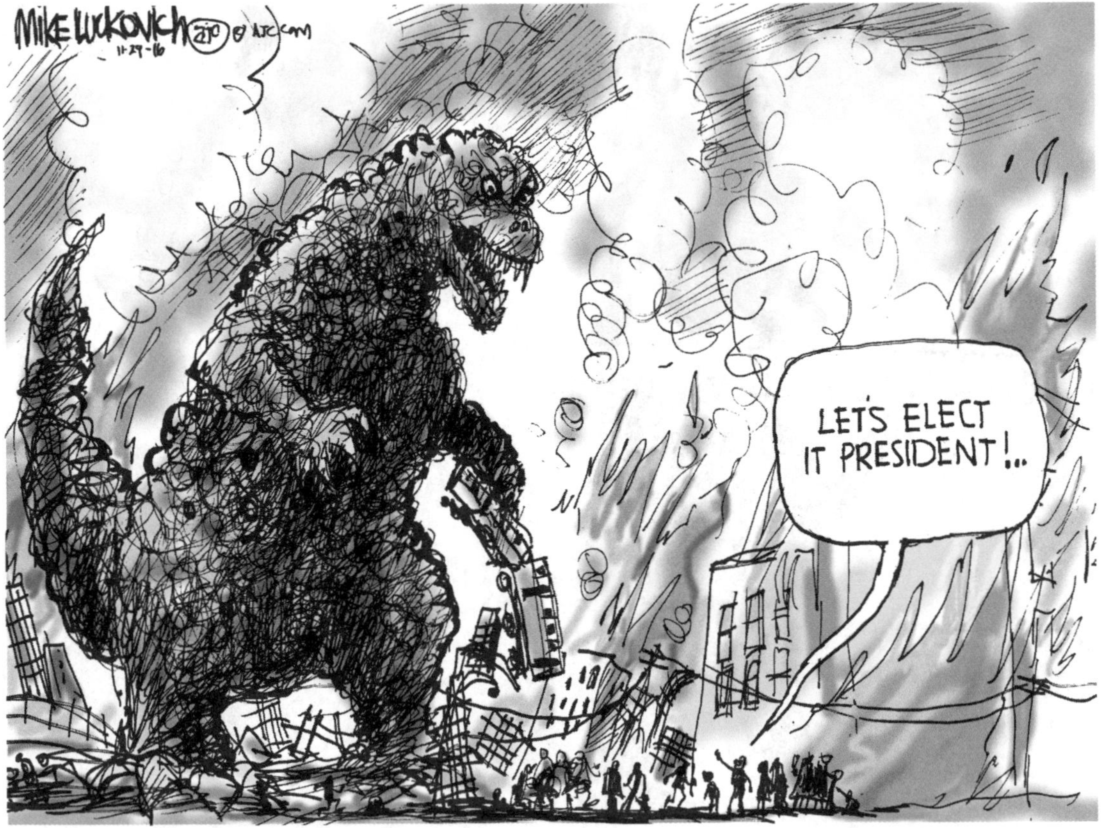
MIKE LUCKOVICH
11-29-16
LET'S ELECT IT PRESIDENT!..

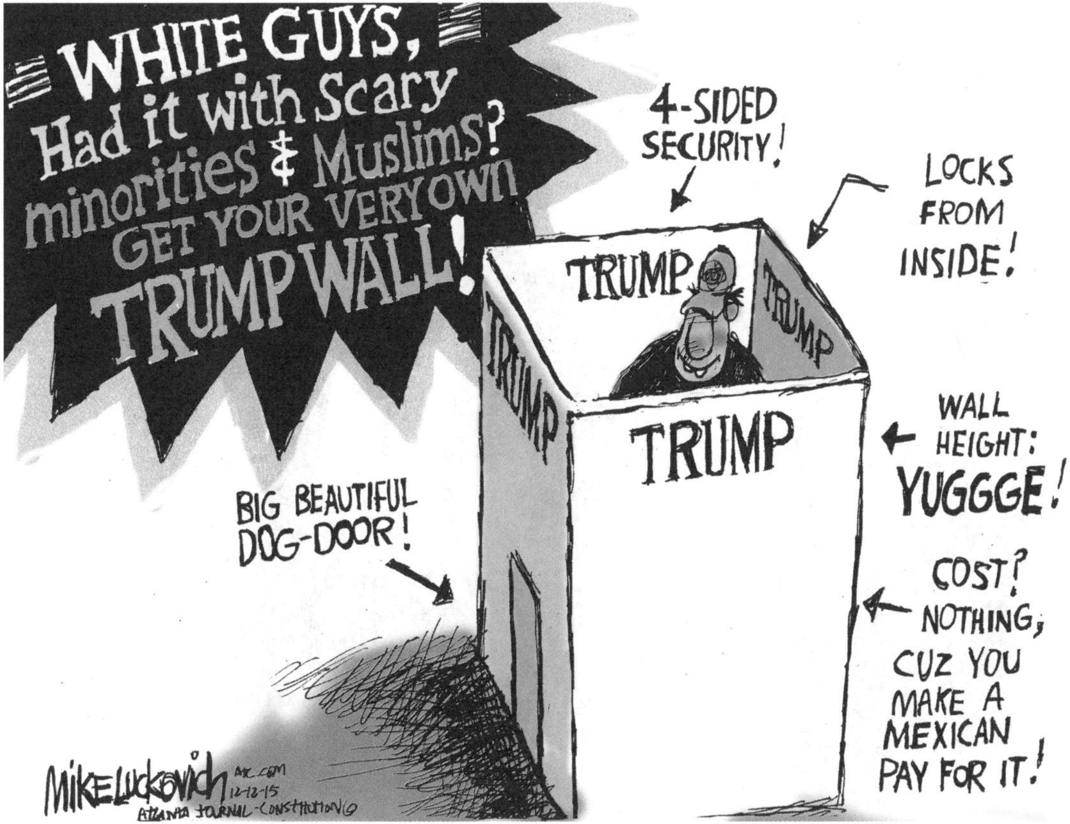
WHITE GUYS,
Had it with Scary minorities & Muslims?
GET YOUR VERY OWN
TRUMP WALL!
4-SIDED SECURITY!
LOCKS FROM INSIDE!
TRUMP
TRUMP
TRUMP
TRUMP
WALL HEIGHT: YUGGGE!
BIG BEAUTIFUL DOG-DOOR!
COST? NOTHING, CUZ YOU MAKE A MEXICAN PAY FOR IT!
MIKE LUCKOVICH
AJC.com
12-12-15
ATLANTA JOURNAL-CONSTITUTION

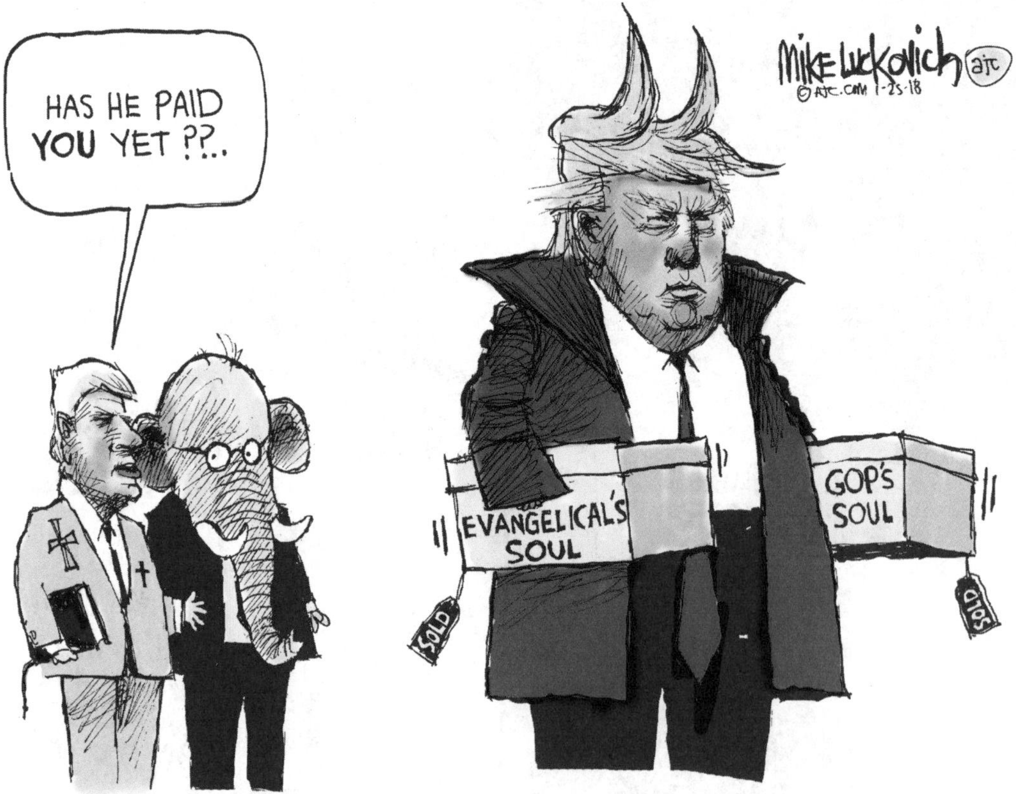
HAS HE PAID YOU YET ??..
EVANGELICAL'S SOUL
GOP'S SOUL
SOLD
SOLD
MIKE LUCKOVICH ajc
© AJC.COM 1-25-18

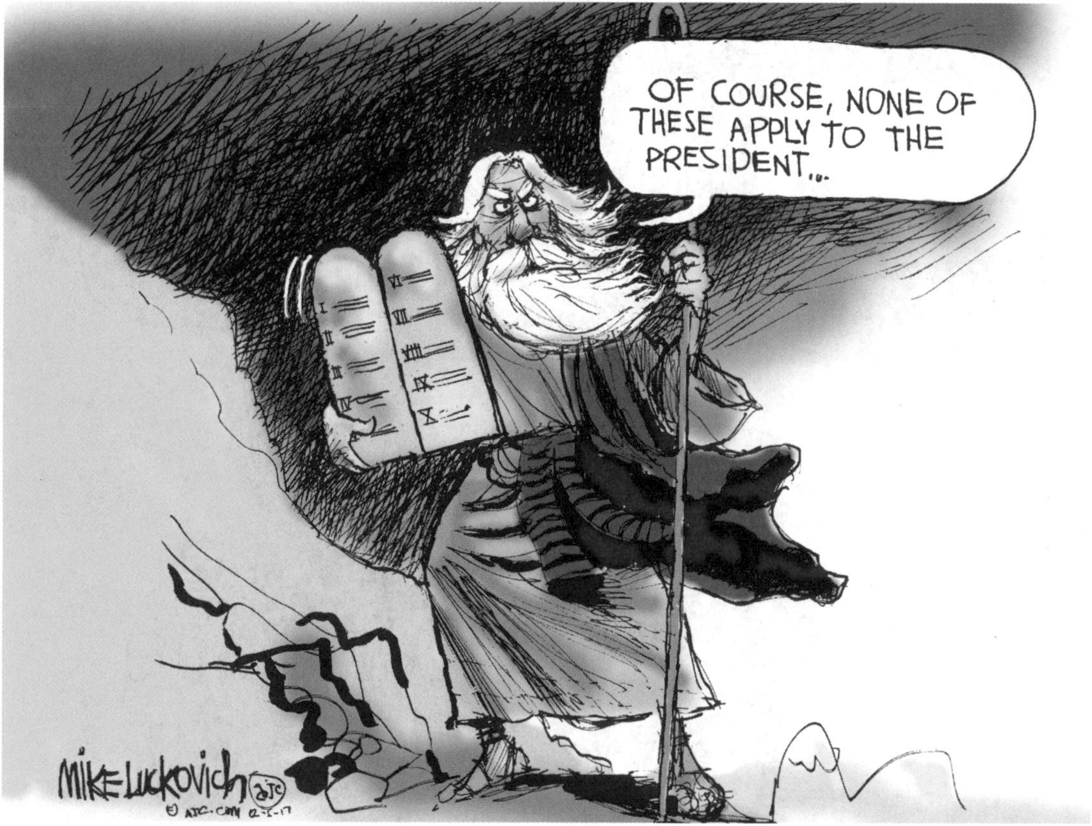
OF COURSE, NONE OF THESE APPLY TO THE PRESIDENT...
MIKE LUCKOVICH

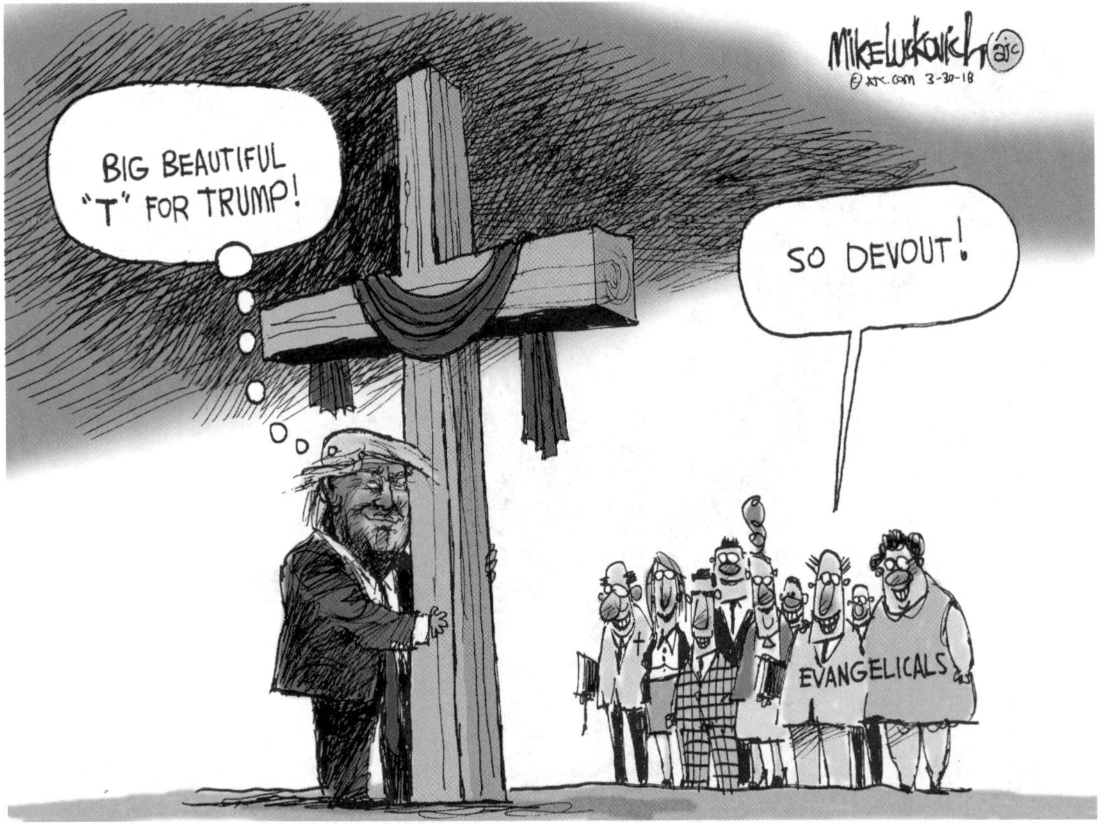
MikeLuckovich ajc
© ajc.com 3-30-18
BIG BEAUTIFUL "T" FOR TRUMP!
SO DEVOUT!
EVANGELICALS

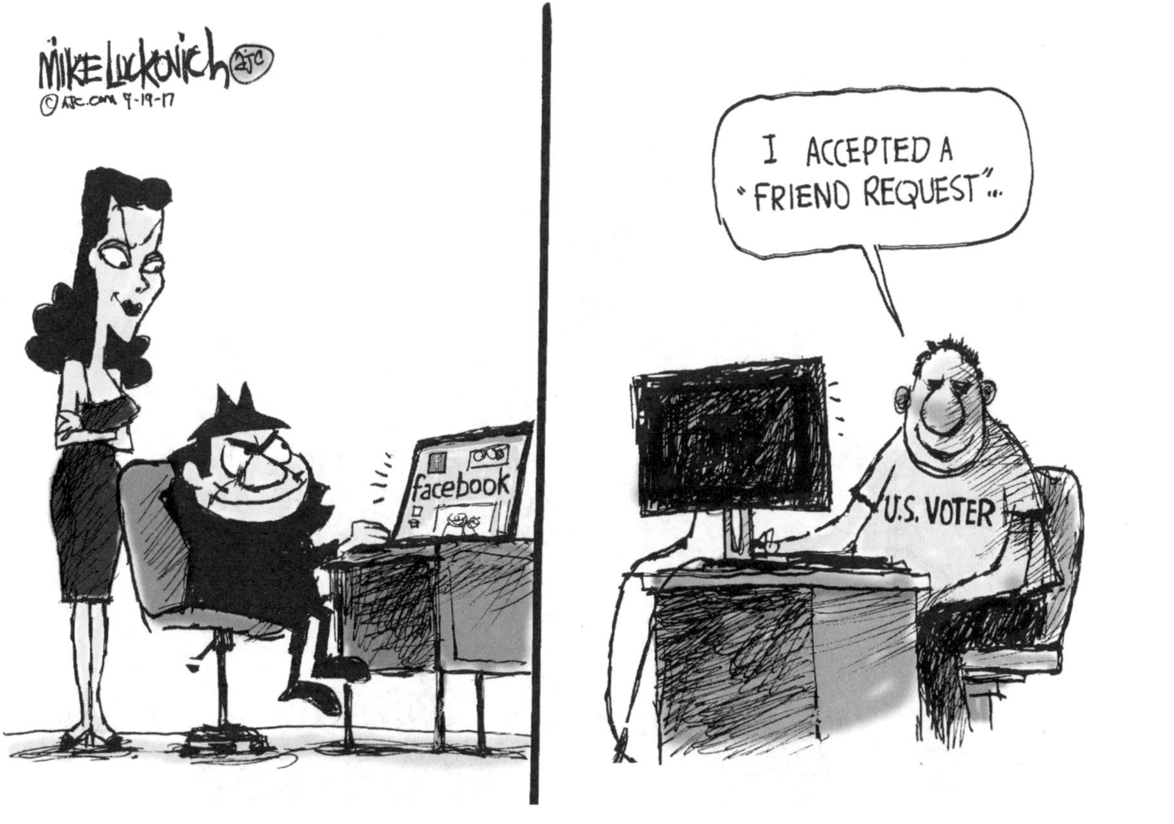
MIKE LUCKOVICH AJC
© AJC.com 9-19-17
facebook
I ACCEPTED A "FRIEND REQUEST"...
U.S. VOTER

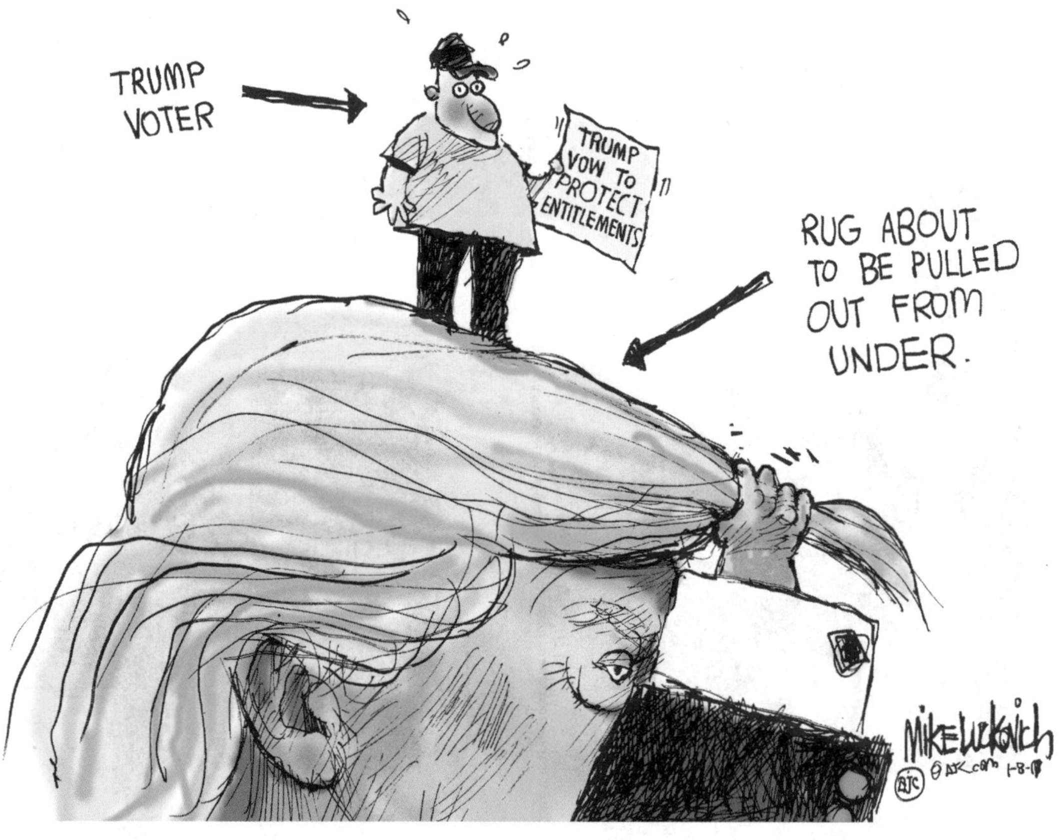
TRUMP VOTER
TRUMP VOW TO PROTECT ENTITLEMENTS
RUG ABOUT TO BE PULLED OUT FROM UNDER.
MIKELUCKOVICH

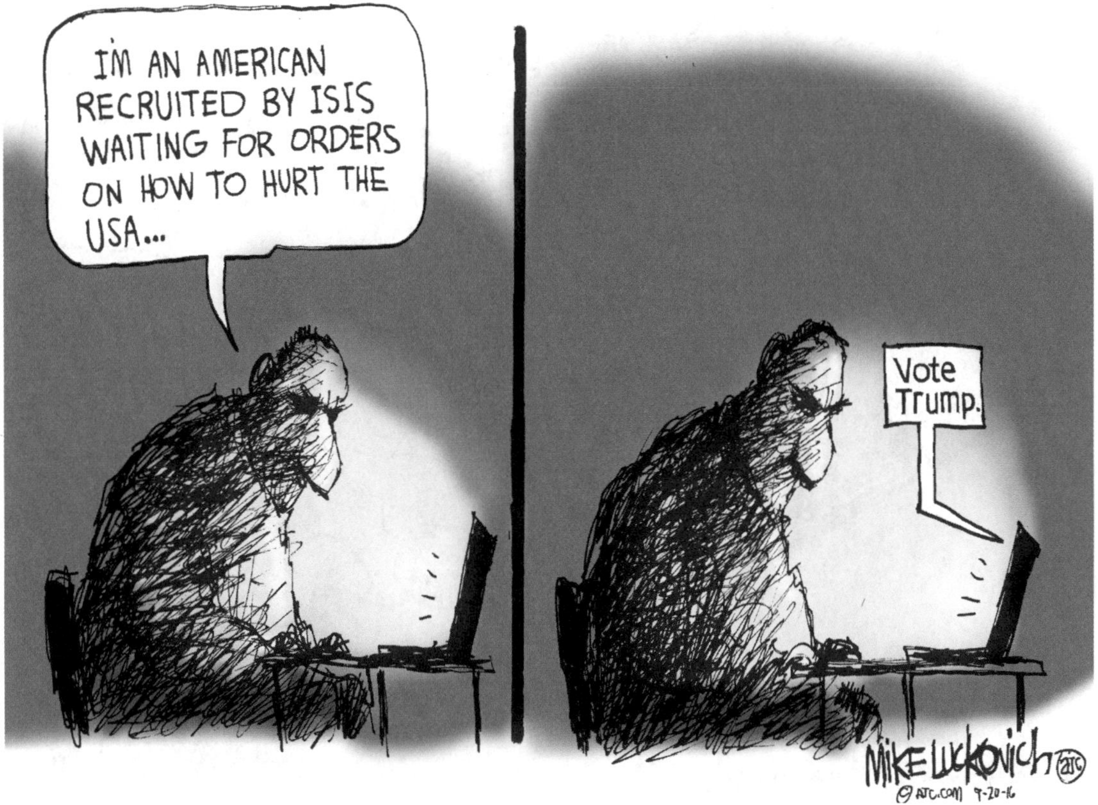
I'M AN AMERICAN RECRUITED BY ISIS WAITING FOR ORDERS ON HOW TO HURT THE USA...
Vote Trump.
MIKE LUCKOVICH
© AJC.COM 9-20-16

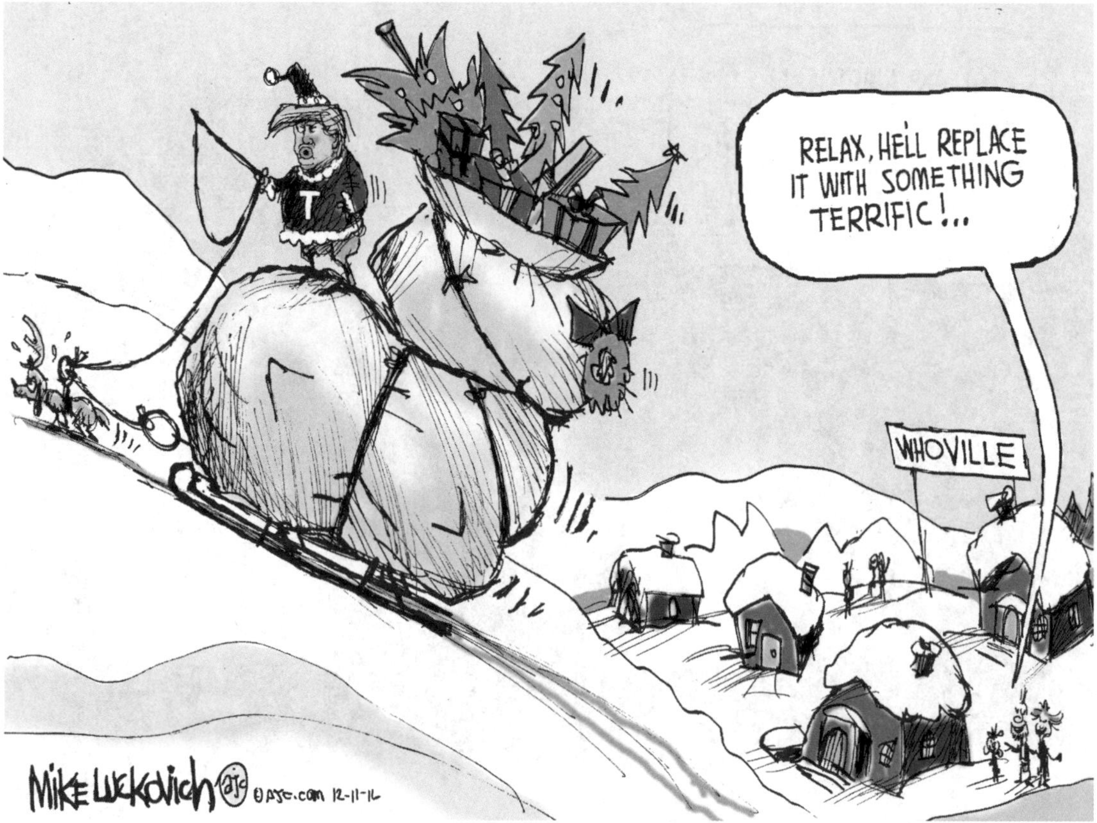
RELAX, HE'LL REPLACE IT WITH SOMETHING TERRIFIC!...
WHOVILLE
MIKE LUCKOVICH
©AJC.com 12-11-16

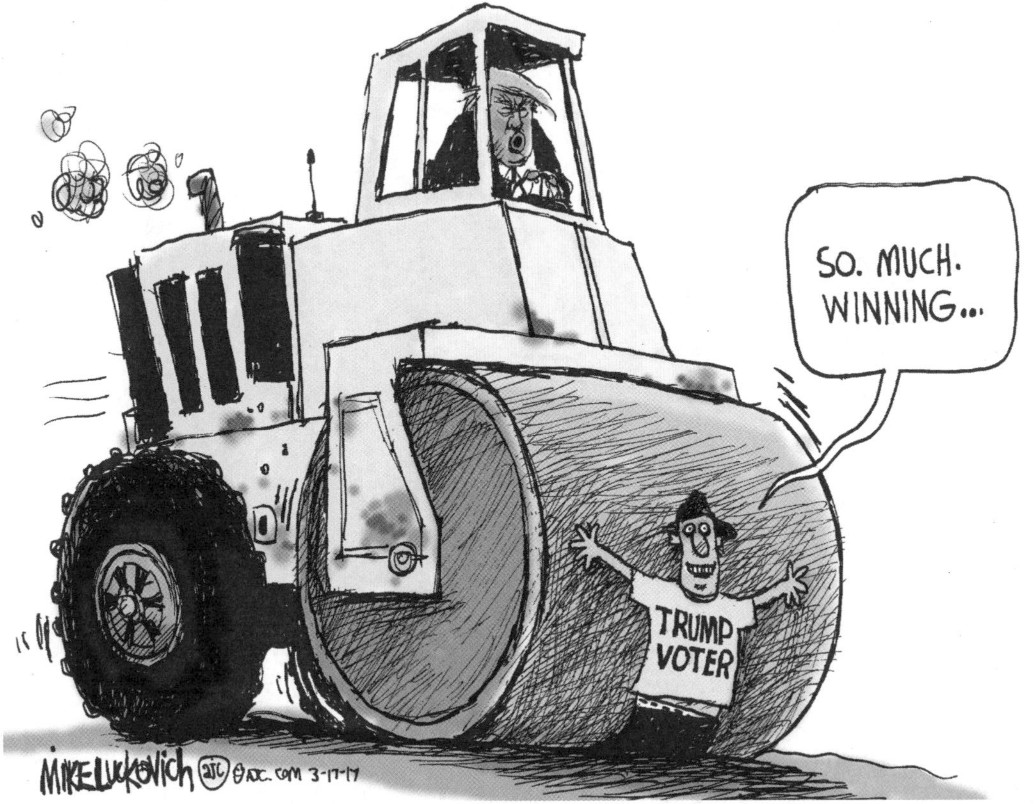
SO. MUCH. WINNING...
TRUMP VOTER
MIKELUCKOVICH

 Donald J. Trump
@realDonaldTrump

 Following

# OUTREACH TO WOMEN

RETWEETS    LIKES
3,582       9,935

🗨 1.7K  🔁 3.6K  ♥ 9.9K  •••

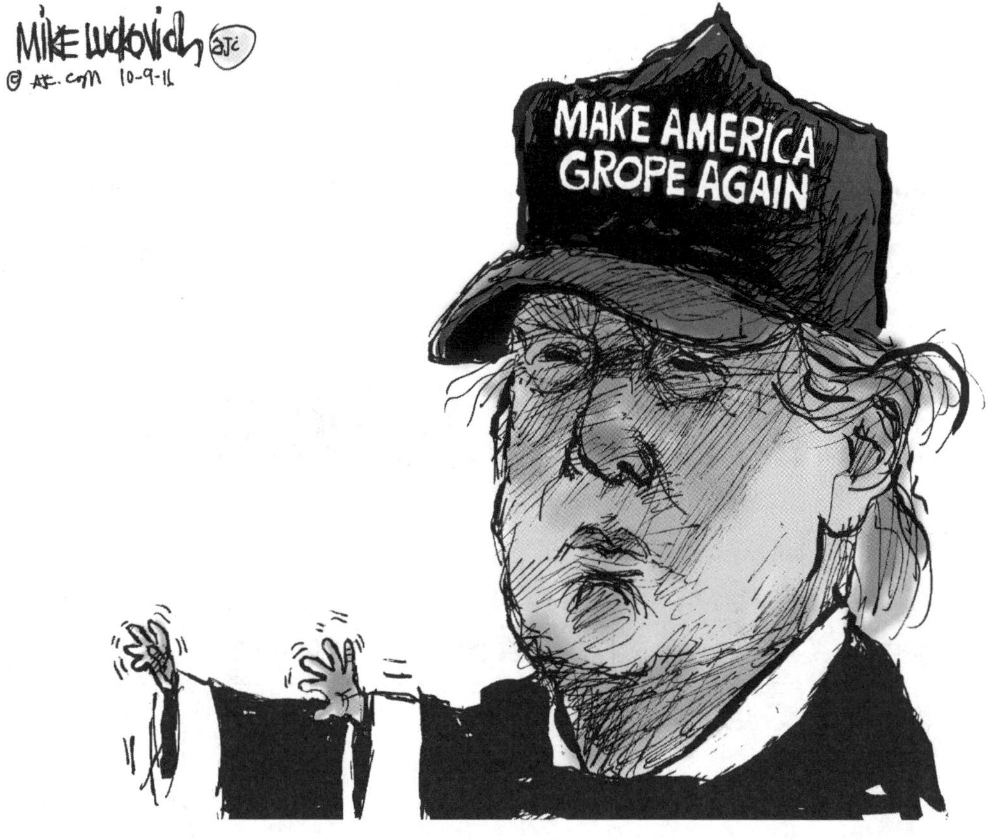
MIKE LUCKOVICH
MAKE AMERICA
GROPE AGAIN

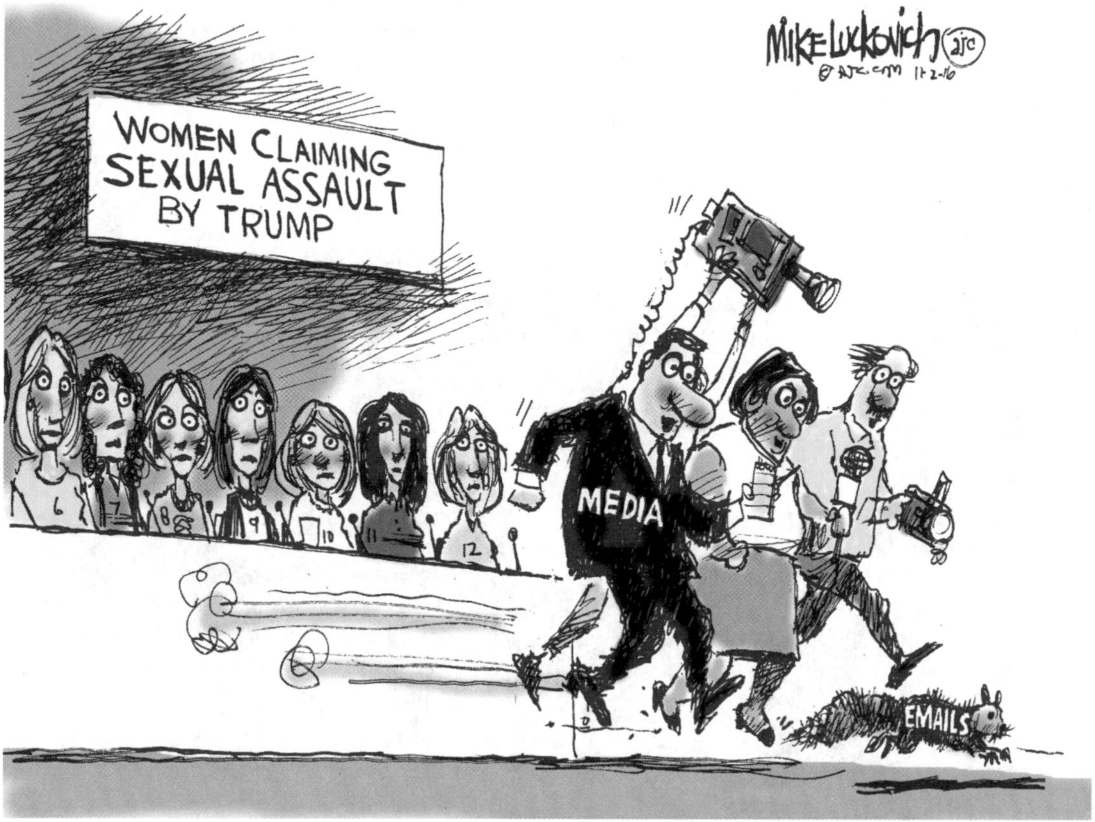
MIKE LUCKOVICH
AJC
WOMEN CLAIMING SEXUAL ASSAULT BY TRUMP
MEDIA
EMAILS

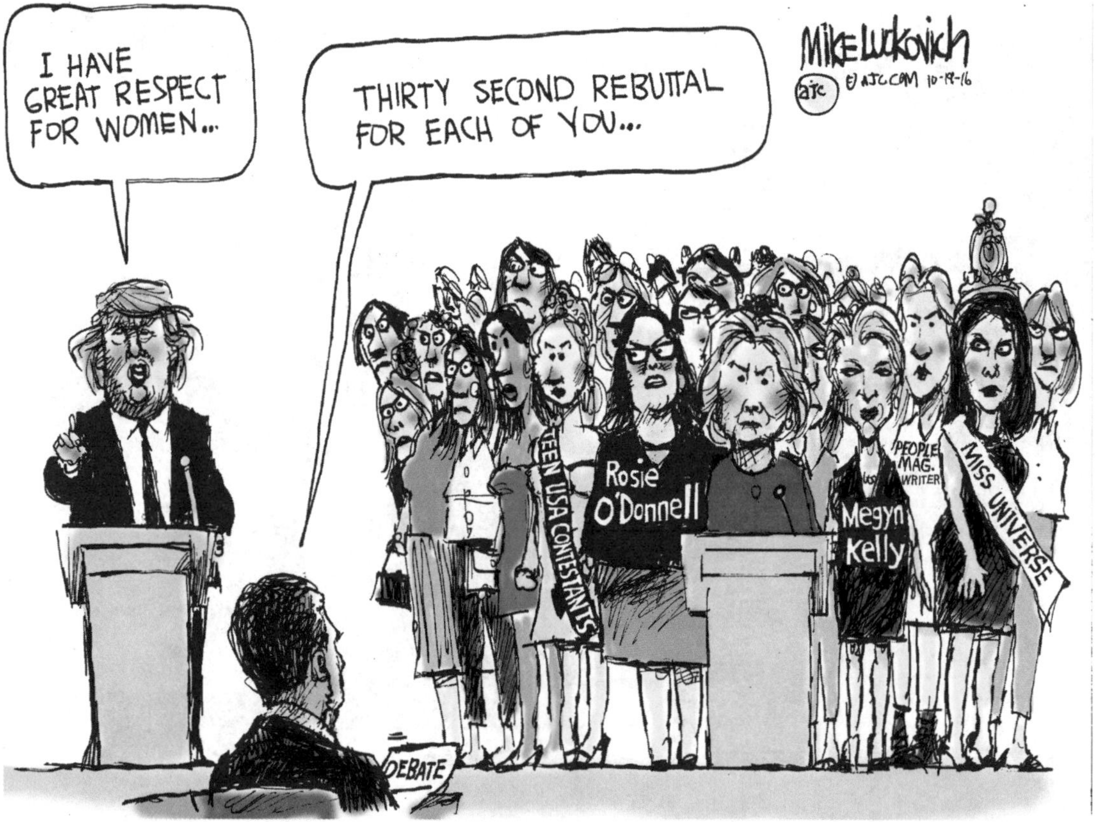
I HAVE GREAT RESPECT FOR WOMEN...
THIRTY SECOND REBUTTAL FOR EACH OF YOU...
MIKE LUCKOVICH
AJC.COM 10-19-16
TEEN USA CONTESTANTS
Rosie O'Donnell
PEOPLE MAG. WRITER
Megyn Kelly
MISS UNIVERSE
DEBATE

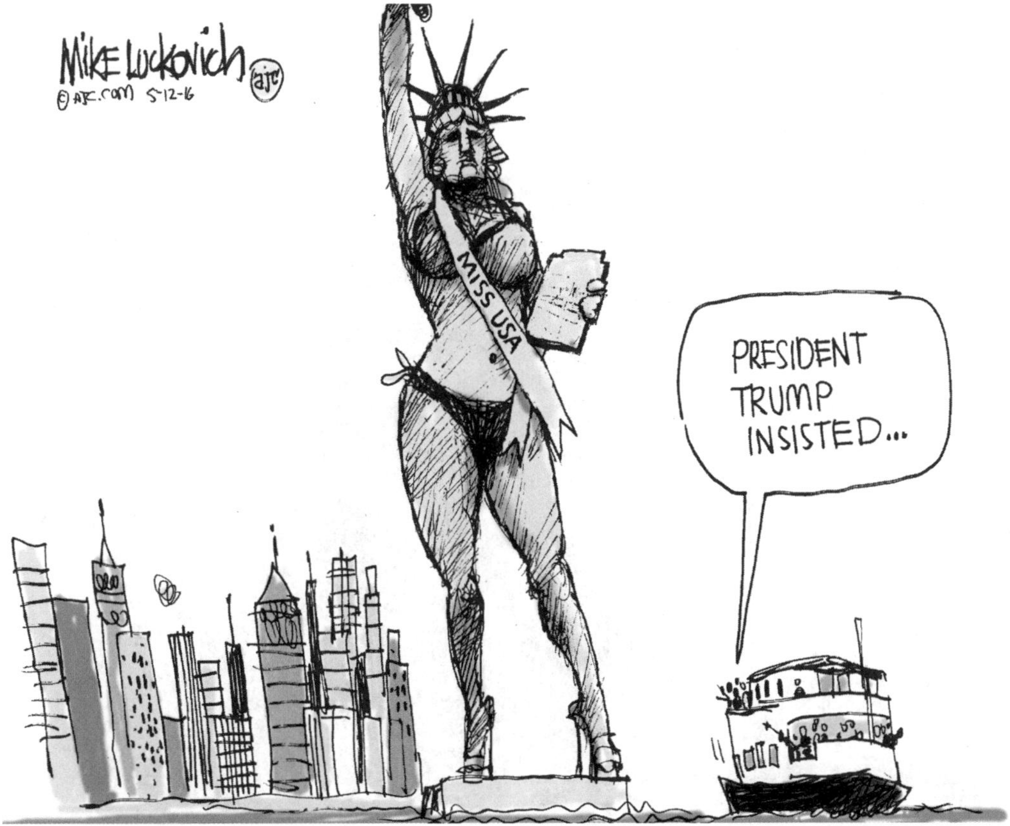
MIKE LUCKOVICH
©AJC.COM 5-12-16
ajc
MISS USA
PRESIDENT TRUMP INSISTED...

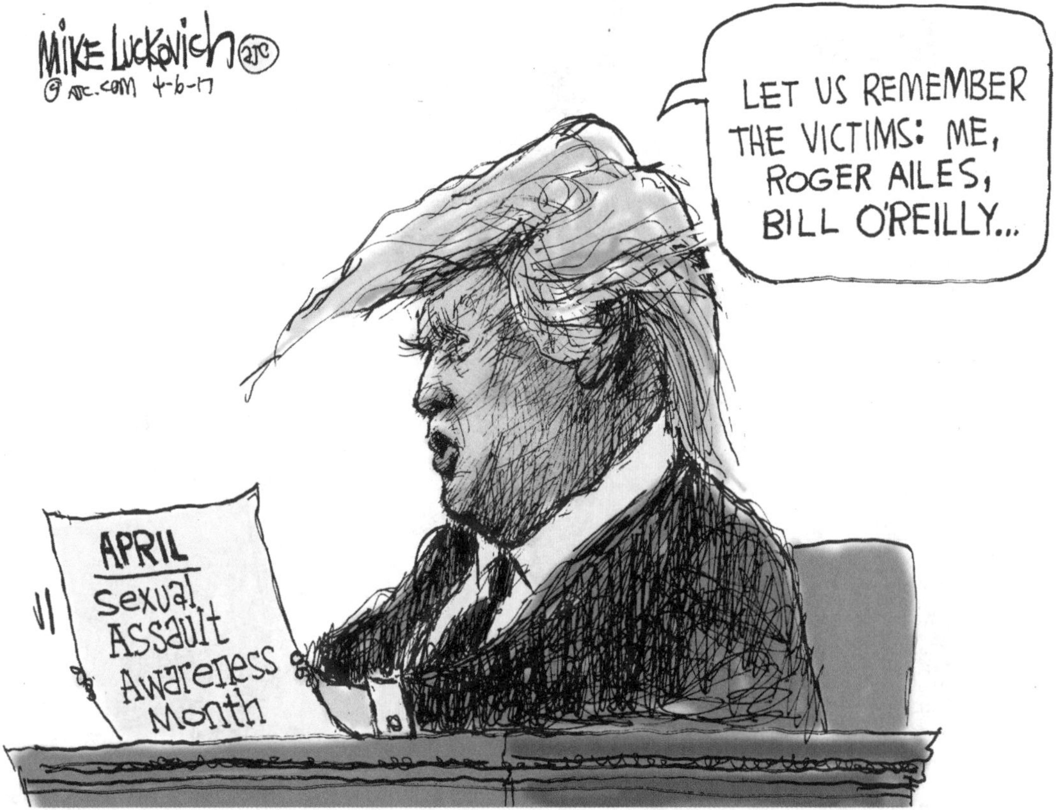
MIKE LUCKOVICH AJC
© AJC.COM 4-6-17
LET US REMEMBER THE VICTIMS: ME, ROGER AILES, BILL O'REILLY...
APRIL
Sexual Assault Awareness Month

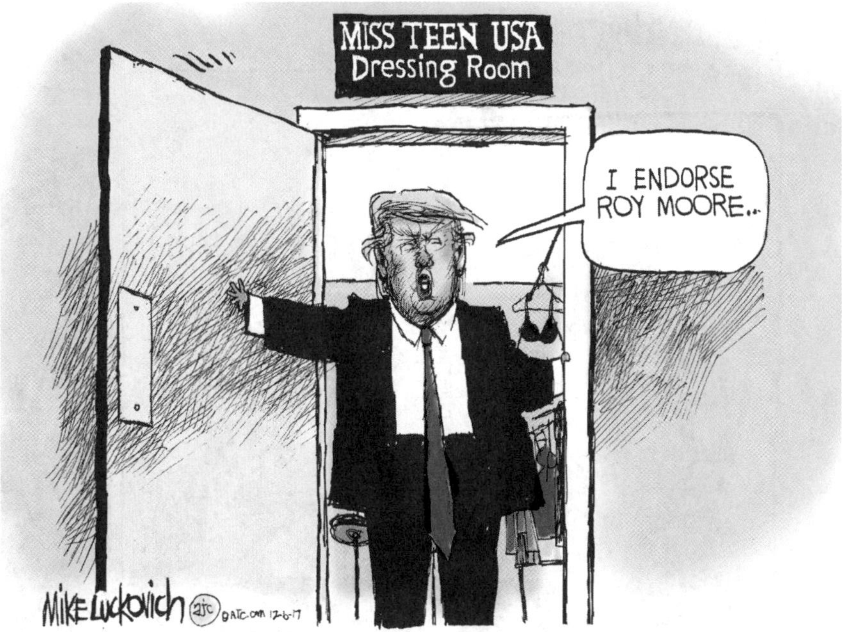
MISS TEEN USA
Dressing Room
I ENDORSE ROY MOORE...
MIKE LUCKOVICH

I sort of admire the producers at Fox News. America has a lying buffoon for a president who's constantly doing irrational, ignorant things. It must take a real gift to make this mess appear competent and presidential to their slack-jawed viewers. It's like filming two hours of a monkey playing piano and editing it down to a minute where it sounds like Beethoven.

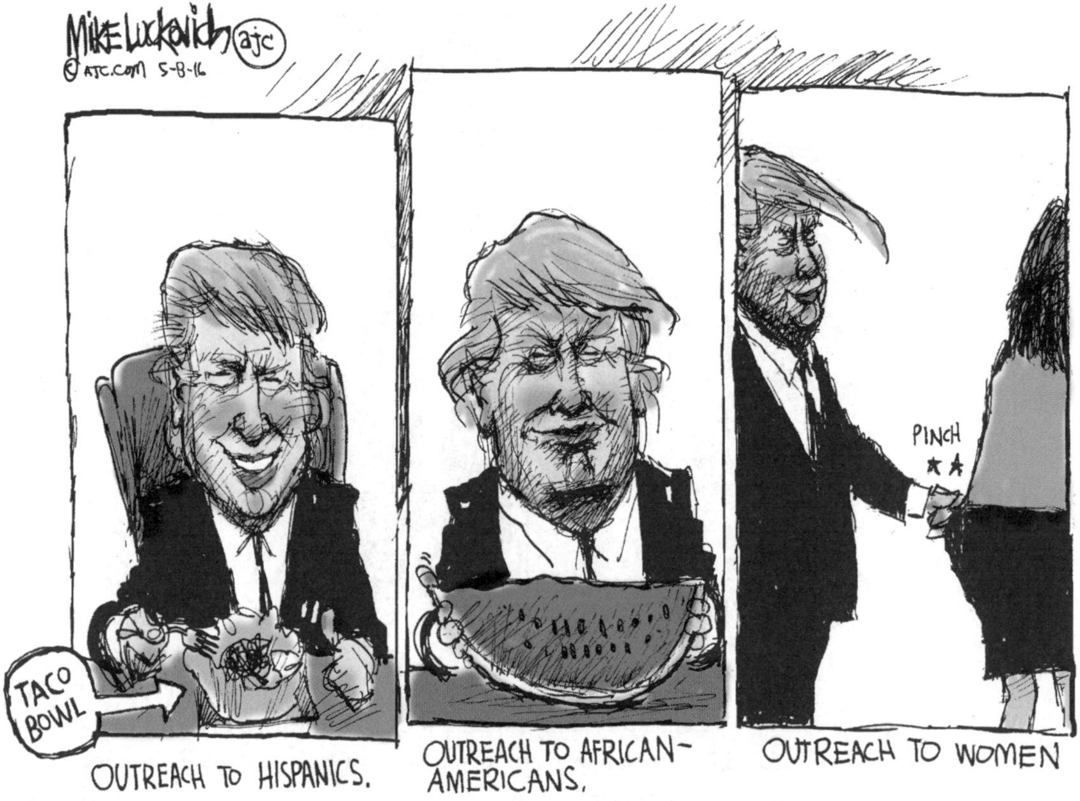
MIKE LUCKOVICH ajc
© AJC.COM 5-8-16
TACO BOWL
OUTREACH TO HISPANICS.
OUTREACH TO AFRICAN-AMERICANS.
PINCH
OUTREACH TO WOMEN

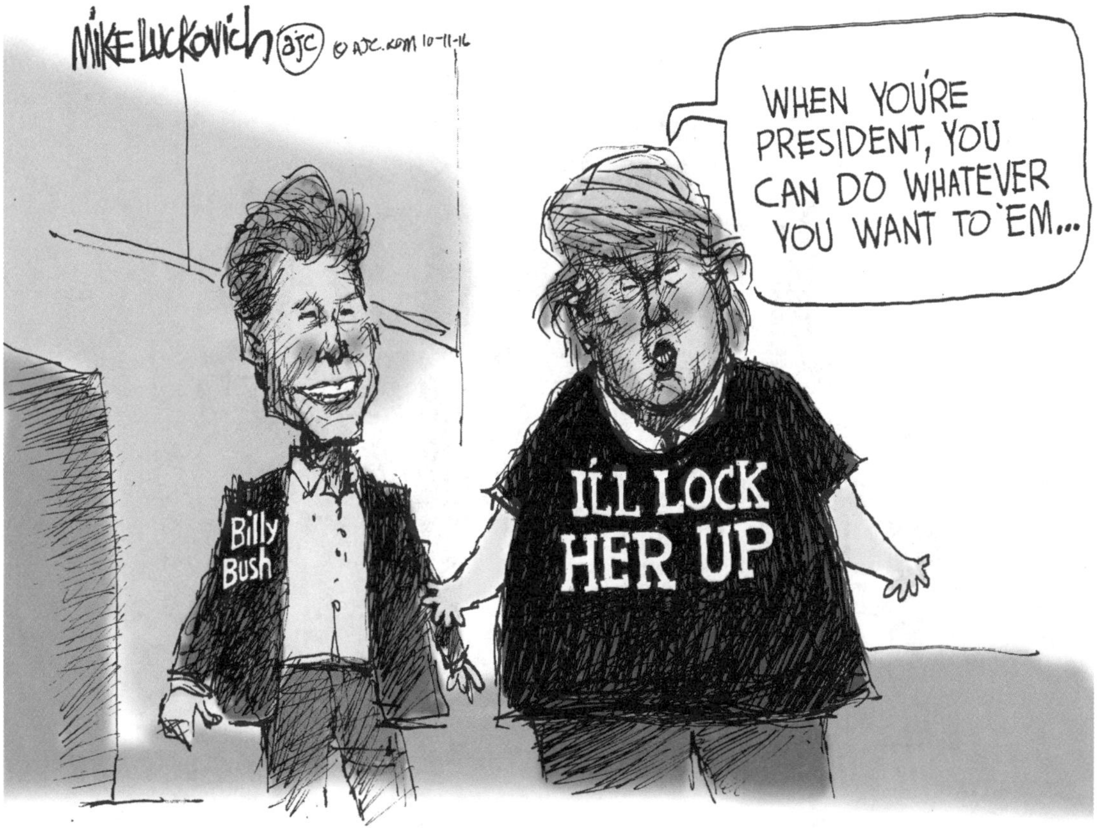
MIKE LUCKOVICH
ajc
© AJC.COM 10-11-16
WHEN YOU'RE PRESIDENT, YOU CAN DO WHATEVER YOU WANT TO 'EM...
Billy Bush
I'LL LOCK HER UP

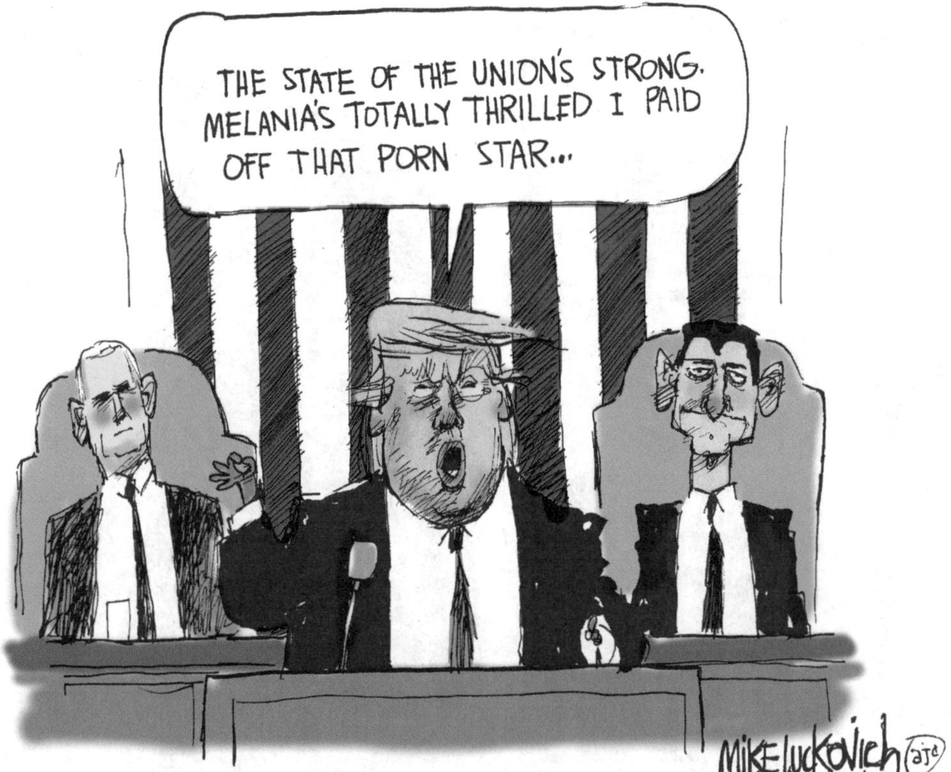
THE STATE OF THE UNION'S STRONG. MELANIA'S TOTALLY THRILLED I PAID OFF THAT PORN STAR...
MIKE LUCKOVICH
© AJC.com 1-30-18

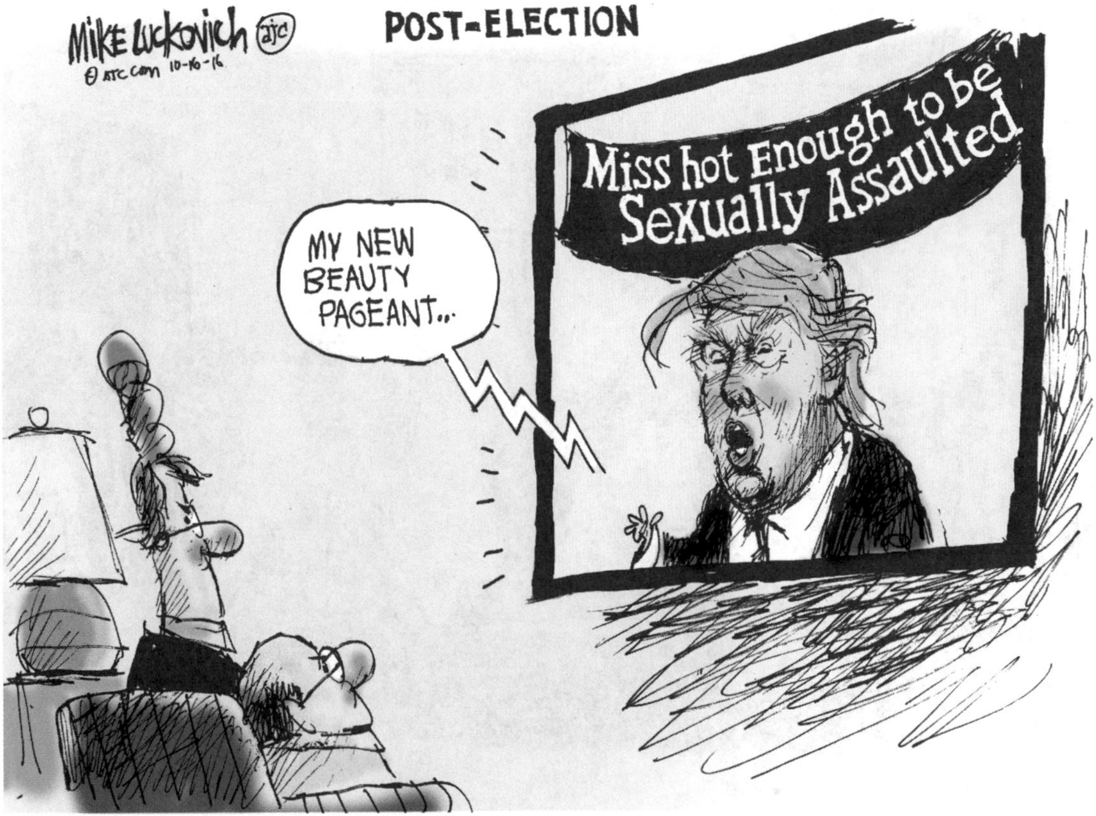
MIKE LUCKOVICH ajc
POST-ELECTION
Miss hot Enough to be Sexually Assaulted
MY NEW BEAUTY PAGEANT...

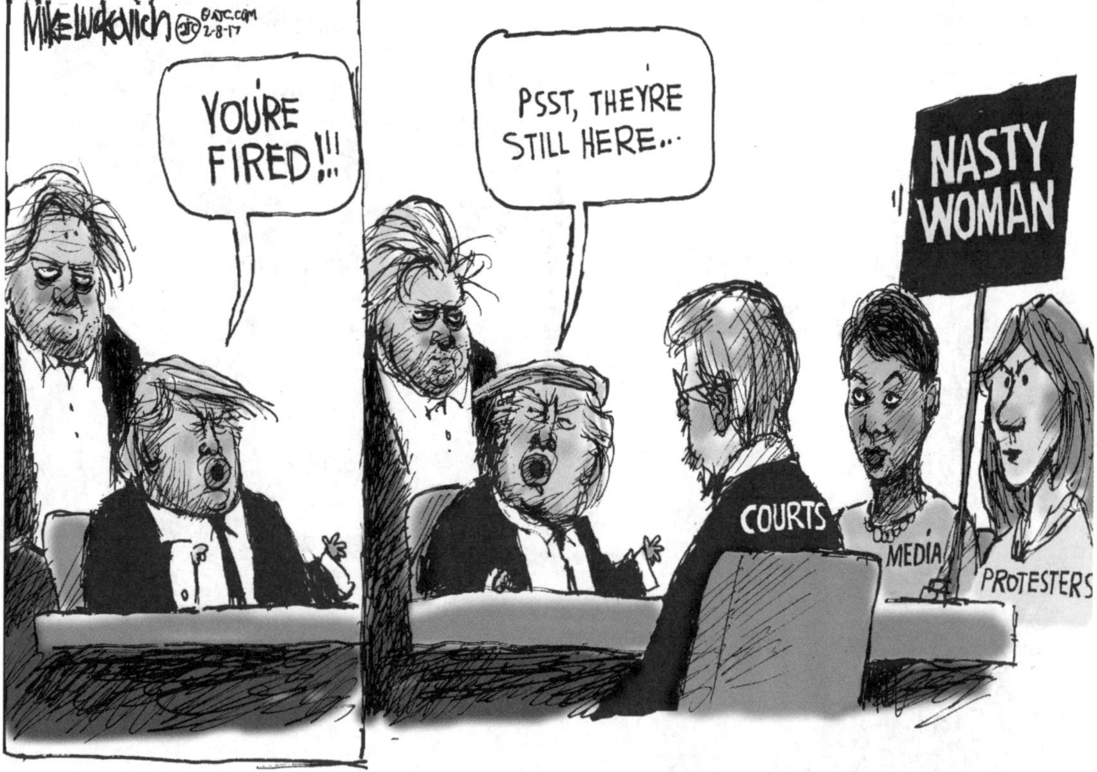
MIKE LUCKOVICH ©AJC.COM 2-8-17
YOU'RE FIRED!!!
PSST, THEY'RE STILL HERE...
NASTY WOMAN
COURTS
MEDIA
PROTESTERS

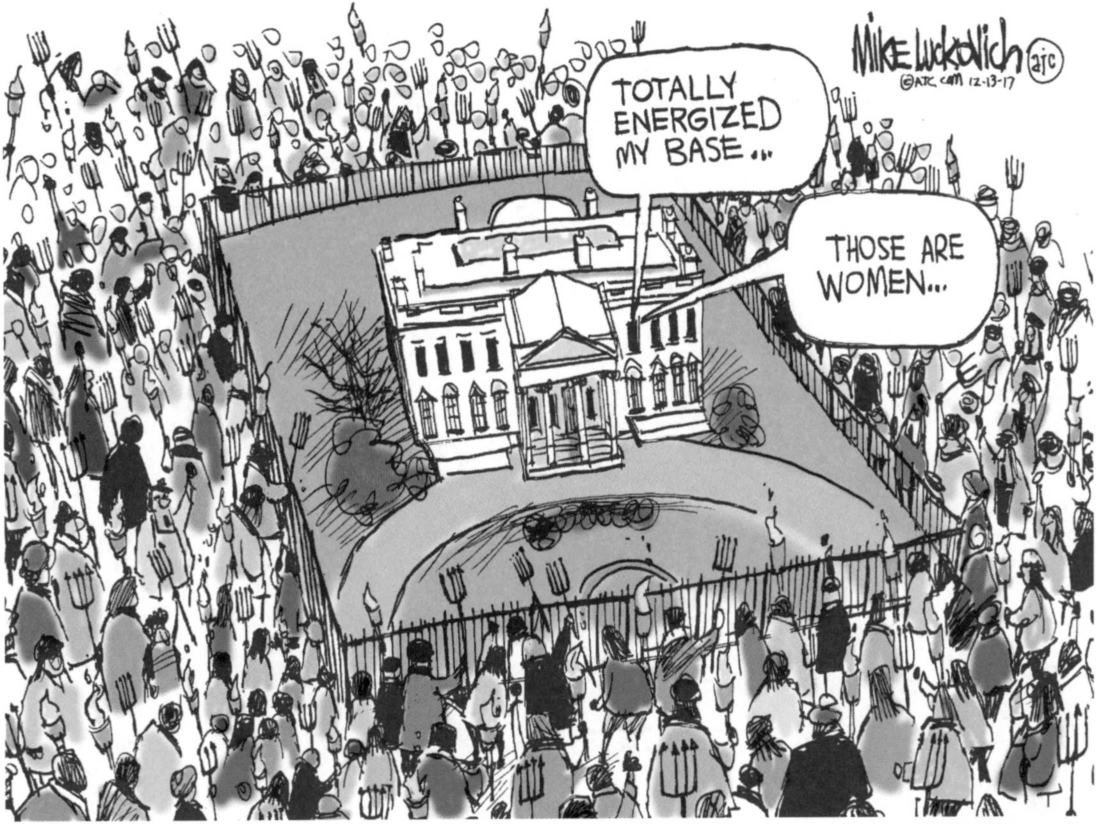
TOTALLY ENERGIZED MY BASE...
THOSE ARE WOMEN...
MIKE LUCKOVICH

 Donald J. Trump
@realDonaldTrump

# PUTIN'S PUPPET

| RETWEETS | LIKES |
|----------|-------|
| 3,582 | 9,935 |

↑ 1.7K   ⇄ 3.6K   ♥ 9.9K  ···

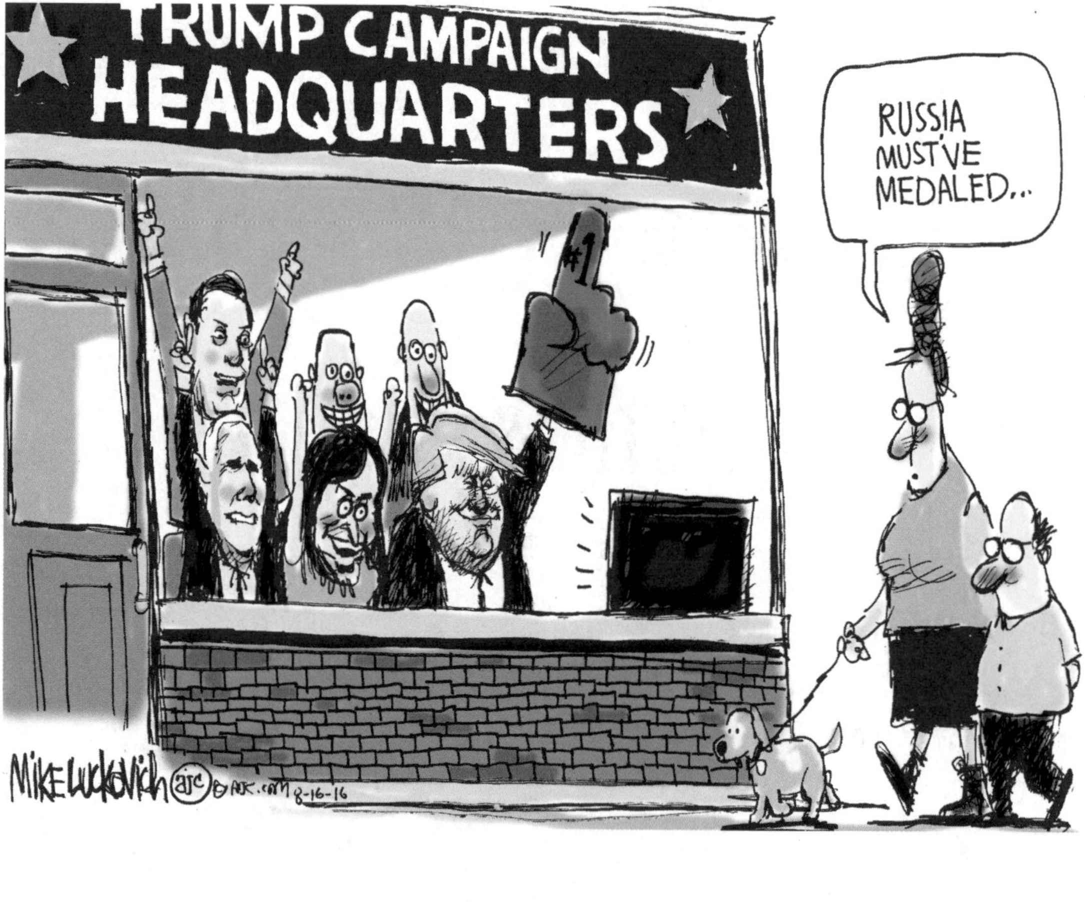
TRUMP CAMPAIGN HEADQUARTERS
#1
RUSSIA MUST'VE MEDALED...
MIKE LUCKOVICH
AJC.com 8-16-16

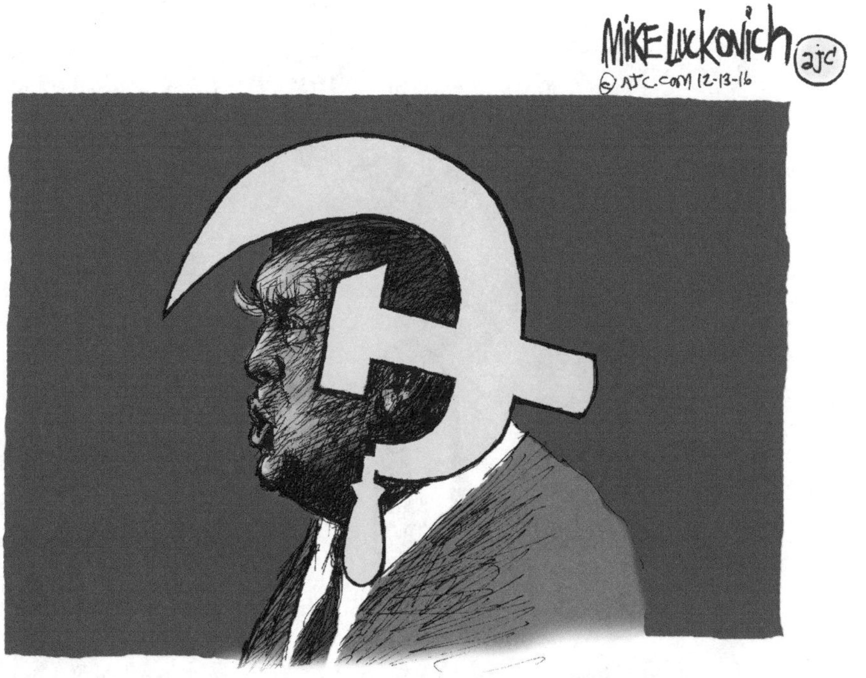
MIKE LUCKOVICH
ajc
© AJC.COM 12-13-16

Trump criticizes everybody. He calls women dogs, criticizes war heroes and mocks a disabled reporter, but he refuses to utter a word of negativity about Vladimir Putin and his interference in our election or his poisoning of British citizens in Britain.

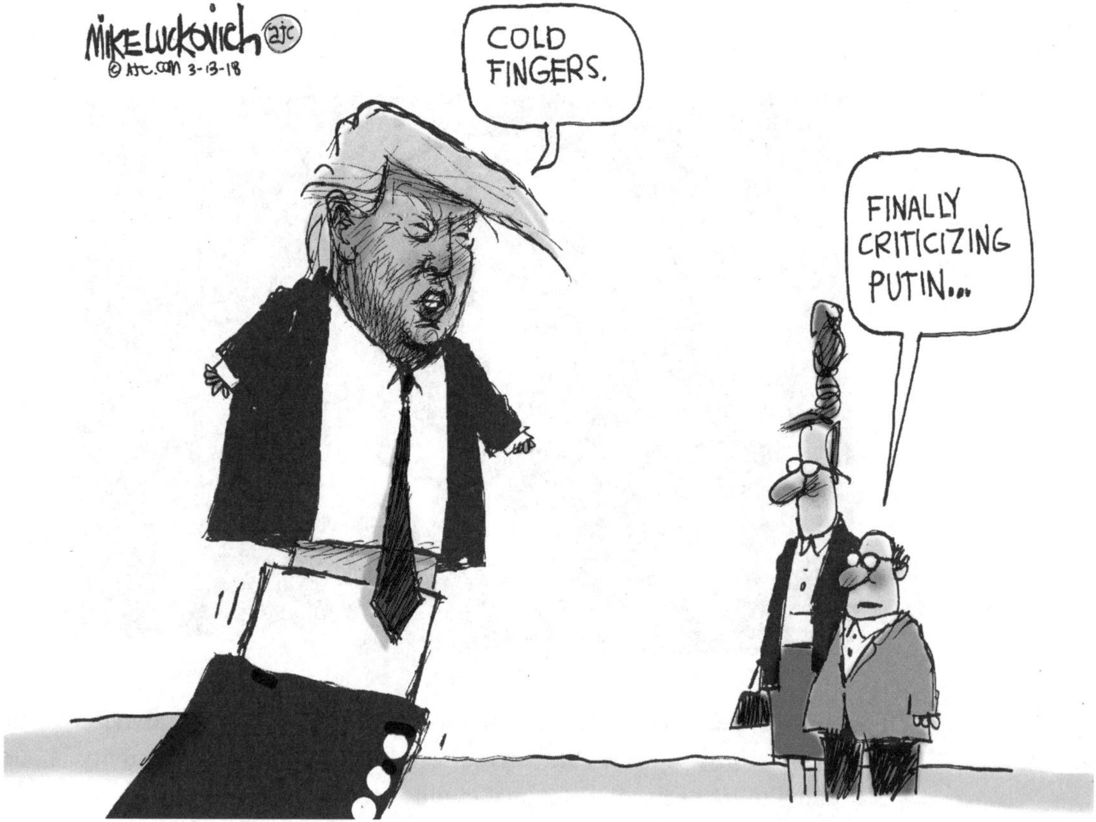
MIKE LUCKOVICH ajc
© AJC.COM 3-13-18
COLD FINGERS.
FINALLY CRITICIZING PUTIN...

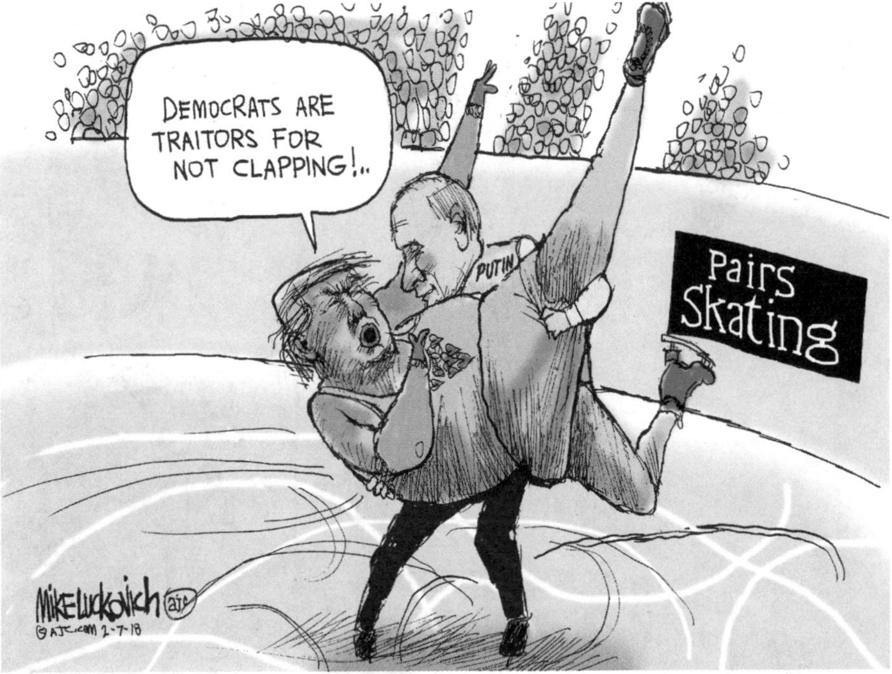
DEMOCRATS ARE TRAITORS FOR NOT CLAPPING!..
PUTIN
Pairs Skating
MIKELUCKOVICH
©AJC.com 2-7-18

I drew this cartoon after Trump's 2018 State of the Union when he claimed that Democrats who didn't clap for him "were traitors." This coincided with the 2018 Winter Olympics.

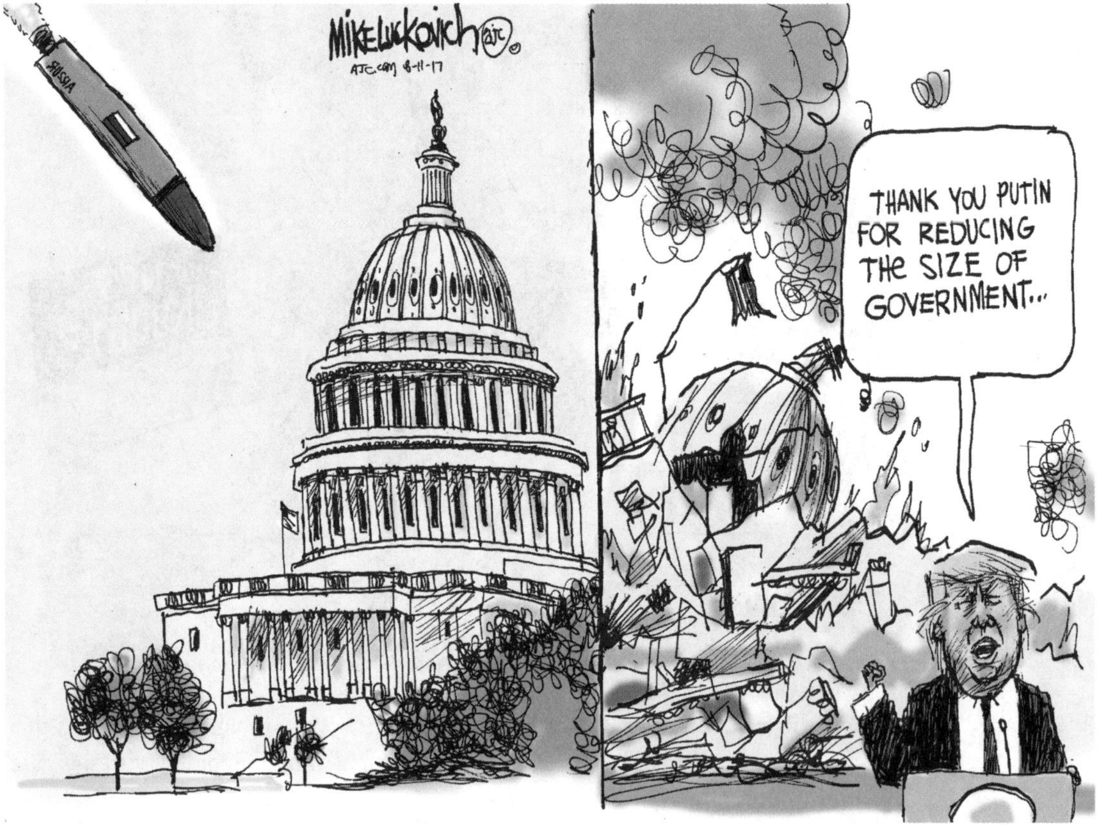
MIKELUCKOVICH
AJC.com 8-11-17
RUSSIA
THANK YOU PUTIN FOR REDUCING THE SIZE OF GOVERNMENT...

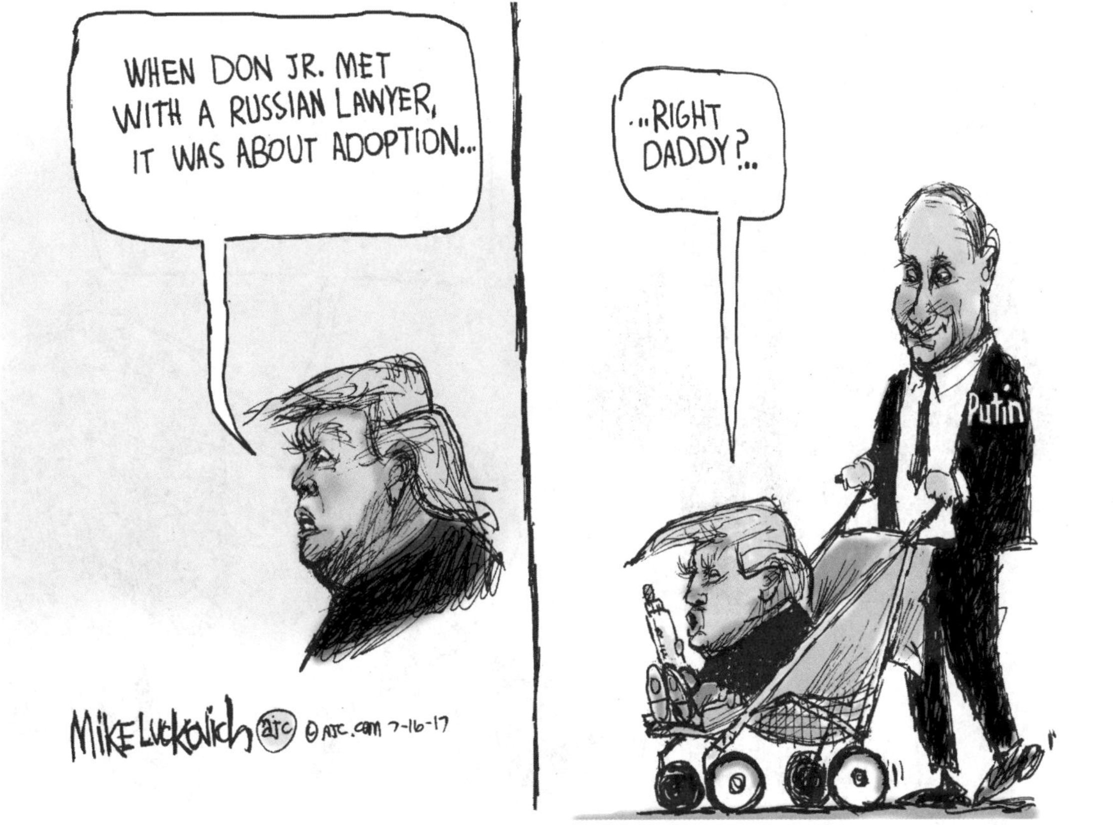
WHEN DON JR. MET WITH A RUSSIAN LAWYER, IT WAS ABOUT ADOPTION...
...RIGHT DADDY?...
Putin
MIKE LUCKOVICH ajc ©AJC.com 7-16-17

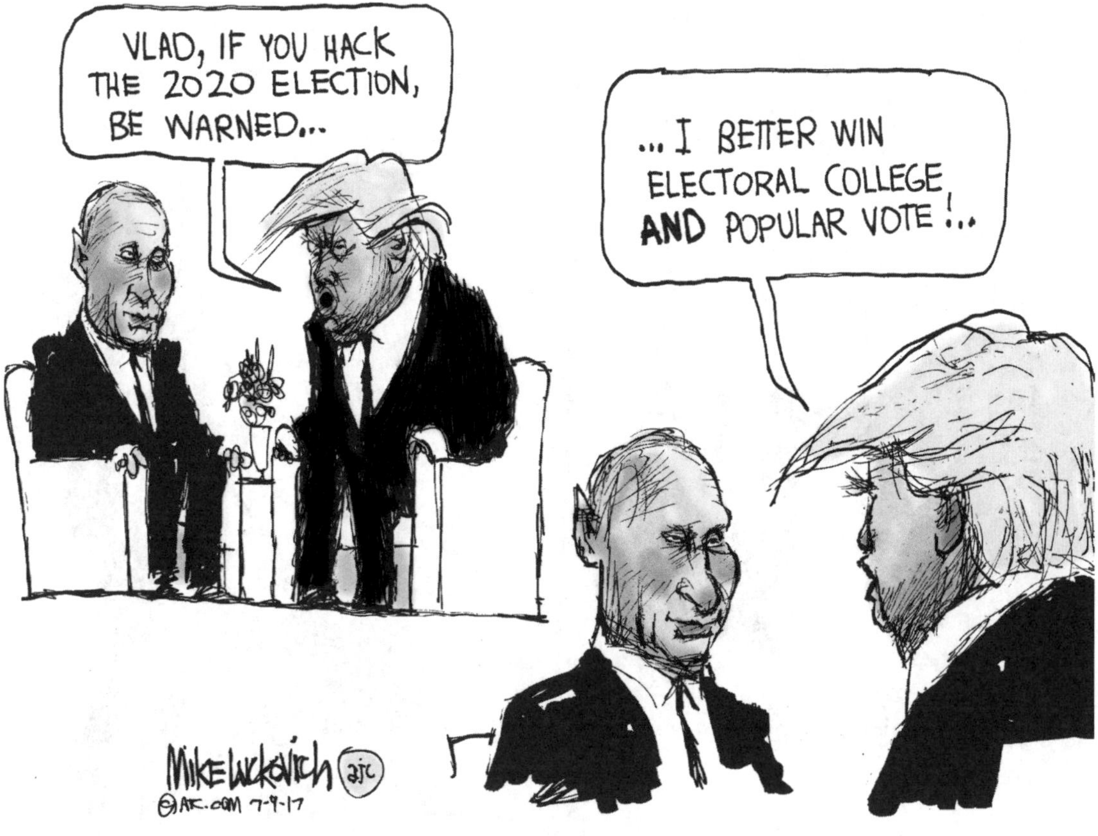
VLAD, IF YOU HACK THE 2020 ELECTION, BE WARNED...
...I BETTER WIN ELECTORAL COLLEGE, AND POPULAR VOTE!...
MIKE LUCKOVICH
ajc
©AJC.COM 7-9-17

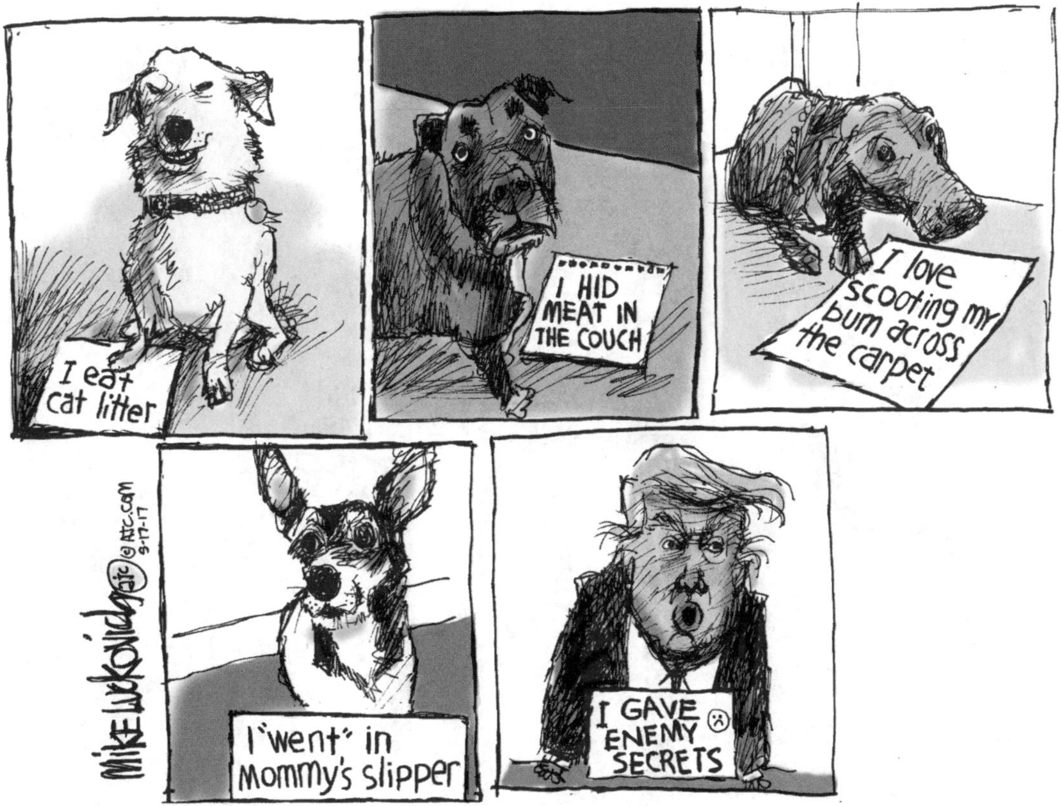
I eat cat litter
I HID MEAT IN THE COUCH
I love scooting my bum across the carpet
I "went" in Mommy's slipper
I GAVE ENEMY SECRETS
MIKE LUCKOVICH AJC © AJC.com 5-17-17

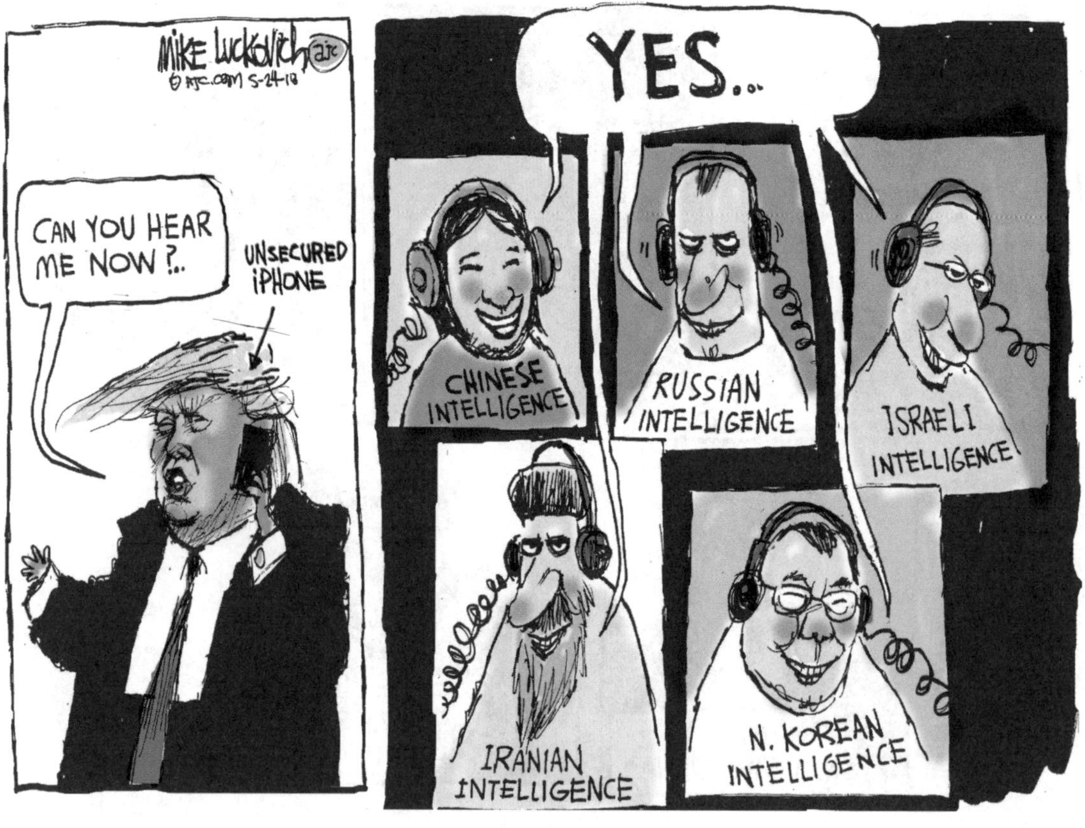
MIKE LUCKOVICH ajc
© ajc.com 5-24-18
CAN YOU HEAR ME NOW?..
UNSECURED iPHONE
YES...
CHINESE INTELLIGENCE
RUSSIAN INTELLIGENCE
ISRAELI INTELLIGENCE
IRANIAN INTELLIGENCE
N. KOREAN INTELLIGENCE

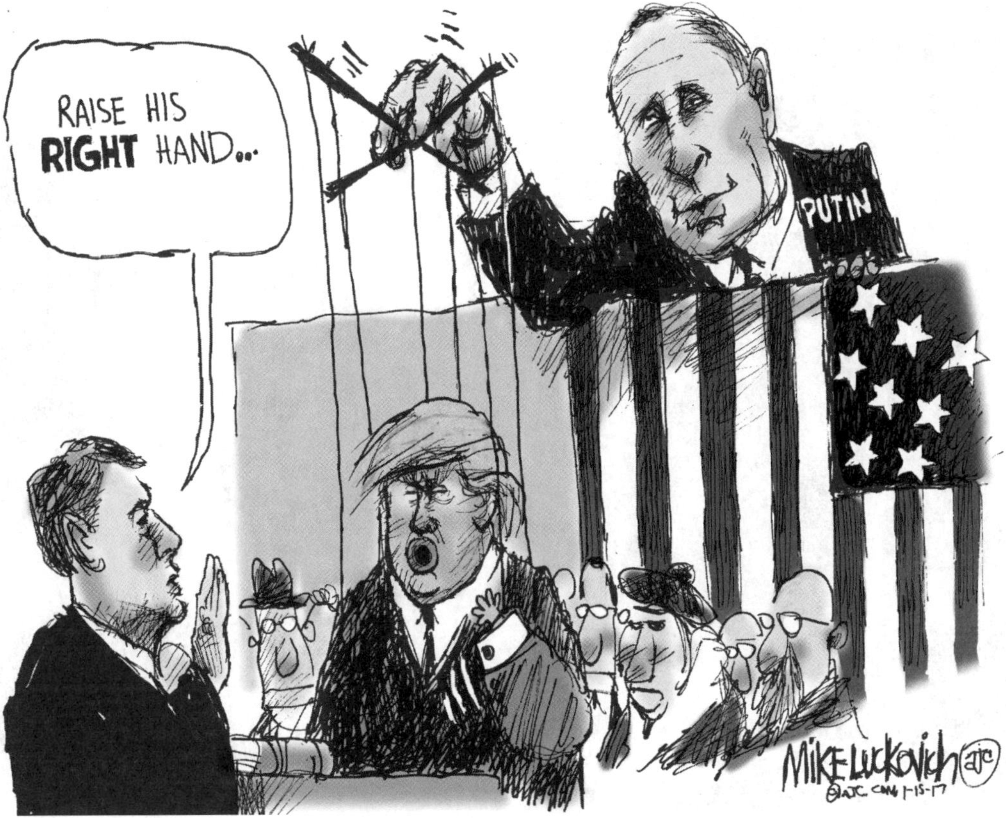
RAISE HIS **RIGHT** HAND...
PUTIN
MIKE LUCKOVICH

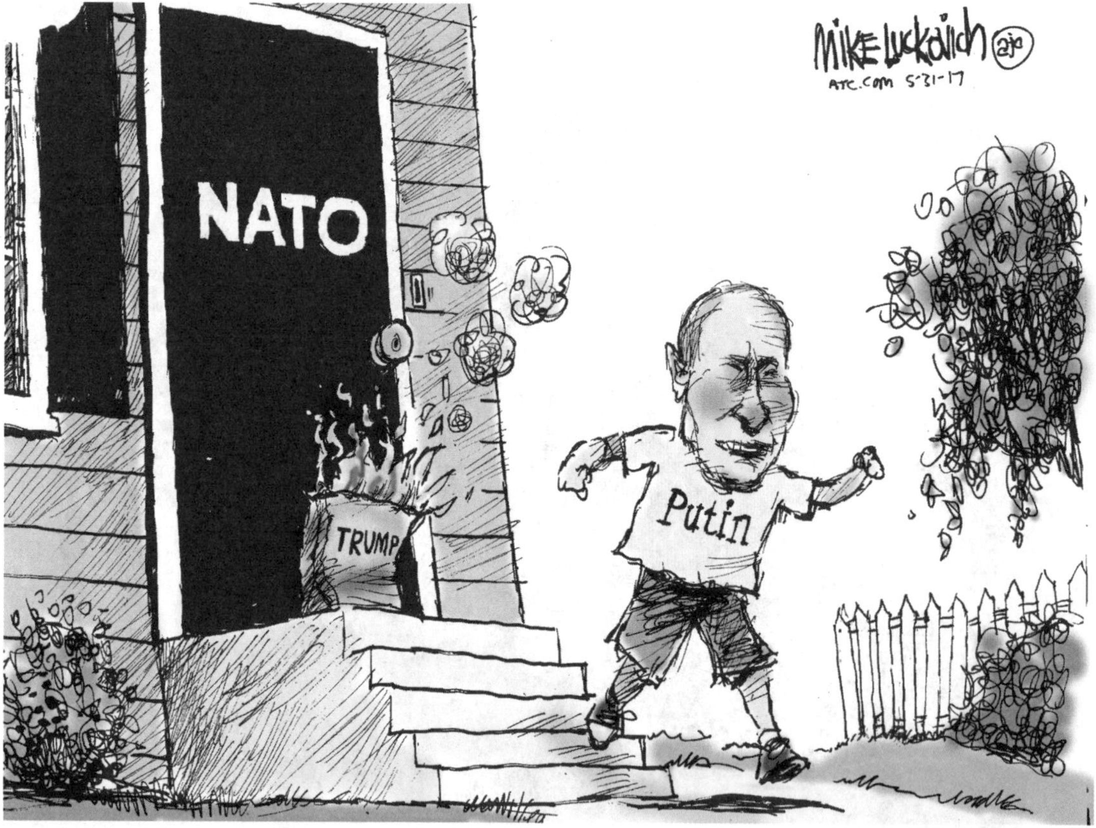
MIKE LUCKOVICH
AJC.com 5-31-17
NATO
TRUMP
Putin

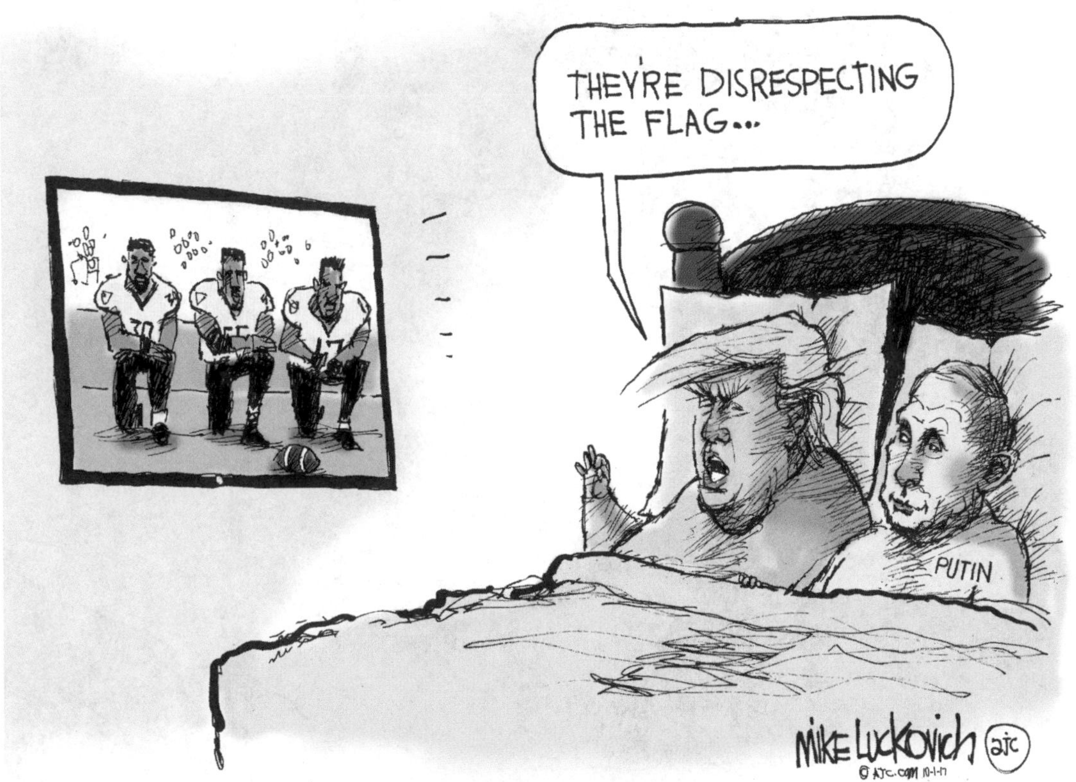
THEY'RE DISRESPECTING THE FLAG...
PUTIN
MIKE LUCKOVICH
ajc
© AJC.COM 10-1-17

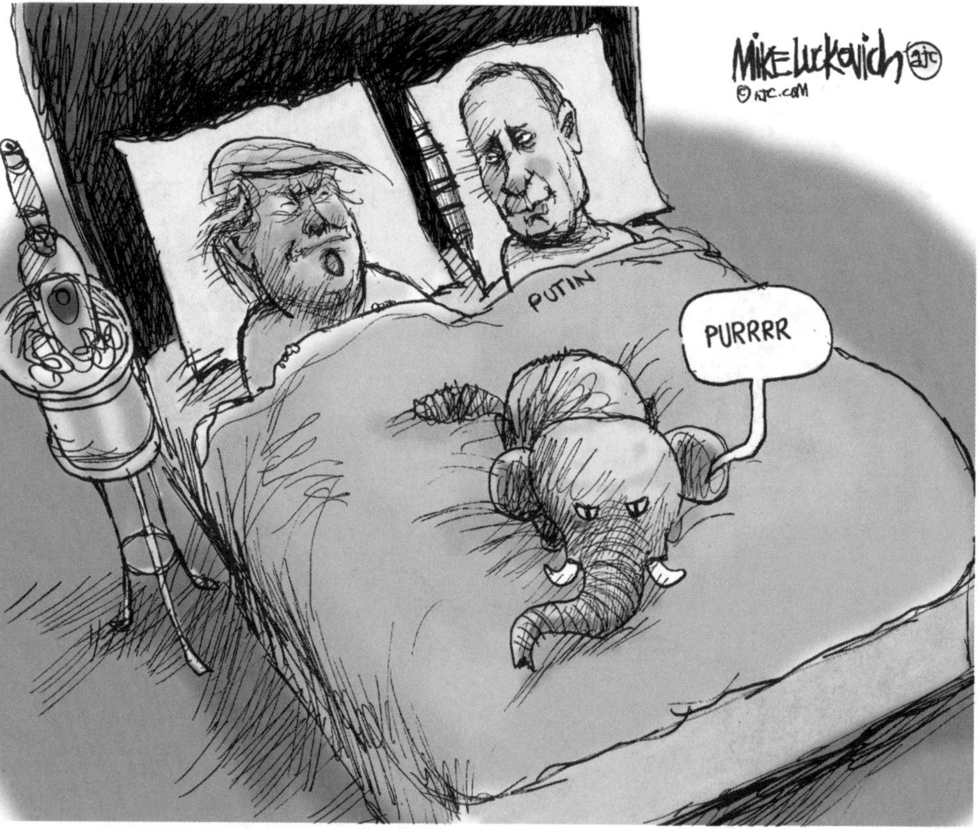
MIKE LUCKOVICH
© AJC.COM
PUTIN
PURRRR

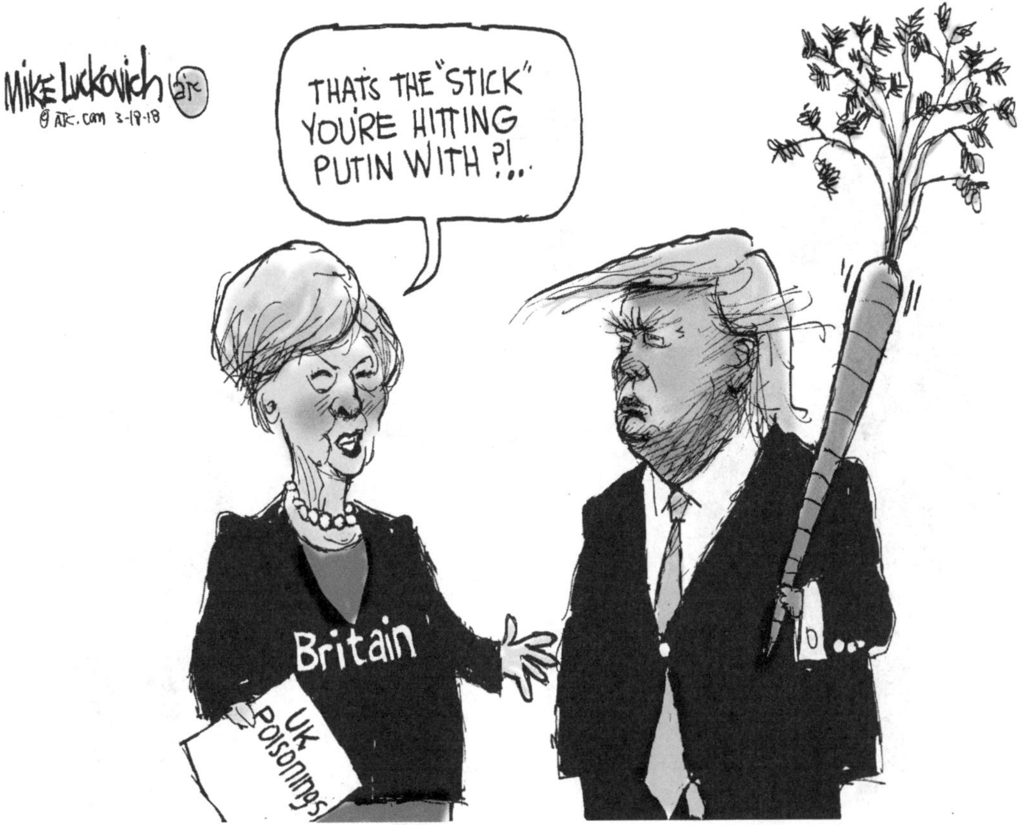
MIKE LUCKOVICH
© AJC.com 3-18-18
THAT'S THE "STICK" YOU'RE HITTING PUTIN WITH ?!...
Britain
UK Poisonings

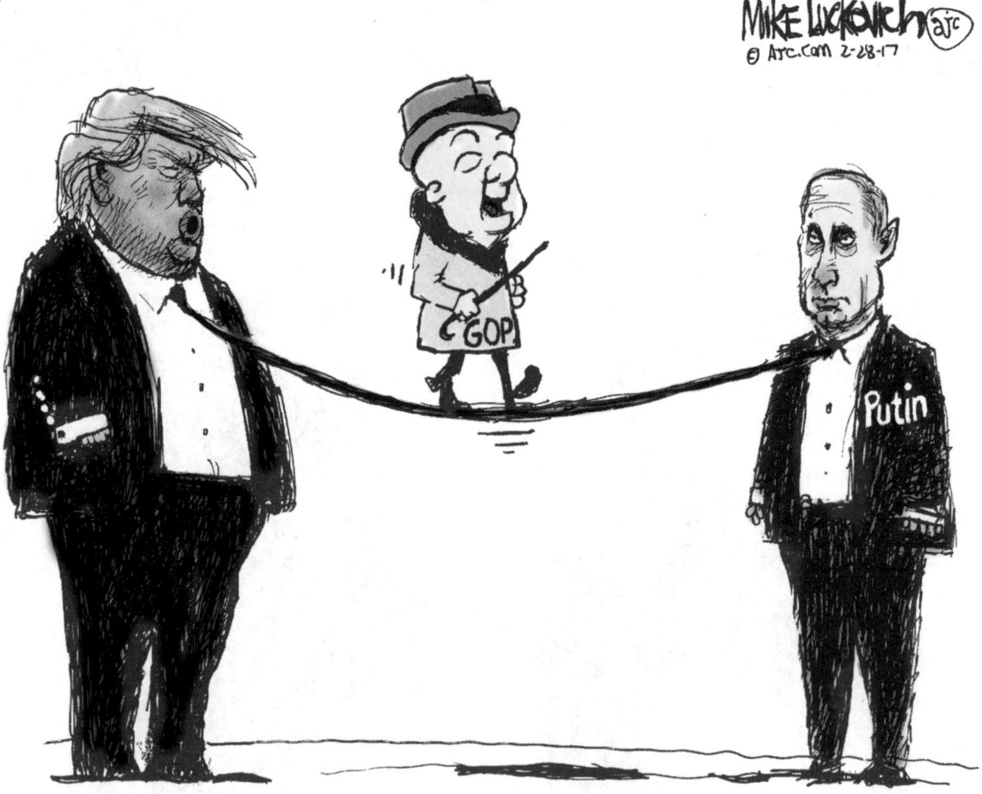
MIKE LUCKOVICH AJC
© AJC.COM 2-28-17
GOP
Putin

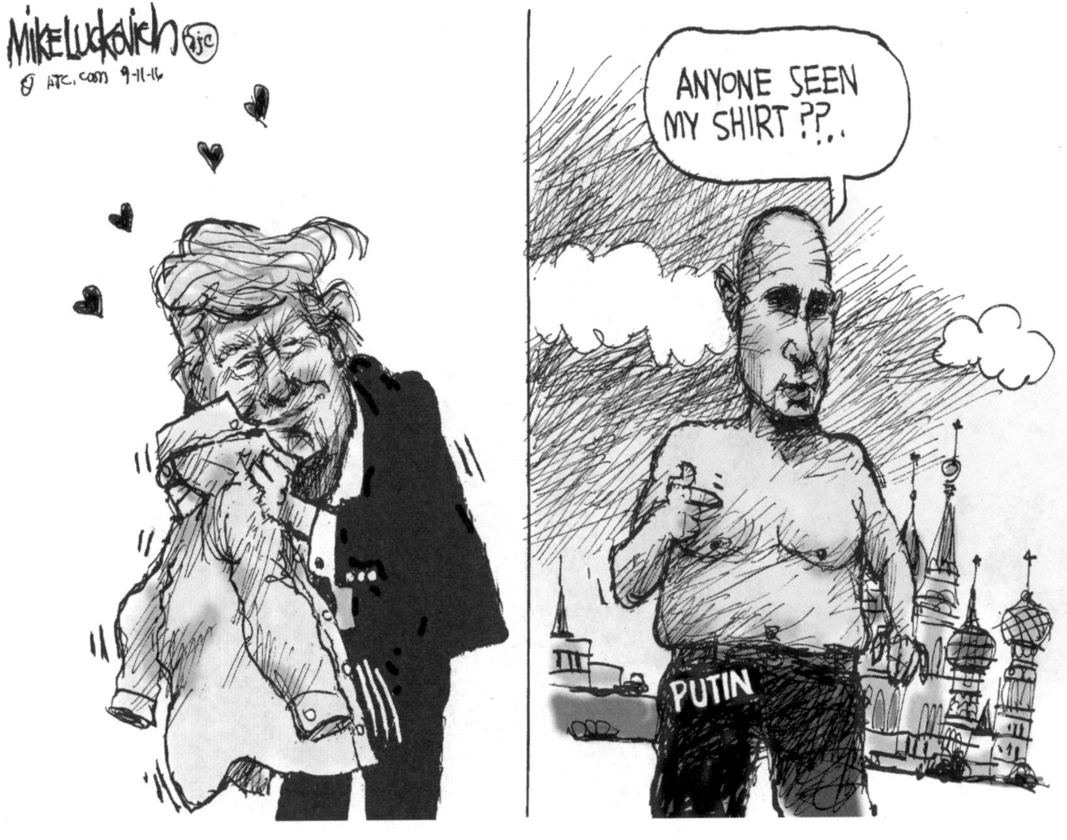
MIKE LUCKOVICH ajc
© AJC.com 9-11-16
ANYONE SEEN MY SHIRT ??..
PUTIN

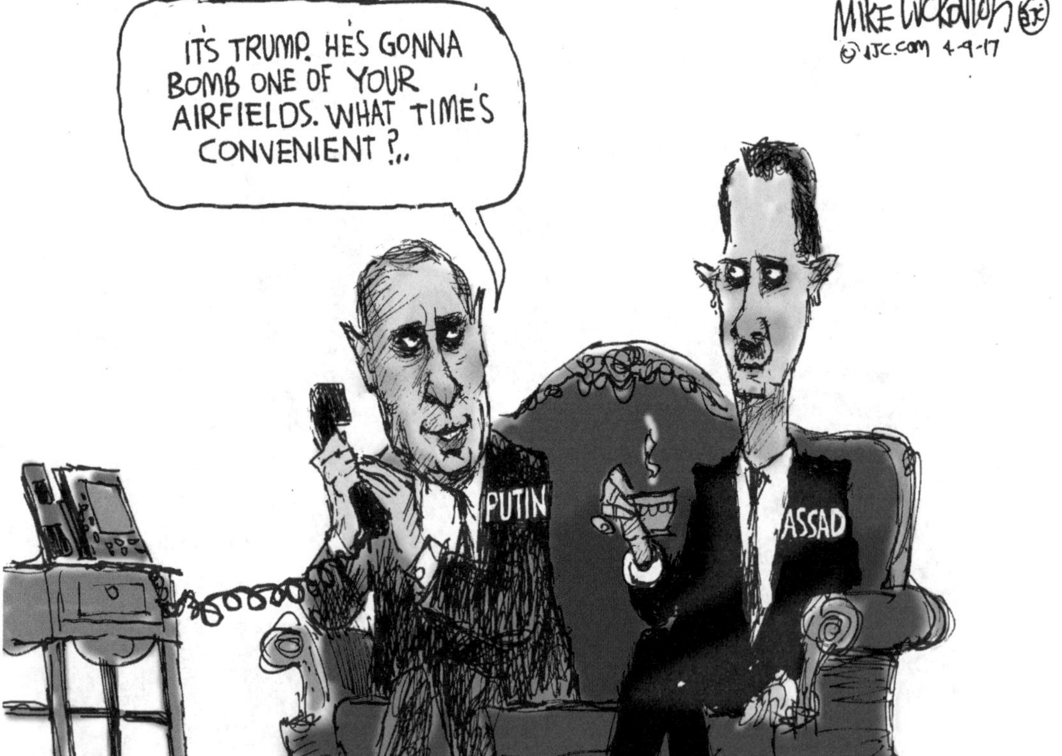
IT'S TRUMP. HE'S GONNA BOMB ONE OF YOUR AIRFIELDS. WHAT TIME'S CONVENIENT ?..
MIKE LUCKOVICH
© AJC.COM 4-9-17
PUTIN
ASSAD

 **Donald J. Trump**
@realDonaldTrump

# COLLUSION?
# WHAT COLLUSION?

RETWEETS      LIKES
3,582         9,935

↑ 1.7K   ⇄ 3.6K   ♥ 99K •••

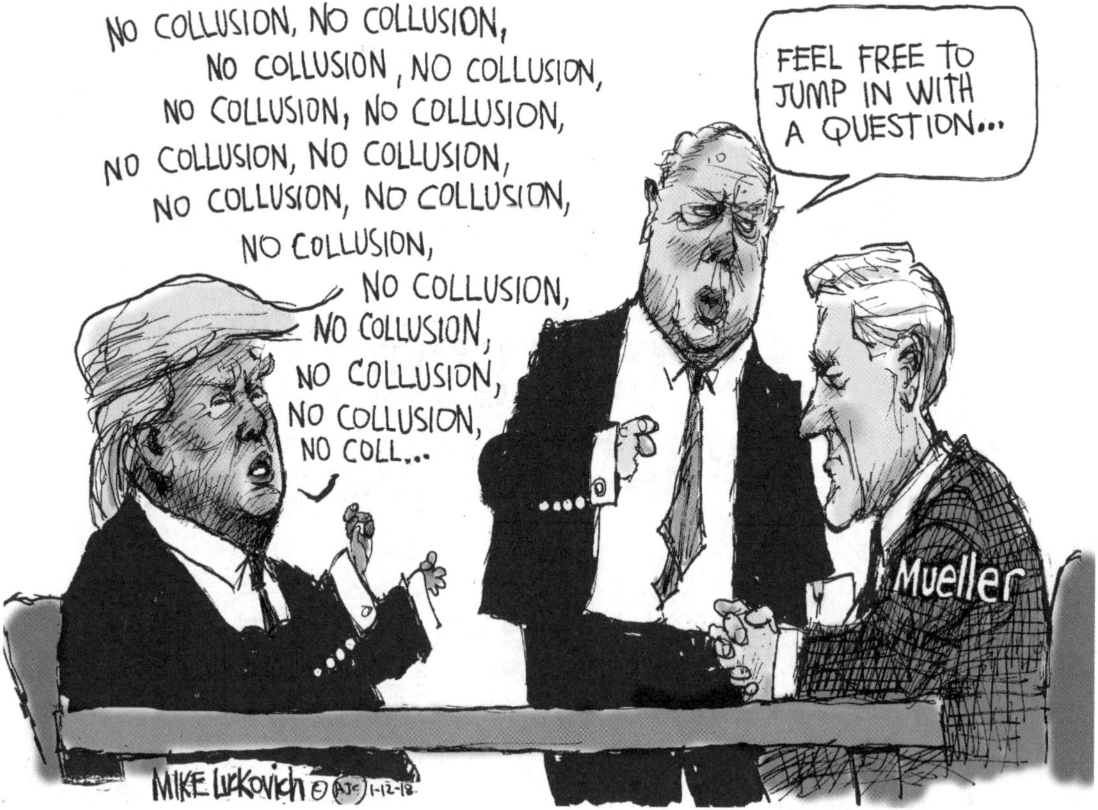
NO COLLUSION, NO COLLUSION, NO COLLUSION, NO COLLUSION, NO COLLUSION, NO COLLUSION, NO COLLUSION, NO COLLUSION, NO COLLUSION, NO COLLUSION, NO COLLUSION, NO COLLUSION, NO COLLUSION, NO COLLUSION, NO COLLUSION, NO COLL...
FEEL FREE TO JUMP IN WITH A QUESTION...
Mueller
MIKE LUCKOVICH © AJC 1-12-18

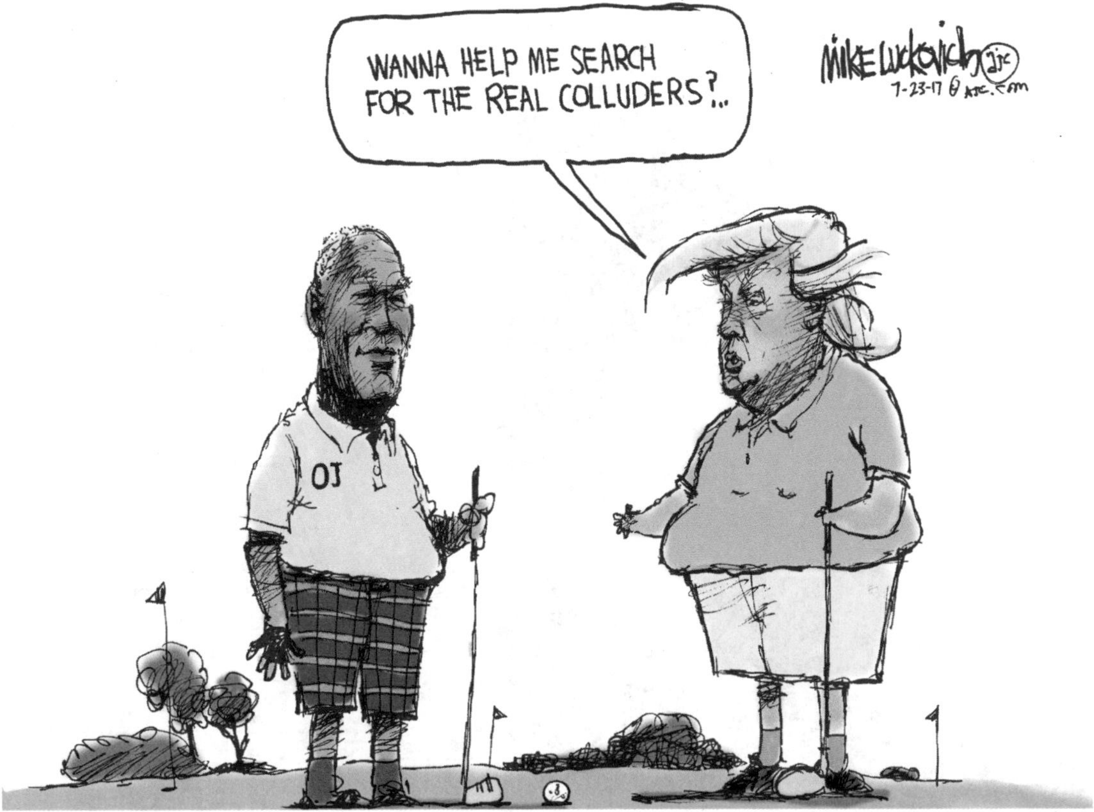
WANNA HELP ME SEARCH FOR THE REAL COLLUDERS?...
MIKE LUCKOVICH AJC
7-23-17 © AJC.com
OJ

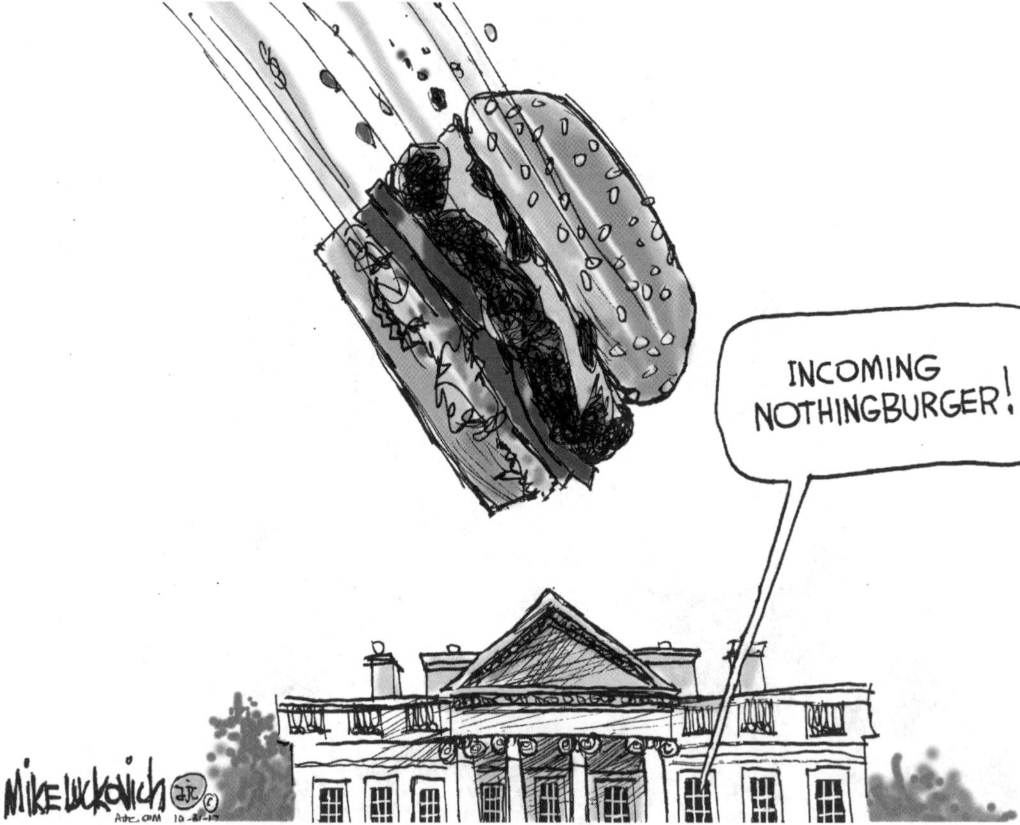
INCOMING NOTHINGBURGER!
MIKE LUCKOVICH

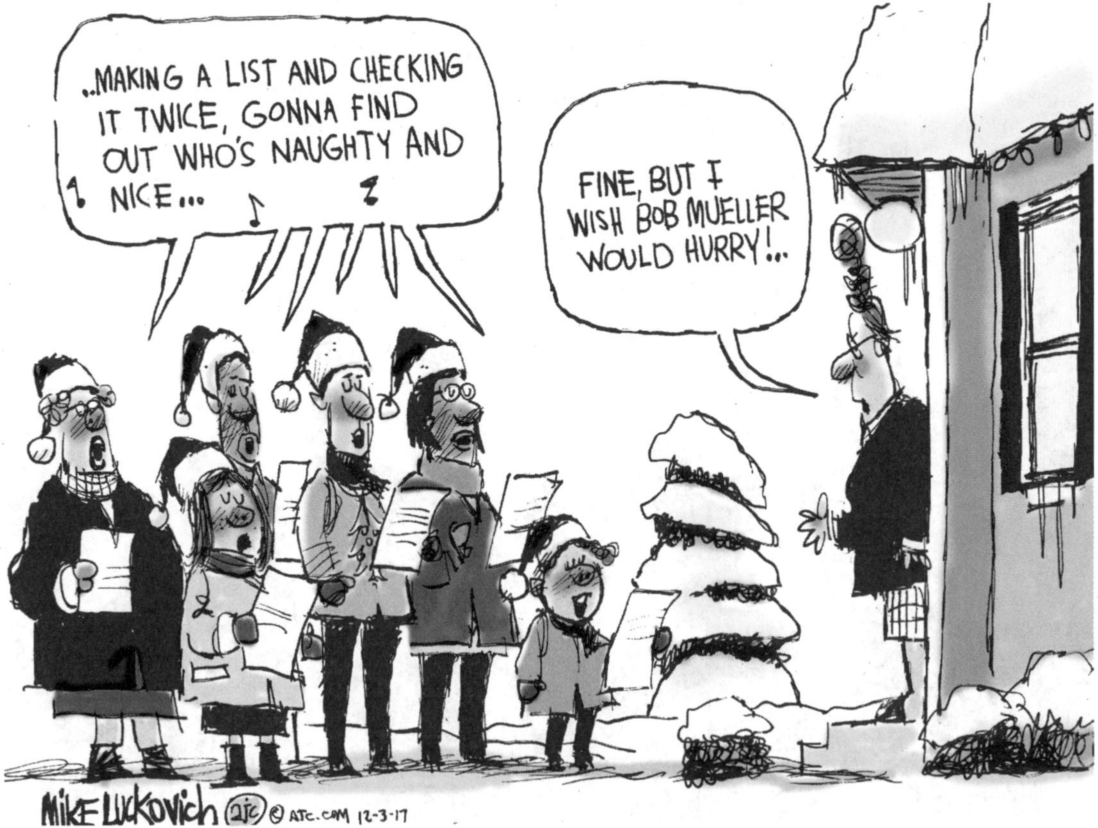
..MAKING A LIST AND CHECKING IT TWICE, GONNA FIND OUT WHO'S NAUGHTY AND NICE...
FINE, BUT I WISH BOB MUELLER WOULD HURRY!..
MIKE LUCKOVICH AJC © AJC.COM 12-3-17

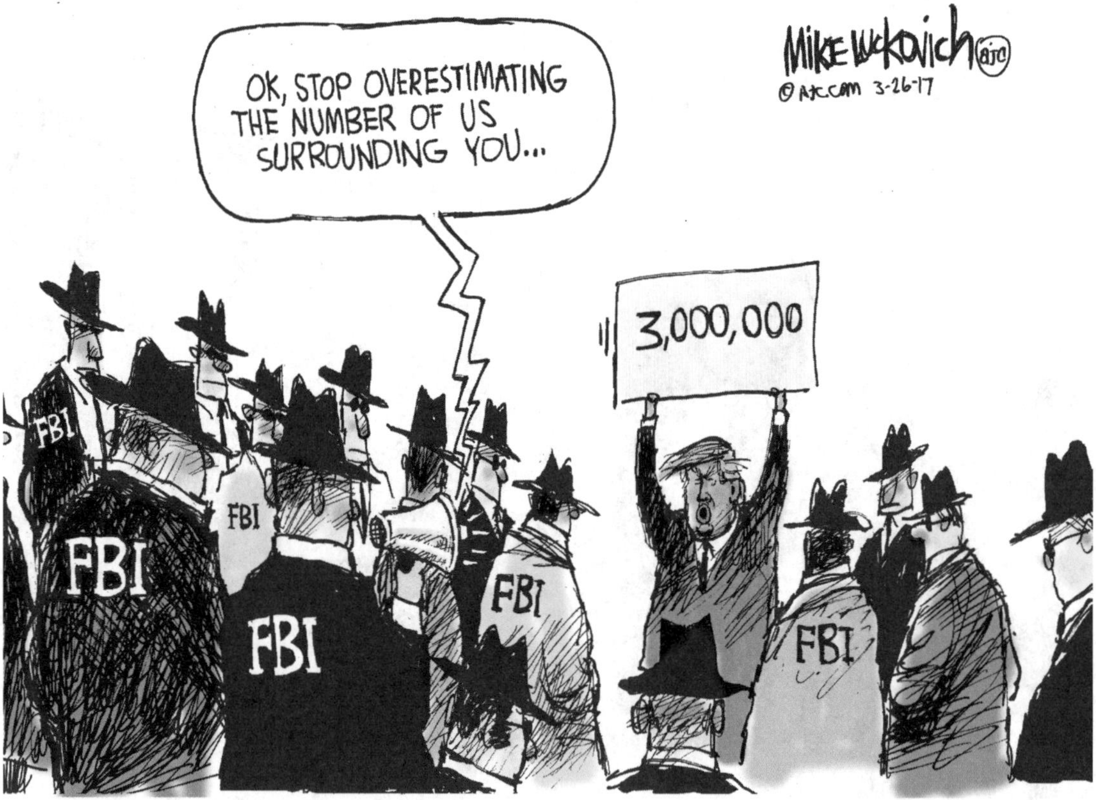
OK, STOP OVERESTIMATING THE NUMBER OF US SURROUNDING YOU...
3,000,000
FBI
FBI
FBI
FBI
FBI
FBI
MIKE LUCKOVICH
© AJC.COM 3-26-17

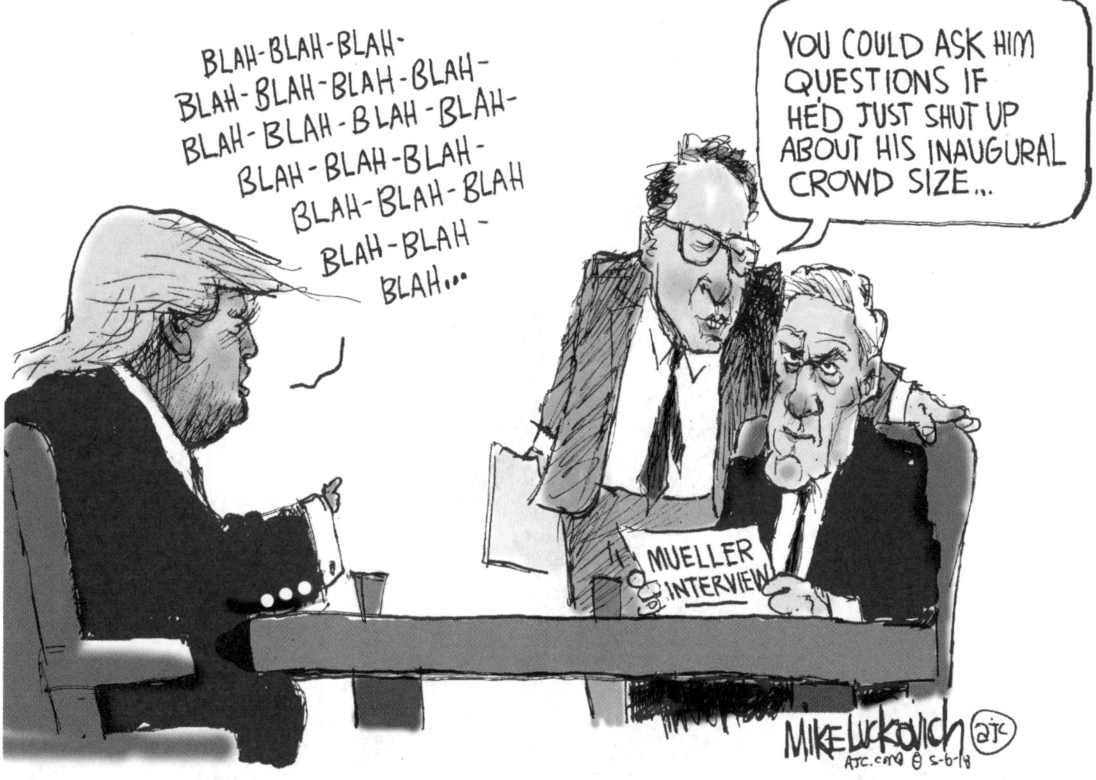
BLAH-BLAH-BLAH-
BLAH-BLAH-BLAH-BLAH-
BLAH-BLAH-BLAH-BLAH-
BLAH-BLAH-BLAH-
BLAH-BLAH-BLAH
BLAH-BLAH-
BLAH...
YOU COULD ASK HIM QUESTIONS IF HE'D JUST SHUT UP ABOUT HIS INAUGURAL CROWD SIZE...
MUELLER INTERVIEW
MIKE LUCKOVICH
AJC.com © 5-6-18

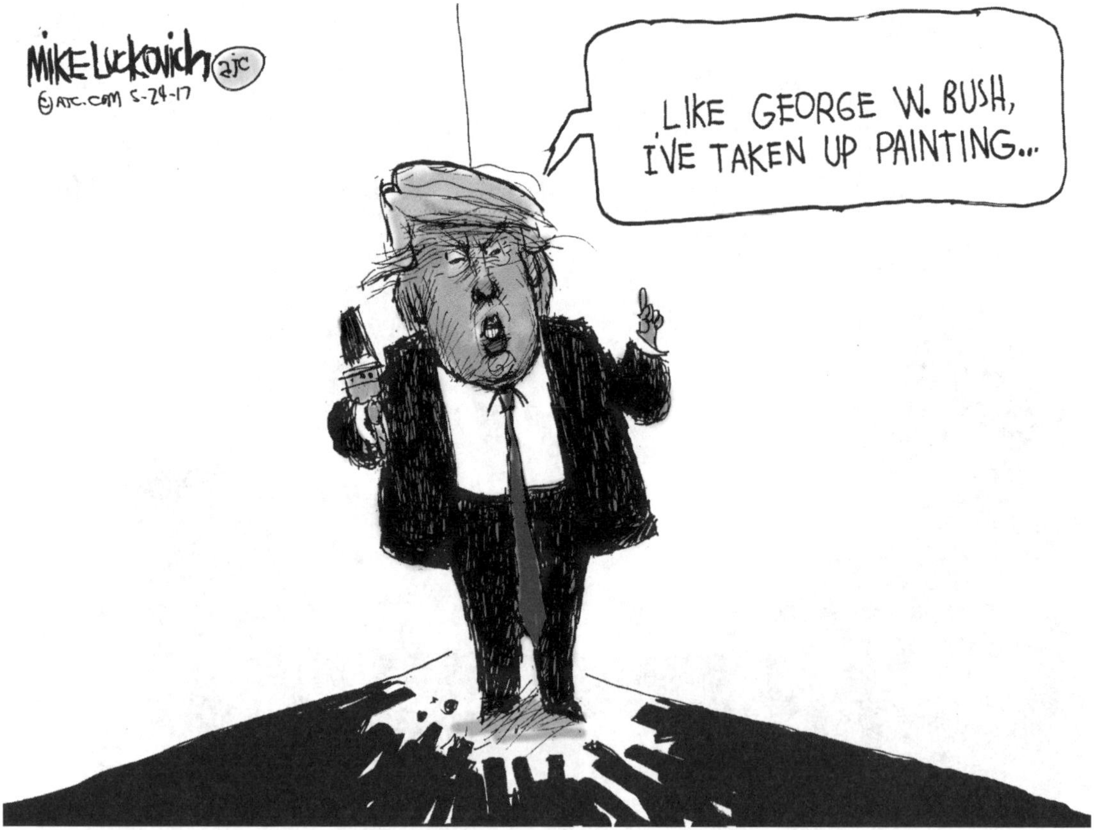
MIKE LUCKOVICH ajc
©AJC.COM 5-24-17
LIKE GEORGE W. BUSH, I'VE TAKEN UP PAINTING...

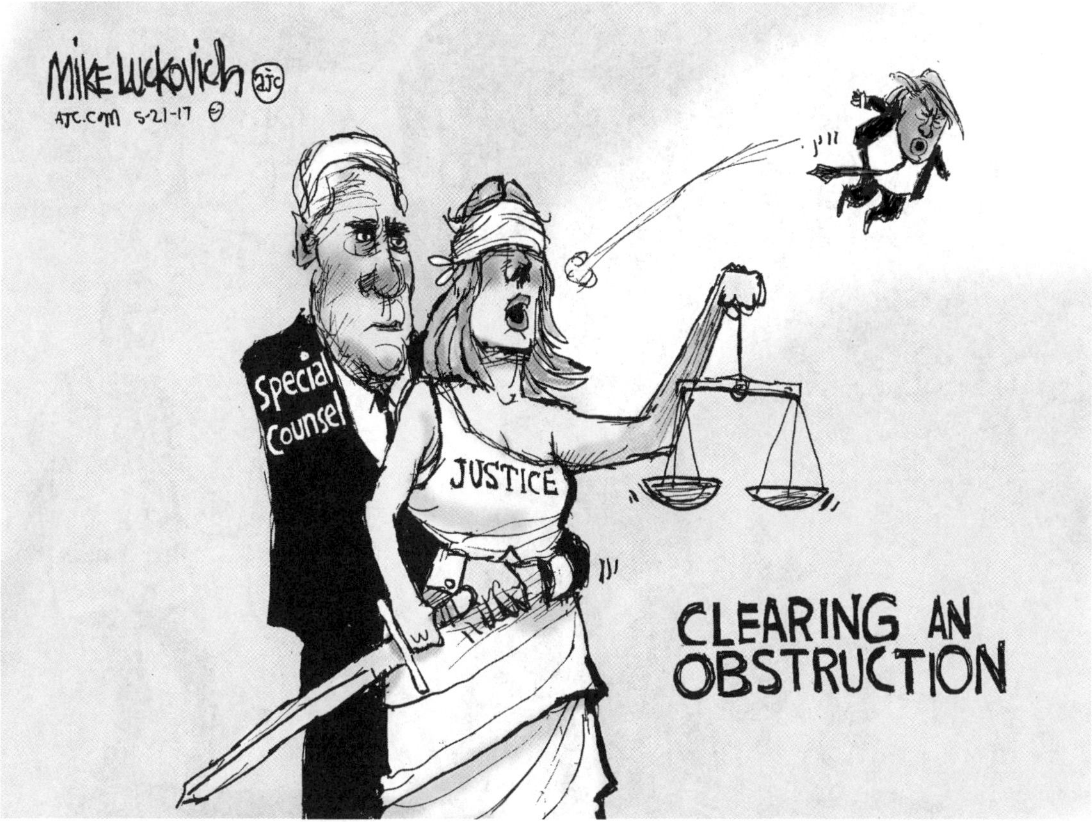
MIKE LUCKOVICH ajc
AJC.COM 5-21-17
Special Counsel
JUSTICE
CLEARING AN OBSTRUCTION

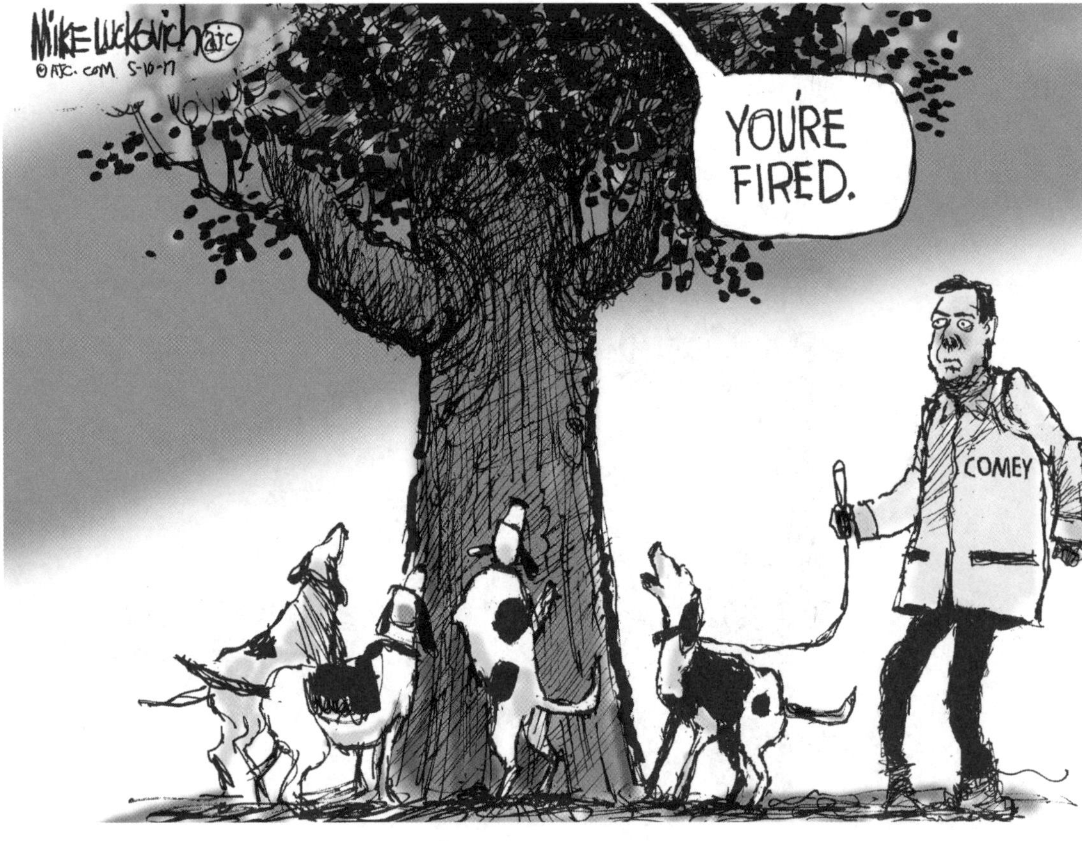
MIKE LUCKOVICH AJC
©AJC.COM 5-10-17
YOU'RE FIRED.
COMEY

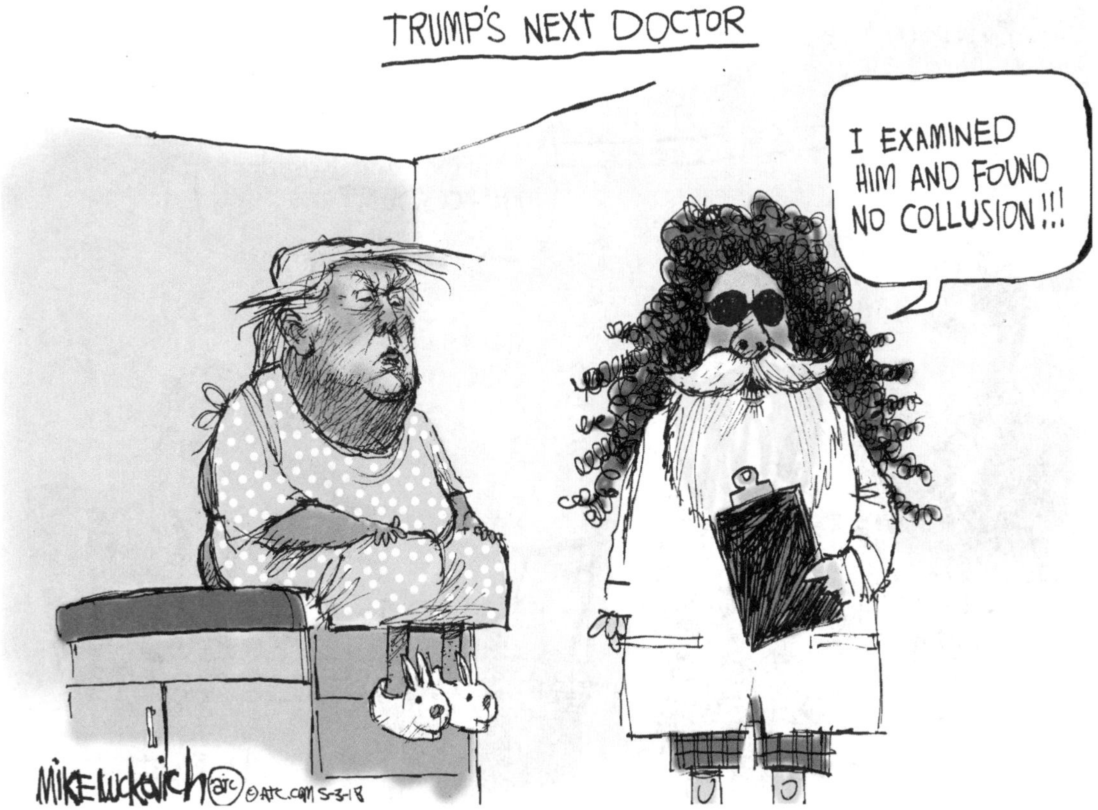
TRUMP'S NEXT DOCTOR
I EXAMINED HIM AND FOUND NO COLLUSION!!!
MIKE LUCKOVICH
©AJC.COM 5-3-18

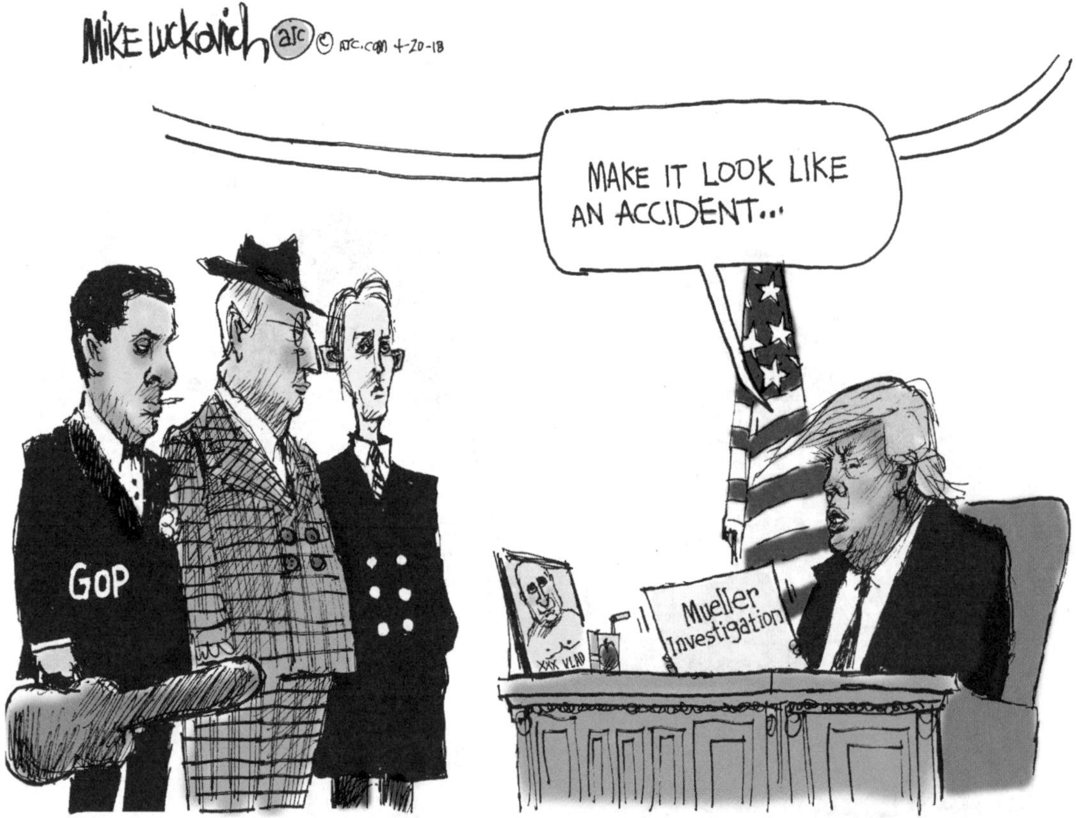
MIKE LUCKOVICH AJC © AJC.COM 4-20-18
MAKE IT LOOK LIKE AN ACCIDENT...
GOP
XXX VLAD
Mueller Investigation

 Donald J. Trump
@realDonaldTrump

# PRAISE

RETWEETS    LIKES
3,582      9,935

🔺 1.7K   ↻ 3.6K   ♡ 99K  •••

My cartoons run daily in the *Atlanta Journal-Constitution* newspaper and online at ajc.com, and they're syndicated to newspapers across the country and around the world, so I get fan mail from all over. I got this email from a couple in Atlanta.

Dear Mr. Luckovich,

We have received home delivery of the *AJC* since our retirement four years ago. The first thing we do every morning, even before we pour our first cup of coffee, is to open the *AJC* to the editorial page, to see your cartoon.

There are some that are poignant, like "Liftoff" for Stephen Hawking; there are some that say everything with very few words, like the bare statue of liberty pedestal, with the words from a sightseeing boat "she resigned." Our personal favorite is "time to start shooting myself in this foot!" Unlike the cable news pundits, your opinion sums up our "stormy" American environment beautifully, in our opinions!

We have papered the inside of our kitchen cabinet doors with our favorite Luckovich cartoons.

Thank you for enlivening our lives!!!

You can also find my cartoons on social media, so I get hate mail from everywhere too. This doesn't bother me. It's kind of fun to think people take time out of their day to call me names. "Luckovich" rhymes with some nasty words, so most of the emails, posts and letters criticizing me aren't that original. Irate readers stick to the tried and true names I've been called since third grade.

## Luckovich, Michael (CMG-Atlanta)

**From:** ████████████████████
**Sent:** Thursday, September 21, 2017 1:26 PM
**To:** Luckovich, Michael (CMG-Atlanta)
**Subject:** FW: You and muck fuckovich

**From:**
**Sent:** Wednesday, September 20, 2017 6:09 PM
**To:** .
**Subject:** You and muck fuckovich

Each time I see that low life fucking far left, muck fuckovich aka mike luckovich aka G D useless m fkr and his so called, fucked up cartoons against President Trump, I curse him to the ends of this earth!! I also curse your fake news, bull shit, trash paper for paying that low life cock sucker!!
The ajc and fuckovich can hopefully burn in hell!!   THE ABOVE IS HOW ONE ADDRESSES USELESS TRASH AND GARBAGE!!!!!!!!!!!!!!!!!!!!!

# CONCLUSION

In my entire life, I've never met someone as racist as Trump. Or someone as narcissistic. Or someone who lies so effortlessly. Or someone totally without shame. Or someone so corrupt. Or someone so stupid that thinks he's smart. We found one of the worst people in the country and made him president. It'll take a long time before the world trusts us again.

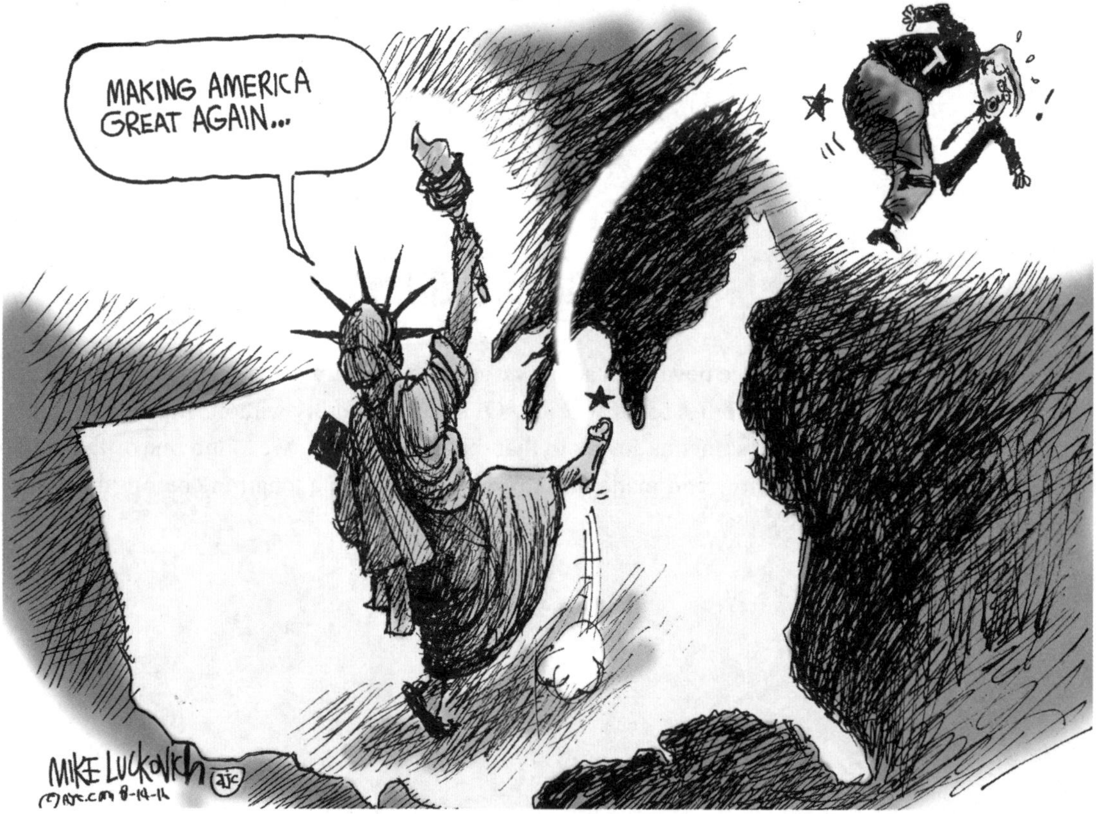
MAKING AMERICA GREAT AGAIN...
MIKE LUCKOVICH